W9-BBS-927

THE ARCHAEOLOGY OF ANCESTORS

UNIVERSITY PRESS OF FLORIDA

Florida A&M University, Tallahassee
Florida Atlantic University, Boca Raton
Florida Gulf Coast University, Ft. Myers
Florida International University, Miami
Florida State University, Tallahassee
New College of Florida, Sarasota
University of Central Florida, Orlando
University of Florida, Gainesville
University of North Florida, Jacksonville
University of South Florida, Tampa
University of West Florida, Pensacola

The Archaeology of Ancestors

Death, Memory, and Veneration

EDITED BY ERICA HILL

AND JON B. HAGEMAN

Foreword by Patricia A. McAnany

University Press of Florida

Gainesville · Tallahassee · Tampa · Boca Raton

Pensacola · Orlando · Miami · Jacksonville · Ft. Myers · Sarasota

Printed in the United States of America on acid-free paper

This book may be available in an electronic edition.

21 20 19 18 17 16   6 5 4 3 2 1

Library of Congress Cataloging-in-Publication Data
Names: Hill, Erica, editor. | Hageman, Jon B., 1967- editor. | McAnany, Patricia Ann, author of introduction, etc.
Title: The archaeology of ancestors : death, memory, and veneration / edited by Erica Hill and Jon B. Hageman ; foreword by Patricia A. McAnany.
Description: Gainesville : University Press of Florida, [2016].|
Includes bibliographical references and index.
Identifiers: LCCN 2015038626 | ISBN 9780813062518 (alk. paper)
Subjects: LCSH: Archaeology—Social aspects. | Archaeology—History. | Ethnoarchaeology. | Funeral rites and ceremonies—History.
Classification: LCC CC175 .A734 2016 | DDC 930.1—dc23
LC record available at http://lccn.loc.gov/2015038626

The University Press of Florida is the scholarly publishing agency for the State University System of Florida, comprising Florida A&M University, Florida Atlantic University, Florida Gulf Coast University, Florida International University, Florida State University, New College of Florida, University of Central Florida, University of Florida, University of North Florida, University of South Florida, and University of West Florida.

University Press of Florida
15 Northwest 15th Street
Gainesville, FL 32611-2079
http://www.upf.com

Contents

Figures

Foreword

Dead or alive! The stark polarity of this phrase resonates with the lethal violence of nineteenth-century western expansion in the United States. The social death of captivity was tantamount to biological death—the two were interchangeable. Contributors to *The Archaeology of Ancestors* tell a different story by interrogating how biological death, in the words of Nancy Scheper-Hughes, "does not destroy personhood but often intensifies it." Ancestralizing practices have a way of extending the boundaries of personhood and stretching the perceived temporal limits of life cycle–linked agency. The powerful lock of mortality implodes with the construction of ancestors around whom there is always much jockeying for position and access to origins. Our medicalized approach to life and death frames these conditions within a measured tolerance, which we internalize only partially. Another part of us recognizes the blurring, the carryover, and the potential longevity of sociality long after the breath of life has ceased. Some social analysts claim that current medicalized and hyper-essentialized approaches to life/death account for the twenty-first-century fascination with zombies and vampires—hybrid life forms that blur the distinction between life and death.

Each chapter in this book can be viewed as an exploration of the materiality of immortality. Although alterity emerges alongside the inescapable biological decay that accompanies death, the residual hard parts of the body—bone and teeth—as well as belongings and place of interment provide unmistakable flash points for memory, resistance, and movement. I use the term "movement" here to encourage a sense of doing and becoming and to emphasize the ways in which things that evoke ancestors—sometimes quite literally—can materialize the identity and wealth of a social collectivity, including points of friction and lines of fracture. Through the reflexivity of ancestralizing practices, we hold up a mirror on ourselves and, depending on what we see, we choose a path forward. In contrast to the claim that such practices valorize the past at the expense of the future, the chapters of *The Archaeology of Ancestors* provide ample evidence that ancestor veneration constitutes an active way of moving forward—by "leveraging" the powerful persuasive force of ancestors—by refusing to forget the past.

Only the intersubjectivities of personhood can render comprehensible how the dead linger and display such staying power as a fulcrum around which networks of connections—what Bruno Latour would conceive of as an assemblage of heterogeneous materials—form, replicate, and transform. Temporally dynamic and historically contingent, ancestralizing practices can dramatically shift in meaning and use. By destabilizing the dichotomy between the living and the dead—between the animate and the inanimate—the authors of *The Archaeology of Ancestors* bring us closer to lived practice and to an archaeology of death that recognizes and respects the vitality of personhood and how a revered ancestor can continue to animate social collectivities long after the heart has stopped beating.

Patricia A. McAnany
Kenan Eminent Professor
Department of Anthropology
University of North Carolina, Chapel Hill

PART I

Revisiting Ancestors

1

Leveraging the Dead

The Ethnography of Ancestors

JON B. HAGEMAN AND ERICA HILL

> . . . the ancestors do not die, but only slowly fade away as they are replaced by their more numerous descendants.
>
> David N. Keightley, "The Making of the Ancestors," 42

Since the late nineteenth century, American and European scholars in history, sociology, and anthropology have speculated on and debated the roles that the spirits of the dead play in societies both ancient and modern. Some—but not all—of those dead are ancestors. Why a select group of the deceased became ancestors, the ways those ancestors were honored and remembered, the ways that ancestors manifested in the lives of their descendants, and the identification of ancestors in archaeological contexts are the subjects of this book. In the simplest terms, an ancestor is a deceased forebear, a member of one's lineage, clan, or house who is no longer among the living. In some societies, ancestors are vital, powerful entities in the daily lives of those who fear, venerate, and propitiate them. These ancestors represent a select subset of the deceased—those kin who, for various reasons, remain part of the collective consciousness of their descendants. Such ancestors may demand sacrifices, offerings, and libations, provide protection and good health, or bring illness, grief, and disaster.

Ancestor veneration is not a religion per se; rather, it is one set of beliefs and practices within a larger cosmological system that explains origins, structures relationships, and conveys information about group membership. While the term "veneration" is used here, earlier scholars often described the worship of the deceased as an "ancestor cult" or a "cult of the dead." In its original sense, the term "cult" generally referred to the rites, beliefs, and *sacra* used to pay homage to supernatural or divine beings. Although ancestors may be perceived as divine in some ethnographic contexts, far more often they occupy ambivalent positions vis-à-vis their descendants. That ambivalence is negotiated through prayer, sacrifice, and other ritual acts that memorialize the deceased, affirm kin relations, and reinforce status, authority, and access to resources. Although anthropologists today understand ancestors as part of the fabric of social organization—as historically contingent and temporally variable—nineteenth-century scholars looked to ancestors in their reconstructions of the earliest forms of human religion and social structure.

Working within the paradigm of cultural evolution and firmly situated within the colonial enterprise, Edward B. Tylor sought the origins of human belief in African and Australian Aboriginal societies. These supposed primitives appeared to Tylor to be relics of an earlier stage of human cultural development. Through the study of their beliefs in animism, totemism, and ancestor worship, he hoped to reconstruct humanity's earliest attempts to explain the world. While Tylor sought answers in Aboriginal beliefs, his contemporary, French historian Numa Denis Fustel de Coulanges, explored the classical world for clues on how religion influenced the social development of Greece and Rome. Despite temporal and spatial distance, "modern primitives" and ancient Greeks appeared to share a similar preoccupation with the ancestral dead, a subject pursued into the twentieth century by Émile Durkheim and James G. Frazer.

Although Victorian era cultural evolution has long since been abandoned as an organizational schema, ancestors and their veneration became firmly entrenched in anthropological understanding of the social and political organization of societies throughout Africa and East Asia during the 1940s and 1950s. In the 1980s and 1990s, the abandonment of structural-functionalist perspectives, with their emphasis on kinship, led to the marginalization of ancestors as a subject of anthropological study in Africa. In spite of this marginalization, ancestors stubbornly maintained their presence among peoples studied by ethnographers. Twenty-first-century cultural anthropology is seeing interest in ancestors emerge in new ways: in colonial and historical critiques, in studies of postcolonialism and modernity, and in transformations of gender roles.

In this chapter, we review the historiography of ancestors, beginning in the late nineteenth century with classical historians and sociologists. We then highlight the work of twentieth-century ethnographers who more fully developed studies of ancestors, and we track the development of the concept through the influential ethnographic debates of the 1960s in which African ancestors became the prototypes for those in other world regions. Forays into China and, briefly, into Madagascar explore how research from these regions simultaneously expanded the breadth of material on ancestors and contributed to the establishment of two primary and distinct traditions of ancestor studies, African and East Asian.

We conclude with a list of ten key points we have derived from this comparative study of ancestors, including the common roles that ancestors fill and the cultural domains in which they operate. Ancestors do many things around the world, but they are consistently associated with agency, power, authority, descent, inheritance, resources, memory, and identity. Finally, we provide a brief overview of the chapters in this volume, which are divided into two parts: "Revisiting Ancestors" in the core areas where their study began (China, Greece, and Africa) and "Discovering Ancestors" in the archaeological records of Europe, Peru, and Mesoamerica.

Defining Ancestors

One of the most influential definitions of "ancestor" to appear in the anthropological literature is that of Meyer Fortes:

> a named, dead forbear [*sic*] who has living descendants of a designated genealogical class representing his continued structural relevance. . . . such an ancestor receives ritual service and tendance [by descendants] [Fortes 1965:124].

As Fortes's definition makes clear, not everyone who dies is or can become an ancestor. "Death has no deifying virtue," wrote Durkheim (1964:62 [1912]); it is a necessary "but not sufficient condition for the attainment of ancestorhood" (Fortes 1965:125). Creation of an ancestor requires the living to engage in some ritual act that separates some of the deceased from the "crowd of the profane" (Durkheim [1964:62 (1912)]). Such acts may be components of mortuary rites or completely separate, occurring months or years after death. Once select deceased have achieved ancestorhood, they remain active among the living. Some inspire fear and require constant propitiation through offerings; other, more benign ancestors are the source of good fortune and lineage prosperity. They, too, require veneration. In contrast to funerary and mourning rites occasioned by death, relations between ancestors and their descendants are reciprocal and periodic; rituals intended to maintain good relations are celebrated at regular intervals on some quotidian or calendrical basis (1964:63 [1912]).

Following Durkheim, Fortes distinguished between ancestors and the dead more generally. He understood funerary rites as rites of passage—acts that resolved the disruption and assuaged the grief resulting from the death of a community member (1965:128). His perspective was similar to that of Max Gluckman[n] (1937:125), who differentiated between ancestor veneration and a more general concern with the spirits of the dead, noting that an "ancestral cult" involves "belief in the continued interference of ancestral ghosts in the affairs of their living kin and continual ritual behavior by the latter to the former." Distinct rites were required to transform the deceased into an ancestor: "The dead has first to be 'brought back home again,' re-established in the family and lineage, by obsequial rites, and will even then not receive proper ritual service until he manifests himself in the life of his descendants and is enshrined" (Fortes 1965:129). From that point on, the deceased becomes "a regulative focus for . . . social relations and activities" (1965:129) through which lineages and other corporate groups are organized and constituted.

A broader definition of "ancestor" is provided by Newell (1976b:18–22) based on comparative work using East Asian materials. First, ancestors are named deceased who successfully undergo a rite of passage. Second, some form of continuity must exist between the ancestor and his former life, usually a family relationship, genealogy, or pedigree. This establishes for the ancestor living relations who may identify and worship him. Ritual, therefore, is an essential part of Newell's definition (1976b:21). Finally, ancestors must be understood to have some existence separate from that of the body. Newell (1976b:20) finds Fortes's definition too restricted; he charges that it reduces ancestor worship "to almost purely structural significance."

A more diffuse definition is offered by John Middleton (1960:33), based on his work among the Lugbara of Uganda:

> Ancestors thus include all the dead and living forebears of *ego's* lineage. . . . They are both male and female. . . . The dead among them are important in ritual as the objects of sacrifice. They are thought

> of as forming a collectivity, in which individual ancestors are not significant *qua* individuals. They send sickness to the living, but they send it collectively, and shrines are erected for them as collectivities also.

In contrast to the Tallensi ancestors described by Fortes, those among the Lugbara may be unnamed, collective, and even childless, though the childless are distinguished as a collectivity separate from that of the patri- or matriline. Despite the diversity of Lugbara ancestor types and their associated shrines, the most commonly recognized ancestors are those belonging to a select collectivity of the male deceased in ego's minimal lineage who have begotten children. Such ancestors are "'just ancestors' without qualification . . . [and] form a collectivity in which individual personality, responsibility, and kin relationship to living people are irrelevant" (Middleton 1960:52).

A component of these definitions critical to the archaeological understanding of ancestors is the fact that veneration is materialized through periodic ritual acts, that is, Fortes's (1965:124) "ritual service and tendance." Middleton (1960:33) noted that the dead "are important in ritual as the objects of sacrifice," while Durkheim (1964:63 [1912]) included periodicity in his definition of venerative rites. Similarly critical to identifying ancestors archaeologically is their link with corporate groups. In his study of Chinese kinship, Watson (1982a:594) identified ancestors as the "original founders of the corporation" and the basis for the "ritual unity" of the lineage celebrated in rites conducted in halls and shrines. He concisely identified those features that distinguish ancestors and their veneration from a concern with the dead more generally: death rituals tend to be *inclusive*; they involve non-kin; serve as rites of passage for the community, the mourners, and the soul or spirit of the deceased; and function as venues for competition and intergroup negotiation. In contrast, beliefs and rituals associated with ancestor veneration emphasize lineage unity, exclusivity, and resource control. This concern with lineage and resources is evident in Stephan Feuchtwang's (1974) succinct definition of ancestor worship as "the use of the biological fact of birth selectively for social classification and for claims on certain kinds of social relationships."

In Ghana and Nigeria, ancestors and their shrines incorporate an additional conceptual component—they represent the domestication of space, their presence proof that the bush has been transformed and incorporated

(Kopytoff 1987; McCall 1995). Ancestors are those who came first, who cleared the land for farms, constructed the first shrines, and were interred beneath the floors of houses. McCall understands ancestors as the conceptual foundation of cultural space, their veneration and the maintenance of shrines as social and material acts that establish links between the living, the dead, and the land. Ancestors are also part of what makes one human; those who cannot claim kin and bear no responsibility to ancestors exist beyond the bounds of society (Middleton 1960). Thus remembering and propitiating ancestors are profoundly human acts; shrines, like houses, distinguish place from space, the village from the bush.

In sum, "ancestors" is a highly diverse category that includes some, but not all, of the deceased of a corporate group that is usually, but not always, unilineal. Ancestors may be named, as they are among the Tallensi of northern Ghana (Fortes 1965), or they may form part of a more nebulous collective presence, as do some long-dead Merina of Madagascar (Bloch 1971) and the most common Lugbara ancestors (Middleton 1960). Their remains may be curated individually for ritual use, or their bones may be deposited en masse in a lineage ossuary. Ancestors may be men or women; they may be fractious shades of elders or childless and dissatisfied. Beliefs about deceased kin are materialized through periodic rituals that seek to access the ancestors for the purposes of revering, propitiating, or gaining favor from them. Such rites tend to have spatial components and leave material residues that are commonly represented in the form of architecture and landscape modifications, curated or modified remains of the deceased, and structured deposits involving sacrifice, offerings, and libations.

A History of Ancestors

Early Ancestors

Ancestors have figured prominently in anthropological and historical literature since the late nineteenth century. Their Victorian era study was part of a larger intellectual project to understand the origins of human civilization and identify the evolutionary stages of its advancement. Religion was of particular interest, as the complexity and sophistication of a society's belief system was thought to be indicative of its overall level of cultural progress. Through the study of funerary rituals and beliefs about death, nineteenth-century scholars learned how people in non-Western societies perceived souls, spirits, and the afterlife. Ancestors proved to be a common component of some of these "lower theologies" (Tylor 1958a:22 [1871]). Comparison of the patterns in their veneration across cultures could therefore illuminate the development of more enlightened religions, such as Christianity.

Fustel de Coulanges (1874:24, 28) described ancestors among the ancient Greeks and Romans as the souls, or *manes*, of the deceased. The family of the deceased made offerings and sacrifices in his memory and asked for aid, strength, and prosperity. Clearly, Fustel de Coulanges observed, the dead could not do without the living nor the living without the dead (1874:44). Failure to provide nourishment to the ancestors in the form of sacrifice was extremely impious and considered "parricide, multiplied as many times as there were ancestors in the family" (1874:43). Untended ancestors became malevolent, punishing their descendants with disease, blight, or drought (1874:23).

Significantly for archaeology, Fustel de Coulanges argued that the structure of the ancient family and concepts of property were built upon the veneration of dead ancestors (1874:51–52; see also Morris 1991 for a critique). Families maintained tombs for deceased paterfamilias who, according to Fustel de Coulanges, were located on the family's agricultural fields (1874:49). This placement of the tomb—"the second home of [the] family"—ensured that the ancestors were involved in the day-to-day affairs of the living and materialized the family's claim to the land.

Edward B. Tylor (1958b:199 [1871]) expanded the discussion of "manes worship," characterizing it as one of the "great branches of the religion of mankind." Gleaning evidence of the practice from travelers' accounts from across the globe, Tylor attributed worship of the dead to societies as varied as the Malagasy, Tongans, Natchez of Louisiana, and Camacans of Brazil. The deceased, "passed into a deity" (1958b:199 [1871]), protected his own family and received service from them. Tylor emphasized the connection between the living and the dead in West Africa and China, where aged family members were highly respected and death gave them even more influence over the living. Descendants not only provided food and drink for the dead, asking for help and good fortune, but also strove to glorify the ancestors by living exemplary lives (1958b:201–205 [1871]).

Like Fustel de Coulanges, scholars of comparative religion, such as Frank B. Jevons (1908:199 [1896]), noted the close correlation between ancestor veneration and family structure, specifically patrilineality and "the filial piety of the patriarchal family." Working within the cultural evolutionary paradigm of the era and elaborating on the link between ancestors and land, Jevons observed that offerings of food by family members to the dead only came about with the development of agriculture (1908:194–195 [1896]). He agreed with Edward Clodd (1895:113) that ancestor worship was not, therefore, the primal religion of humankind; it was contingent upon the recognition of kinship—a "comparatively late" occurrence (1908:195*n*1, 199 [1896]). Jevons argued that ancestor worship existed side by side with worship of the gods (1908:197–198 [1896]), but that the public worship of the gods tended to "assimilate" the private cult of ancestors (1908:195–196 [1896]).

Herbert Spencer, following Jevons, emphasized the tie between a sedentary farming lifestyle and ancestor veneration. In contrast to Jevons, however, he believed that ancestor worship was the "root" of every belief system, an evolutionary stepping-stone in the history of religion, with ancestors being transformed into deities along the way (Spencer 1916:293–294). Citing cross-cultural examples, Spencer 1916:303) argued that "nearly all [societies] . . . have a belief, vague or distinct, in a reviving other-self of the dead man." "More advanced" peoples demonstrated "persistent" ancestor worship; of these, some differentiated between "distinguished" and "undistinguished" ancestors. Spencer related forms of ancestor worship to phases of cultural evolution, with "primitive" tribes making few distinctions among the deceased. For members of advanced societies, "once-similar human souls" diverged in character and importance until their original forms became "scarcely recognizable" (1916:303).

In *The Elementary Forms of the Religious Life*, Émile Durkheim took issue with the idea that ancestor cults were the earliest form of religion. Like Jevons, he believed that ancestor veneration was a cultural development that occurred after the origin of agriculture, since groups such as the Australian Aborigines, who represented the "simplest form of social organization," practiced totemism rather than ancestor worship (Durkheim 1964:63, 64 [1912]). Durkheim defined "ancestors" as those kin who become the object of veneration after death; therefore, the mythic forebears found in totemic societies—those who exercised superhuman or divine powers during life—occupied a separate conceptual category. They were not ancestors but rather "sacred beings of a wholly different nature" (1964: 64 [1912]). For Durkheim, ancestor cults were restricted to advanced societies, such as ancient China or Egypt (1964:63 [1912]) where a "system of diverse rites, festivals, and ceremonies . . . reappear periodically." Periodicity was key to distinguishing between irregular death rituals and ancestor cults, which Durkheim (1964:63 [1912]) defined as rites, sacrifices, or libations performed in honor of select dead on a regular basis.

Like Durkheim, Freud viewed totemism, rather than ancestor worship, as the earliest form of religion. In *Totem and Taboo*, he identified totems as "tribal ancestors" among the Australian Aborigines and explored taboos related to the dead, their belongings, and the treatment of mourners (1918:9, 35, 87–89). He suggested that the dead aroused ambivalent, contradictory emotions, both hostility and tenderness. The living repressed their unconscious fear of and hostility toward the deceased and, through the mechanism of projection, transformed the deceased into evil demons who rejoiced in human misfortune and death (1918:99–108). As humans developed, however, Freud (1918:109–110) suggested that the same ambivalence that gave rise to the fear of demons gave rise to ancestor veneration. Fear of demons disappeared as grief lessened and the mourning period ended. The same spirits that had been feared earlier were now "revered as ancestors, and appealed to for help in times of distress" (1918:110).

James G. Frazer published three volumes examining the relationship between the living and the dead in Australia (1913), Polynesia (1968 [1922]), and Micronesia (1968 [1924]). The dead in the South Pacific were feared, and a variety of practices were undertaken to prevent the dead from returning to the world of the living. Frazer emphasized that those in greatest danger were the immediate descendants of the deceased. In *The Fear of the Dead in Primitive Religion*, Frazer also considered evidence from the Americas, Asia, and Africa. His exhaustive review of the available data led him to believe that, with a few exceptions that established the rule, fear of the dead was universal (1933:13–14).

Like Durkheim and Freud, Frazer drew many of his examples from the Aboriginal societies of Australia. However, in contrast to Durkheim's rejection of any association between totemism and ancestor worship, Frazer argued that

> dead forefathers viewed as beings perfectly distinct from and far superior to the living, might easily come to receive from the latter the homage of prayer and sacrifice, might be besought by their

> descendants to protect them in danger and to succor them in all the manifold ills of life, or at least to abstain from injuring them [1913:115].

In Frazer's view, ancestor worship was one aspect of a more general cult of the dead (1933:66). African societies were of particular interest, as beliefs in ancestral spirits were "widely spread and more deeply rooted" there than elsewhere (1933:51). Frazer's ethnographic examples demonstrated the often idiosyncratic and vengeful nature of ancestors, who were feared and propitiated with offerings and sacrifices. Recalling Freud's idea of ambivalence toward the dead, Frazer asserted that while relations with the deceased may initially be friendly, they become "decidedly hostile" after mourning ends (1933:66; see Leach 1966 for a critique). Frazer's evidence indicated that relations with the deceased were materialized in food offerings, such as the beer and porridge provided in household shrines, and in activities at the site of interment. In a Micronesian example, he noted that the dead were buried beneath the floors of houses. The graves were periodically reopened and skulls removed for anointing with coconut oil. Family members slept and ate beside the skulls and in some cases entire skeletons were disinterred so that they might be appealed to for good luck "in fishing, war, or love" (1933:19). Though Frazer's subject was fear of the dead rather than their veneration, many of his examples show that the living attributed great powers to their ancestral kin and expected to receive aid from them as well as misfortune.

Ancestors in Africa

Max Gluckman's structural-functionalist work in Africa represents a radical departure from the evolutionary and comparative studies of the late nineteenth and early twentieth century. He approached burial practices and beliefs about ancestors among Bantu speakers of southern Mozambique in terms of conflict and cohesion. While death ritual was about the "readjustment of social relationships" (1937:124) involving the entire community, sacrifice and commemoration of ancestors concerned only the kin group. Ancestors were deceased elders who affected their descendants by sending "illness . . . fertility or barrenness, pestilence, rain, good crops" (1937:123). These ancestors were approached at their places of interment in either a cattle *kraal* or sacred grove (see also Insoll 2007, 2008). When a village was relocated and the remains of the deceased were left behind, the ancestor could be accessed in a "temple of the village" in the new location (Gluckman 1937:127).

Gluckman made three primary points concerning the nature of ancestor veneration among the Bantu and related peoples. First, he identified a correlation between ancestor veneration and the level of concern a society had with the condition of the soul in the afterlife. Societies that worshipped ancestors "have a very inchoate picture of the afterlife" (1937:125), whereas societies that did not placed greater emphasis on culturally coherent beliefs about the journey and destination of the soul of the deceased. This observation may have originated from Gluckman's comparison of Bantu practices with Bronislaw Malinowski's account (1916) of the Trobriand feast of the dead; Trobrianders had a well-articulated and shared cultural vision of the soul's journey to and existence in the netherworld.

Gluckman's second point was the distinction between ancestor veneration and a more generic "cult of the dead" (1937:129–130). His definition of ancestor veneration as "the belief in the continued interference of ancestral ghosts in the affairs of their living kin and continual ritual behavior by the latter to the former" (1937:125) is in clear contrast to Malinowski's pointed observation that Trobrianders had no fear of or concern with the *baloma* (spirit) of the deceased except during their annual feasts. Gluckman further suggested that social bonds were strongest among those descended from a common ancestor, in part because such kin groups, which were both patrilineal and patrilocal, tended to live in close proximity. Gluckman thus linked ancestors to the social cohesion of the lineage and viewed veneration as a cult embedded in kinship that reminded lineage members of their social bonds. Because ancestor worship was "compulsory" (1937:128), rites functioned effectively even in societies with large and complex systems of kinship. Among the Xhosa, Gluckman (1937:128) noted, obligations to attend ancestral rites superseded Christian beliefs, lest converts "be expelled from their families" (cf. Meyer 1999).

Gluckman's third point was that ancestor veneration entrenched the social position of elders within kin groups. Elders alone had the privilege of sacrificing to the ancestors, and thus they reinforced their authority with every ritual act. They also negotiated relationships between and among ancestors and living kin. Like ancestors, elders could curse and punish erring relatives. Younger members of the lineage who quarreled or made trouble had no choice but to "make amends" with elders (1937:128).

Meyer Fortes's ethnography of the Tallensi ancestor cult in Ghana is framed by considerations similar to those of Gluckman; his definition of an ancestor as a "named, dead forbear" (1965:124) with living descendants has become a standard in anthropology. Fortes understood ancestors as members of a distinct social category created by the death of an elder, usually a parent or lineage head. While mortuary rituals "disincorporat[ed]" the deceased from the social group, specific "obsequial rites" were required to confer ancestorhood and establish the ancestor in family and lineage organization in his reconstituted form (1965:128–129). This "reincorporation" was made tangible to the living through shrines (Fortes 1949:329, 1965:128–129, 1976:7), which symbolized the unity and corporate identity of lineage members (Fortes 1945:55).

The extent to which ancestors were interwoven with the daily life of the Tallensi is one of Fortes's key points: the entirety of social life was predicated on the ability to trace descent from a known and named ancestor along a putatively continuous male line (Fortes 1945:30–33). This is evidenced not only in religion but also in the beliefs and practices associated with marriage and landownership (Fortes 1959:346, 1965:137). Though all males of the lineage had the right to inherit corporate land, control was vested in the head of the lineage by right of seniority (Fortes 1945:178). Lineage headship was marked by succession to the custody of the ancestor shrine. The custodian was, by definition, an elder or senior male who accepted the role of shrine custodian and sacrificer irrespective of his personal relations with a given ancestor (Fortes 1965:133). The authority of the lineage head was, in turn, based on privileged access to the ancestors through his possession and tendance of the shrine. The shrine was located within the house of the lineage head and linked status, authority, and ancestors in both material and spatial terms (Fortes 1959:32). To Fortes, shrine ritual served two purposes: it promoted lineage cohesion and maintained social inequalities by affirming the status of the lineage head. When he died, specific rites were performed to decouple him from the shrine and inaugurate a new headman (Fortes 1945:227–228).

Shrine construction and "ritual service and tendance" operated at multiple scales. The erection of a shrine honoring patrilineal ancestors marked the establishment of a household at the family scale, while lineage shrines and the burial of select deceased in sacred groves materially and spiritually tied larger kin groups to specific localities (Fortes 1945:143; see also Insoll 2007, 2008). Together, shrines and graves fixed lineage origins on the landscape and demarcated ancestral lands and sacred places from the surrounding bush (Fortes 1945:208; see also Kuba and Lentz 2002:386; McCall 1995).

The ancestral cult as a whole was based on parental duty and filial piety (Fortes 1961). The authority of the ancestors was, in Fortes's view, analogous to the authority of a father over a son, but infinitely magnified and sanctified (1959:59–60). As children were dependent on their parents for survival, so living descendants were dependent on the ancestors, who could either punish or reward them. Like parents, ancestors antedated their descendants and made their existence possible; thus the living owed the social order in its entirety to the ancestors (Fortes 1945:68). Both sets of relationships were marked by ambivalence, with the parent or ancestor perceived as alternately protective and benevolent or demanding and persecutory (Fortes 1949, 1959, 1965). It behooved a son to construct shrines and make offerings to his forebears "irrespective of his sympathies or aversions, and without regard to his character or achievements" (Fortes 1965:134). Thus "the experience of filial dependence . . . provides the material for the code of symbolism and ritual by means of which reverence for authority can be regularly affirmed and enacted" (1965:139). Fortes's interpretation of ancestor worship is explicitly psychoanalytic; his focus on the ambivalent and arbitrary nature of ancestors is suggestive of Freudian perspectives on parenthood. In Tallensi beliefs about ancestors, Fortes found a culturally constructed psychological matrix that reproduced the parent-child relationship and reinforced social norms regarding kinship, descent, and authority.

Similar themes emerged in Jack Goody's (1962) monumental study of the LoDagaa (Dagara) of northwestern Ghana, in which he explored how social organization and authority were materialized through ancestor worship, death ritual, and inheritance. Goody argued that unilineal genealogies were flexible mnemonics of social relationships past and present (1962:381–382). The construction and maintenance of ancestor shrines provided "a material counterpart to the patrilineal genealogy" (1962:389). These shrines were wooden and impermanent, unlike those of the Tallensi. They were sometimes consumed by fire or grew "smaller and smaller as the termites [ate] into them" (1962:389). In contrast to the durable descent relationships and authority structures that Fortes described, Goody emphasized the malleable nature of kinship and memory and the negotiable custody and maintenance of shrines.

Ancestors were ideally tended by the eldest son (Goody 1962:384), but in contrast to the Tallensi, any male in the direct agnatic line could make offerings (1962:388). Offerings were obligatory; they were not gifts but rather a "fulfillment of obligations to those who . . . provide the living with earthly goods" (1962:414). Typically, important events were conducted in close proximity to shrines, which were portable and so could be carried to births, marriages, harvest festivals, and occasions of property transfer (1962:390–393). Thus offerings to the ancestors, in the form of blood sacrifice or water libations, tracked the stages of the life cycle.

Goody identified ancestors as agents of social control (1962:407). Like Fortes, he emphasized the relationship between descent, authority, and shrine custody. "A man has the power of life and death over his agnatic descendants not only when he is dead, but also while he is still alive, a power that is reinforced by his position as custodian of his own dead father's shrine . . . [this] gives a father's curse such potency" (1962:408). Ancestors thus served as "standardized projections" of the father's role, the weight of their authority analogous to his position as shrine custodian and "socializing agent" (1962:408). These hierarchical relations were buttressed by the threat of mystical retribution in the form of sickness or death.

Goody makes it clear that the ancestors are concerned with a specific type of authority—that related to the control of money and livestock and vested in the heir and sacrificer. This man may be the source of considerable tension within the family or lineage as he is "head of the household, master of the shrines, controller of the food supply, upbringer as well as holder" (1962:410). Hostility directed at him could be diffused or managed, then, through ancestor veneration, which supported the authority of the heirs, the senior members of the descent group (1962:412).

Ancestors in China

Though Africa was where the anthropological concept of "ancestor" was initially developed, ancestors found a large measure of their ethnographic variation in Asia. Traditions of ancestor veneration in China, Korea (e.g., Janelli and Janelli 1982; Kendall 1985; Kendall and Dix 1987), and Japan (e.g., Newell 1976a; Smith 1974; Traphagan 2004) have received the most scholarly attention, although anthropologists are increasingly exploring ancestors elsewhere in Asia (e.g., Friesen 2001). Though Asian ancestors share a number of similarities with their African counterparts, major geographic, ethnic, and temporal differences structure how, when, where, and by whom they are venerated. Maurice Freedman's work established the foundation for the study of Chinese ancestors in British and American anthropology in the 1950s and 1960s. He took a structural-functional perspective on family structure, kinship, and marriage among both traditional and mid-twentieth-century Chinese in southeastern coastal provinces.[1]

Freedman's work became the paradigm for research on Chinese kinship and lineage organization, but reliance on ethnographic materials derived from the southeast belies the incredible variation in practices and beliefs about ancestors across China (Cohen 1990). Nadeau and Chang (2003:287) neatly summarize Freedman's idealized Chinese family structure as

> a unified, patrilineal organization with wealth in trust, ancestral lands, an ancestral temple and shared cemetery, and carefully maintained genealogies. For Freedman, the common worship of a single ancestor reinforces the conviction that the members of the clan belong to a common group. Ancestor veneration is a reflection of deeper principles of lineage organization, and lineage organization is the basis and model of social organization in general.

Freedman (1958, 1966) was interested in the extent to which asymmetrical lineage segmentation was related to ancestral property. His research showed that internal descent hierarchies and lineage fissioning were marked through ritual practice. The choice of grave site, establishment of ancestral halls, and the transfer of tablets throw "the differentiation of the lineage community into relief" (Freedman 1958:77). Work in other regions in China confirmed his findings. Potter, for example, found that the various branches of a maximal lineage in Hong Kong reflected major differences in wealth, status, control of ancestral property, and concern with ancestral halls. The lineage branches with the most property were also those that were most internally differentiated and concerned with the performance of venerative rites at the graves of ancestors and the preservation and recitation of genealogies. Because both hall construction and sacrificial rites were financed by corporate property, the elaboration of ancestor worship directly reflected wealth (Potter 1970a).

Elsewhere and for other ethnic groups, Freedman's lineage model was less applicable. Ethnographers suggested that it overemphasized lineage fission and that segmentation was offset by diverse aggregative processes (Pasternak 1973; R. S. Watson 1982). In Taiwan, lineage systems differed significantly from the Freedman model, with concomitant differences in the importance of genealogy and ritual practice. Ancestor veneration was often focused on domestic shrines rather than ancestral halls, for example (Nadeau and Chang 2003). In northern China, Myron Cohen (1990:509) described patterning in burial places, ancestral scrolls and tablets, and corporate groups that differed significantly from Freedman's descriptions of Guangdong and Fujian.

Freedman's work and that of successive scholars have demonstrated that traditional (twelfth through nineteenth century) forms of ancestor worship in China reflected major ethnic and regional differences and degrees of influence of Confucian, Daoist, and Buddhist beliefs. More recently, these distinctions have been complicated by conflict, urbanization, Christianization, war, communism, and pressures to modernize. Post-1949 funeral reform, in particular, banned ancestral hall rites and mandated compulsory cremation rather than burial. Many halls were destroyed, others abandoned, and still others repurposed (Goossaert and Palmer 2011; Whyte 1988; Zhou 2002). Given internal variation in beliefs and practices, the following section addresses only a few of the most influential studies of ancestor veneration in China, describing how ritual practices in the home, in the ancestral hall, and at the grave reinforce unequal access to prestige and property or present opportunities for display and competition.

Traditional Chinese ancestor veneration was part of a complex eschatology involving beliefs in souls, supernatural beings, and geomancy (Cohen 1988; Harrell 1979; Jordan 1999; Potter 1970b; Wolf 1974). The archetypal ancestor in China was one who left property to his patriline, was owed gratitude and obeisance, and who, through the auspicious placement of his grave, might favor his descendants with health and good fortune. Ancestors provided for their agnates in the form of heritable wealth and in return expected to be fed, thanked, and honored through periodic rites. Wolf (1974:168) characterized the reciprocal relationship between the ancestors and those responsible for their veneration as one of "common welfare and mutual dependence."

Shrines to ancestors typically took two forms—one in the home, one in the ancestral hall—though there are regional differences in the presence and elaboration of each form (Freedman 1979 [1970]). Not all lineages had ancestral halls, since their construction and maintenance were dependent upon corporate resources. In the Taiwanese village studied by Jordan (1999), ancestral halls were relatively uncommon (see also Cohen 1969). A similar situation existed in Hebei province in northern China, where veneration occurred at graves rather than at shrines (Cohen 1990; see also Naquin 1988). In southeastern China, the domestic shrine contained ancestor tablets representing the most recently deceased (Freedman 1958:84–85). Tablets were wooden plaques about 15 to 30 centimeters tall upon which the name of the deceased was painted or engraved (Jordan 1999:chap. 5). Tablets were inherited on the principle of primogeniture in some regions; elsewhere they might circulate among members of the patriline. In southeastern China, the tablet was either enshrined in the ancestral hall, burned, or buried after three or four generations (Freedman 1958:85–87, 1979:276 [1970]). Emily Ahern (1973:149) noted that making an ancestral tablet was associated specifically with the inheritance of land. While other deceased might receive offerings indicative of some sort of debt or obligation, tablets were not carved in their honor. Freedman's (1979:275 [1970]) work on the mainland, however, indicated that tablets were made only for those who had attained parenthood, though this could be achieved posthumously or through adoption. Tablets were rare in Hebei and were only found in wealthier families; instead, most people used scrolls (Cohen 1990). Women were the primary caretakers of tablets in the home; worship of ancestors in the hall was the domain of men (Freedman 1958:85–86, 1979:285–286 [1970]).

Ancestral halls were much larger than domestic shrines and contained tablets memorializing ancestors for as many generations as the lineage tracked. The condition of the ancestral hall reflected lineage prosperity (Ahern 1973:100–101; Freedman 1979 [1970]). The construction of a new hall occurred when agnates formed a distinct faction and the lineage segmented (Freedman 1958), although in the Taiwanese villages studied by Ahern (1973:106–115), such segmentation rarely occurred and then only with the settlement of new territory. Ancestral tablets were the locus of veneration within the ancestral hall. Though the physical remains of ancestors were elsewhere, their souls were thought to visit or inhabit the tablets bearing their names. Access to the ancestral hall and its rituals was a marker of status and an expression of the lineage hierarchy (Freedman 1958:90–91). In contrast to the domestic cult, which facilitated a more intimate connection with the dead and permitted all members of the household to participate, veneration in the ancestral hall was restricted to specific male agnates in order of seniority (Newell 1976b:23). In communities without household shrines, where veneration occurred exclusively in halls and at grave sites, women might be completely excluded, as Ahern (1973) found in Taiwan. In Freedman's (1979:285 [1970]) words, "This is a world of men . . . wives enter the hall only as tablets—a dumb and wooden fate."

The head of the patrilineal descent group was also the leader of venerative rites by virtue of his seniority and genealogical proximity to the apical ancestor. His privileged status and that of other descent-group elites was reinforced by auspiciously locating the final resting place of each ancestor on geomantic principles. Ideally, standard southern Chinese burial practices were tripartite, involving initial interment in a coffin, exhumation after a period of five to ten years, and entombment of a pot containing the cleaned bones on a hillside (Ahern 1973; Nelson 1974; J. L. Watson 1988b; R. S. Watson 1988). Even in southern China, however, not all the deceased received the full complement of secondary burial rites; those who left substantial property were much more likely to survive in the memory of their descendants, be entombed in a secure location, and receive routine tendance (R. S. Watson 1988:209).

Geomantic concerns influenced the site of the initial grave in Taiwan (Ahern 1973) and of the final tomb made of brick or concrete in southern China (Freedman 1968; R. S. Watson 1988). Freedman emphasized that favorable tomb locations assured descendants of good fortune (1958:77, 1968, 1979:286–288 [1970]; see also R. S. Watson 1988:206n18) and suggested that the bones of the deceased passively facilitated or conducted geomantic benefits. In contrast, Ahern (1973:178–182) found that the comfort of the deceased within the geomantic landscape determined whether the living prospered or suffered misfortune. An ancestor unhappy in tomb placement might bring illness or poor crops; an ancestor who had a comfortable site with a good view and fresh air would be happy and refrain from making trouble. Conditions that might upset the ancestor included a tomb with dripping rainwater or one with an unstable foundation. Such conditions were occasionally remedied by retrieving the pot and moving the site of the tomb (Ahern 1973:183–186), actions that may be identifiable archaeologically.

Communal rites conducted at the grave or tomb site included food offerings and veneration; other activities involved routine care and cleaning or personal appeals. Communal activities were often highly formalized, with ritual structured in ways that conveyed information about both individual and lineage status. For example, members of different lineage branches assembled around the tomb according to seniority (Nelson 1974:275). Material evidence of such activities may include dishes for offerings and food detritus, in addition to archaeological features representing the original interment and subsequent tomb placement. Tsu (2000) describes in detail the handling of the bones of the deceased after initial disinterment in South Taiwan; defleshing may occur in order to ensure complete skeletonization, as partially decayed corpses are viewed with fear and suspicion (see also J. L. Watson 1982b, 1988a). Furthermore, all teeth of the deceased were extracted and thrown away at the gravesite, apparently to neutralize the danger of the ancestor "consuming" the good fortune of his descendants.

Prosperity of descendants, internal lineage competition, and landscape considerations all influenced frequency and degree of elaboration of graveside rites. Placement and condition of the remains of the deceased therefore represent the intersection of a number of variables, only some of which reflect social persona in a Saxe-Binford sense. In Freedman's view (1958), the conduct of rites in ancestral halls, in particular, while nominally focused on ancestors, in actuality highlighted and perpetuated descent hierarchies, in which distributions of economic and ritual privileges, including corporate properties, were vested in the lineage head. The inherent conservatism of hall rites, emphasized by Freedman, contrasted with the opportunities presented by graveside ritual to alter existing social relationships. While care and tendance of the ancestor at his grave ensured the well-being of his direct descendants, veneration of the hall tablet benefited the descent group more generally (R. S. Watson 1988:207).

Cohen found that burial patterns, rather than tablets, were the key markers of common descent in northern China where "the common graveyards of lineages contrasted with the dispersed burial characteristics of much of south China." As a "permanent public display," the cemetery in northern China expressed genealogical relationships in the positioning of individual graves, with the founding ancestor—in the form of a stone, brick, or board—at the apex of a triangle (Cohen 1990:513). Burton Pasternak (1973:272) observed that burial location and configuration among Hakka of Taiwan reflected processes of lineage fission and aggregation. Changes in burial patterns "signal[ed] departures of relevance to the development and structure of . . . descent groups as well as to the nature of relations within them."

The tendance of ancestors, whether it occurred at home, at the grave site, or in the ancestral hall, took the form of prayers and offerings (Freedman 1979 [1970]). Incense or pieces of paper representing money (Ahern 1973) or clothing (Cohen 1990:519) might be burned as offerings or rice wine and various sorts of food proffered. Pork was especially valued (Potter 1970b), though dumplings, sweets, or fruit were also used (Cohen 1990:520; see also Thompson 1988; Wolf 1974:177).

In sum, ancestor veneration and burial practices in China are marked by regional, ethnic, and temporal variation—what James L. Watson (1988b:17) has described as "chaotic local diversity" that gives "great scope for regional and subethnic cultural displays." Major variables include the location of veneration, its scale, and frequency. Recent or apical ancestors were remembered and venerated individually, while more distant ancestors joined an anonymous collectivity. The rites celebrated at the grave, ancestral hall, or shrine created powerful focal points for expressions of lineage unity or exclusivity and reflected multiple social variables, including seniority, status, wealth, and genealogical proximity to the deceased.

Rites minimally differentiated the lineage from other lineages, but could also mark membership in a specific branch, surname association, or household (Feuchtwang 1974:118). Women's roles in ancestral rites varied across China, but were often limited to domestic contexts (Freedman 1979 [1970]; R. S. Watson 1981) or were completely absent (Ahern 1973; J. L. Watson 1982b:179). Ancestors conferred good fortune on their descendants when pleased by routine rites and tendance and when their graves were well sited. In spite of regular prayer and sacrifice, however, ancestors could be punitive and capricious or their anger roused by misbehavior, bringing illness, misfortune, and death (Ahern 1973; Otake 1980; Wolf 1974). As in West Africa, descent ideology and venerative ritual in China expressed the interests of the patriline, which was constituted at multiple levels of inclusiveness. While the investiture of ritual authority and corporate control in senior males was an implicit feature of studies of Chinese ancestor veneration, Marxist anthropologists and others working in Africa and Madagascar in the 1960s and 1970s made explicit links between descent ideology, elder males, and power.

Elders and Ideologies: The Rise and Fall of African Ancestors

In the late 1960s and early 1970s, anthropologists influenced by Marxist perspectives increasingly viewed ancestors and venerative ritual as components of ideologies that naturalized inequalities within hierarchical social systems. One approach viewed ancestors as a way to legitimize the privileged position of elders in agricultural societies. Meillassoux (1981:82) noted that the "sublimation" of the father and the ancestors he represented is the primary ideological resource for an elder, who controlled both production (surplus) and reproduction (access to women). The annual growth cycle of crops and the need to store produce and seed from year to year meant that younger farmers were indebted to earlier generations—the elders and their ancestors—who had previously harvested and stored seed and surplus. Agrarian life therefore fostered an ideology of descent and a cult of the ancestors that privileged age and senior social rank. Meillassoux thereby linked the emergence of ancestor veneration with domestication (1972:99–100).

An alternative approach was provided by Friedman's reevaluation of Leach's (1954) study of the shift from an egalitarian to stratified social system among the Kachin of Burma (Myanmar). Friedman suggested that lineage heads leveraged access to ancestors in order to naturalize unequal access to resources, thereby institutionalizing social hierarchies. In short, acquisition of surplus revealed that the lineage head was descended from spirits, who favored him as descendant kin. Supernatural validation bolstered the positions of some lineage leaders and enabled them to become chiefs (Friedman 1975:172). The chief received tribute and corvée, allowing him to reinforce his authority and descent claims through redistributive feasts. Chiefs become responsible for communicating with ancestral spirits, ensuring growth and prosperity for the community. Increasing surpluses justified claims, leading, in some cases, to the development of small, stratified states on the Assam plains (1975:172–194).

The association between ideology, ancestors, and land has perhaps been most successfully articulated in Maurice Bloch's influential work on the Merina of Madagascar. The Merina built megalithic communal tombs and practiced a secondary burial ritual, the *famadihana*, that established the deceased as an ancestor. Bloch identified Merina ancestors as "some past, long dead, unspecified forebear" (1968:100) and described the process through which the Merina transformed named individuals into a "common substance" (Bloch 1982:213). This substance consisted of the collectivity of ancestors, their living descendants, and the agricultural land associated with the tomb. The *famadihana* and other rituals were part of a legitimating "ideology of descent" (1968:100) that promoted a durable, unchanging social order (Bloch 1971, 1982). That order was underpinned by the authority of elders, who acted as critical intermediaries between the living and the ancestors. Elders alone transmitted the blessings of the dead to their living descendants—without which descendants were "impotent in all senses of the word" (Bloch 1982:212).

To the Merina, blessings such as children, crops, wealth, and strength were tied to the integrity of the social group, which in turn was conceptually merged with the land and the ancestors. The monumental tomb served as the central symbol of the Merina kinship community. Located on and defining ancestral lands, the tombs represent shared substance and the regrouping, in death, of dispersed members of the kin group. Although the Merina reside throughout Madagascar, upon death, their remains are returned to their natal villages and installed in the tombs. Rituals accompany both the removal of the body from its location of temporary burial and its interment on ancestral lands, effectively reconstituting the kin group in death and symbolically expressing the antithesis of social division (Bloch 1982:213). Bloch observes that where one's ancestors are entombed is a more significant social marker than where one resides, since the tombs establish group membership and corporate rights. In sum, the Merina ideology of descent is profoundly territorial in nature; it is signaled through ritual acts and in construction of and access to communal tombs. Elders serve as intercessors in ritual between ancestors and their living descendants. By transmitting blessings, elders reinforce an ideology that links well-being with kinship and land and legitimates their authority as critical mediators between past and present (Bloch 1968, 1971).

Like Bloch, Victor Turner sought a nuanced understanding of how ritual worked within the context of sociopolitical transformations. Two issues are especially relevant to the study of ancestors: ancestor cults as markers of social difference and ritual as a means of reconstituting social structure. First, Turner understood that ritual could operate at multiple levels of inclusiveness. He suggested that ancestor cults in West and Central Africa were vehicles for identifying and highlighting the distinctiveness of a lineage or kin group. They represented sectional divisions within society and were associated with "lineage segmentation, local history,

[and] factional conflict" (Turner 1974:185). In contrast, earth cults facilitated the creation of social bonds between groups; they expressed shared values and inclusiveness.

In addition to showing how ancestor cults marked social divisions, Turner's (1969, 1974) work suggests how ritual functions *within* ancestor cults. *Communitas*, a sense of solidarity and shared experience, created through ritual enables integration of group members. In this sense, Bloch's work and Turner's are very similar: both emphasize the role of ritual in creating community and reinforcing the group membership of ritual participants. Further, the liminal feature of ritual enabled the dissolution of social relations and their reconstitution in new form. Ritual made the creation of ancestors possible and facilitated the transition of ritual practitioners from one social status to another—for example, from dependent son to lineage head. While Marxist anthropologists were studying ideologies and inequalities, other Africanists were questioning whether "ancestor" was a meaningful category and scrutinizing emic distinctions between ancestors and elders. These issues fostered a decade of debate in African anthropology.

Elders as Ancestors

On the basis of his work among the Suku of Congo, Igor Kopytoff argued that the term "ancestor" was an ethnocentric imposition by Western anthropologists on African cultures. The Suku had no word for "ancestor." Deceased lineage members were *bambuta*, which refers not only to the select deceased but to all members of the lineage older than ego, whether living or dead (Kopytoff 1971:131). Power and authority among the Suku were based on age and generation rather than strictly on descent from an ancestor. Because of their state, the dead were approached differently than the living, but "they remain in the same structural positions *vis-à-vis* their juniors" (1971:134). In his study of the term "ancestor" in Bantu languages, Kopytoff (1971:135–136) found that the word may also mean "elder," "aged," "antecedent," "long ago," "forebear," and so on. From an emic perspective, Kopytoff argued, there were no significant differences between ancestors and elders; what is perceived as "ancestral" by ethnographers is really a generational distinction.

Brain contested Kopytoff's semantic analysis. While most Bantu languages do not have words for "ancestor," they do have words for "ancestral spirit" (Brain 1973:123). While some support for Kopytoff's position existed, in that there may be semantic overlap between the categories of "ancestor" and "elder," ancestors can do things elders cannot. Deceased ancestors were aware of people's thoughts as well as their actions. Additionally, gifts to elders differed qualitatively from sacrifices to ancestors. To Brain, significant, though subtle, differences existed between "ancestors" and "elders" in practice, though those differences were not always linguistically elaborated.

Also critical of the elders-as-ancestors argument was Victor Uchendu (1976:285), who charged that, by equating the world of living elders with that of the deceased ancestors, Kopytoff "asserts a 'structural fusion' that represents the highest level of reductionism." To illustrate the issue, Uchendu described the relationship of living descendants to deceased ancestors among the Ibo of Nigeria. Ancestors were "creatures of society," subject to manipulation by the living, but also agents of moral authority who facilitated the articulation of Ibo ontology (1976:283).

Based on his study of the Sisala of northern Ghana, Eugene Mendonsa agreed with Kopytoff that "worship" as applied to activities surrounding select deceased was an inadequate term. On the other hand, he supported the use of "cult" and "sacrifice." Mendonsa pointed to a conceptual separation between the world of the living and the world of the dead ancestors, as well as a "subtle comprehension of the similarities between the two spheres" (Mendonsa 1976:63).

C. J. Calhoun (1980) responded to the linguistic analysis and called for a more comparative perspective on ancestors based on authority and power. He suggested not only that the distinction between ancestors and elders reflected the actions taken by the living, but that patterns of descent and postmarital residence affected the extent to which ancestors had power over the living. The Tallensi, for example, practiced patrilineal descent and patrilocal residence; for them, descent and residence were congruent with parental and ancestral authority. The Suku, studied by Kopytoff, practiced matrilineal descent and patrilocal residence. Residential affiliation, rather than descent, was more strongly linked with authority, and hence genealogy was of less significance. Furthermore, among the Tallensi, no living person wielded final authority. Instead, divination and other ritual practices represented collective decision-making rather than a system based simply on authority by age. To Calhoun (1980:312–313), the Tale case warranted the maintenance of the term "ancestor."

In response, Kopytoff (1981:135) noted that Tale terms, similar to those in other sub-Saharan languages, failed to distinguish between living and deceased elders. In some cases, the term for an elder spanned the living/dead divide. Comparative linguistic analysis indicated that terms translated as "living elders" and "dead ancestors" are often cognate and belong to the same semantic field (1981:136). In reply, Fortes (1981) agreed with Calhoun, noting that no ambiguity existed between living elders and deceased ancestors among the Tallensi.

This debate recalls Newell's (1976b) discussion of the variability of ancestors: not all ancestors are like Tale ancestors; the roles of ancestors vary cross-culturally and are influenced by principles of descent, postmarital residence, and degree of political centralization (e.g., Drucker-Brown 1981). The elders-as-ancestors debate highlighted the tension between the twin concepts of ancestor and elder among anthropologists and their informants, as well as the ambiguity that existed between the ancestors and elders themselves (e.g., Helms 1998).

Marginalization and Decline of African Ancestors

During the 1980s and 1990s, the number of studies focusing on ancestors in African anthropology dropped precipitously (Cole and Middleton 2001). First, there was no need to study ancestors if they were, as Kopytoff (1971) suggested, a Western fiction. On the other end of the spectrum was the idea that ancestors were universal, their omnipresence obscured by semantic distinctions between ghosts, shades, souls, spirits, and totems. According to Lyle Steadman and Craig Palmer (1996), attention to the exotic led anthropologists to create distinctions among the dead that masked broader patterns, one of which was the universality of ancestor worship. Using cross-cultural data compiled in the 1960s, they identified ancestor worship as "claims of communication between the dead and their descendants" (Steadman and Palmer 1996:63), basically a conflation of ancestors and the deceased more generally.

Ancestors were also marginalized because structural-functional approaches, which gave them primacy, were in decline. Adam Kuper's (1982) polemic against the lineage model, which up to that point had framed analyses of ancestor veneration in Africa, is cited by McCall (1995:257) as a watershed moment, as ancestors were swept away with lineages. Social structure had previously been seen as a manifestation of the ancestor cult. The shift away from structural-functionalism effectively sidelined ancestors from studies of African religion and consigned a large body of ethnographic data to the theoretical dustbin. Finally, interest in African ancestors declined as the discipline shifted toward studies of postcolonialism and change that were grounded more in history and practice than in structure and function (see also Campbell, this volume).

The ethnography of African postcolonialism focused on topics such as witchcraft, spirit possession, and Protestant Christianity (Cole and Middleton 2001:1). In many of these works, the word "ancestor" is absent, though there are a handful of exceptions. In his study of religion in Zambia, for example, George Bond (1987) described the maintenance of an ancestral cult amid Presbyterian missionization. He noted that individuals and groups used "the religious ideologies of the ancestor cult and the Free Church to promote their interests, obscuring the social changes their actions are producing in the social field" (Bond 1987:56).

In contrast, Birgit Meyer (1999) attributed the decline of ancestors among the Peki of Ghana to the effects of Christian missionaries and the attractions of capitalism. Prior to 1876, ancestor veneration by the patrilineal and patrilocal Peki was "the most common feature of people's religious life" (Meyer 1999:72). Ritual practices included prayers, libations, and the annual yam festival in honor of the ancestors. Between 1876 and 1918, however, evangelizing Protestant groups prohibited "idol-worship" and participation in "heathen ceremonies" (1999:9). Christian Peki no longer made offerings of clothing, jewelry, and cowries at the deceased's grave (1999:10). Instead, material goods became emblematic of prosperity and status in colonial society as capitalism and Christianity supplanted the Peki ancestral dead.

Glazier's investigation of changing mortuary practices among the Mbeere of Kenya linked land tenure and colonial edicts to the "domestication of death" and the emerging importance of named forebears. The Mbeere abandoned corpse exposure in the bush in favor of formal burial, Glazier suggested, because ancestors facilitated the establishment of property rights: the graves of deceased kin forged "new and socially valued links between the land and its claimants," allowing descendants in litigation to "assert continuity in a particular line of descent and the territorial embodiment of that line" (Glazier 1984:144). As products of economic change, the Mbeere ways of death that Glazier documented in the 1970s marked "a new fixity in relationships between social groups and territories" (1984:145).

Return of the Ancestors: Agency, Landscape, and Power

In spite of shifts in research priorities within African anthropology, interest in African ancestors began to reemerge in the late 1990s and early 2000s. New studies integrated the historical and practice-based insights of the 1980s and 1990s, but also recognized that ancestors were alive and well in Africa, albeit often in new or altered forms. Ancestors affirmed group identity and fostered solidarity and emerged as critical variables in studies of agency, space, and power relationships.

McCall (1995), for example, highlighted the role of ancestors in memory practices among the Ibo of Nigeria. Ancestors originally cleared agricultural land and created cultural spaces from the bush. Male ancestors received sacrifices in shrines, while female ancestors were memorialized with pots embedded in the kitchen hearth. Space, material culture, and ritual acts inscribed ancestors in the household, on the landscape, and in the memories of their descendants (McCall 1995:259–262). While profoundly conscious of the importance of history, McCall recognized that the work of Fortes and other early twentieth-century African anthropologists represented part of the daily reality of many sub-Saharan Africans. Privileging one theoretical approach over the other for the sake of argument, he suggested, "diminishes our understanding of the whole" (1995:267).

The relationship between ancestors and the domestication of landscape is also a central theme in Mather's (2003, this volume) study of the patrilineal Kusasi of northern Ghana. Shrines representing founding ancestors demarcate lineage territory and signal descent and group membership (Mather 2003:35); they are maintained by senior males, responsible for sacrifices and libations. Shrine tendance may reify social norms, but the desires of ancestors are also subject to interpretation and manipulation, enabling the living to deploy them in sometimes surprising ways—for example, in support of local political candidates. Ancestors are also implicated in status and power negotiations among the Tuareg of Niger, where offerings and gift-giving establish and maintain links between the living and the dead, present and past, youth and elders (Rasmussen 2000).

In a return to Madagascar, where Bloch's (1968, 1971, 1982) influential work established the Merina in the anthropological imagination, Cole and Middleton (2001) situated ancestors within the context of twentieth-century French imperialism (see also Feely-Harnik 1991). They suggested that the appropriation of colonial symbols revived local ritual practices focused on ancestors. Ambivalent attitudes toward colonial administrators paralleled concerns with ancestors—both were dangerous beings requiring appeasement. In contrast to Bloch, who emphasized the integrative role of ancestors, Cole and Middleton (2001:31) viewed them as points of contention between indigenous groups and foreigners "precisely because they are multi-voiced, permeable, and ambivalent." In concluding this section, we find that, like Malagasy ritual, ancestors embody "multiple, mutable, and contradictory meanings" (2001:31), both to anthropologists and the people they study.

Conclusions

Marginalized in the 1980s and 1990s, the study of ancestors has proven to be extremely relevant to twenty-first-century anthropology. Elements of recent studies would be familiar to ethnographers of the last century, including the links among ancestors, social solidarity, and group identification. Recent studies have also provided a broader perspective on ancestors, including more nuanced interpretations that appreciate variables such as age, sex or gender, and relative status within a lineage. Postcolonial research has shown how ancestors are used to resist and reinterpret power relations and demonstrates that ancestors, often in new, hybrid forms, have strong opinions about politics and modernities. In defining ancestors and outlining their history in anthropology, some major themes emerge:

1. Ancestors are about power, whether social, political, religious, or economic, whether based in a single household or encompassing an entire ethnic group.
2. Ancestors are bulwarks of conservatism and resistance, yet they also shift and hybridize amid the forces of colonialism, Christianity, Islam, the state, and modernity itself.
3. Ancestors reinforce status and authority within the social group, usually that of senior members.
4. Ancestors are also manipulable, not just by elders or powerful

lineages. The care and feeding of ancestors provides an arena in which to cajole, demand, entreat, and berate them.

5. Ancestors are the conceptual domain through which elders or lineages compete, strategize, and negotiate.
6. Ancestors are conceptually tied to the landscape and reference fundamental dichotomies, such as wild/domestic or nature/culture.
7. Ancestors are directly implicated in issues of descent, inheritance, property, and access to resources.
8. Ancestors are fundamental components of individual and group identities, referencing kin groups at multiple scales (e.g., household, family, clan, lineage), as well as age and sex.
9. Ancestors are venerated at multiple scales (e.g., individual, household, lineage) within societies and cross-culturally; their routine care and tendance generate material residues.
10. Ancestors are repositories and reference points for the origins, genealogies, and memories of kin groups.

The rich ethnographic records of Africa and East Asia illustrate the extraordinary variation that exists in beliefs about ancestors and in venerative practices. In chapter 2, we address the ways in which archaeologists have approached ancestors, specifically as they relate to the above themes. In closing, we hope that both the introduction and the volume as a whole will encourage archaeologists to take ancient ancestors more seriously. Clearly not all societies peopled their universe with ancestral "ex-humans" like the Bronze Age Shang (Keightley 2001, 2004). Those that did, however, leveraged ancestors in myriad ways. Ancestors are implicated in politics, social organization, economics, ideology, religion, mortuary practices, architecture, and material culture. In short, the revered dead are critical components of the ethnographic present and archaeological past. Ancestors have a great deal to tell us, and we ignore them at our peril.

The Structure of This Volume

In part 1, we "revisit" world regions in which anthropologists have conducted particularly influential studies of ancestors: China, ancient Greece, and sub-Saharan Africa. Now-classic works on societies in these areas have provided a foundation upon which later studies on ancestors have been built. By returning to these regions and taking a fresh look at the evidence, which has been supplemented with nearly a century of subsequent research, contributors to this volume provide sophisticated interpretations of architecture, cultural landscapes, iconography, and texts.

Chapter 2 focuses on identifying ancestors in the archaeological record. We begin by reviewing the contributions of two landmark studies: *Living with the Ancestors* (McAnany 1995) and *Access to Origins* (Helms 1998). We then provide an overview of the lines of evidence that archaeologists have used to argue for the presence of ancestors in the archaeological record, including architecture and landscape, structured deposits, human remains, art and iconography, and documentary sources.

In chapter 3, Roderick Campbell looks at China, the site of some of the most influential studies of ancestors in cultural anthropology (e.g., Ahern 1973; Freedman 1958, 1966, 1967; Newell 1976a; Watson and Rawski 1988). He demonstrates the contingent nature of Chinese ancestors, showing how their meaning and use have shifted over time—from being inhabitants of a complex medieval thanatological system that involved any number of spectral threats, to the enshrinement of Mao Tse-tung's body in a postrevolutionary version of ancestor veneration. Questioning the utility of an overarching definition of ancestors, Campbell notes that the term "is a translocal placeholder for a variable set of locally constituted [social] relations."

In a case study from the Late Shang site of Anyang, Campbell examines the massive ritual deposits at the royal cemetery, which include bronze vessels, jade weapons, and thousands of human sacrificial victims. Combining the archaeological evidence with oracle bone inscriptions, Campbell suggests that Shang death ritual located ancestors within a politicized and hierarchical kinship system. Ancestors mediated the social landscape where power, status, and memory were constantly under negotiation by the living.

Carla Antonaccio's contribution (chapter 4) deals with the concept of ancestorhood among the ancient Greeks. In addition to a "shadowy collectivity" of dead just beyond the limits of human memory, Greeks of the fifth and sixth centuries BC venerated mythic heroes. In some cases, they visited and reentered ancient Bronze Age tombs in order to establish links with the past. As Antonaccio observes, mythic ancestors were "the ultimate referents for communal and regional identity."

Returning to West Africa, where British social anthropologists such as Meyer Fortes, Jack Goody, and Igor Kopytoff did so much work on ancestors in the mid-twentieth century, Charles Mather (chapter 5) contributes a sophisticated ethnoarchaeological study of ancestor shrines and domestic space among the Kusasi of northern Ghana. Mather argues that the composition and location of ancestor shrines within Kusasi residential compounds reflect and reinforce social organization and the often ambivalent nature of patrilineal and matrilineal relationships.

In part 2, four contributors explore ancestors using data derived from European, Mesoamerican, and Peruvian contexts—places not traditionally associated with ancestors in nineteenth- and twentieth-century anthropological thought. In chapter 6, Murray argues that ancestors were fundamental structuring structures in the landscapes of central Europe during the Iron Age. Taking a phenomenological approach, Murray suggests that Iron Age ancestors reinforced social norms and helped materialize kin relationships. Burial sites, tombs, and their associated features were imbued with agency and functioned as spaces in which performance and discourse occurred between ancestors and their descendants.

Following Alfred Gell, Murray proposes that landscapes existed within a sort of "ancestor time" that melded past, present, and future. He suggests that two sites in Germany, the Heuneburg and the Glauberg, functioned as "landscapes of ancestors" in which movement was choreographed to focus attention on specific tombs and monuments. Variation in grave goods and type of interments are used in conjunction with spatial analysis to identify changes in the nature of political power in Iron Age Europe.

Weiss-Krejci (chapter 7) explores how the central European House of Habsburg deployed ancestors as part of a political strategy to link both the dynasty as a whole and its individual members with the illustrious dead. Taking a liberal view of ancestorhood, Habsburgs such as Rudolph I and Maximilian I publicly visited and reused ancient burial places, intermarried with members of other dynasties in order to increase the prestige of their own, and occasionally manufactured the required genealogical documentation to bolster their kinship-based claims to royal status.

In chapter 8, Hill deals with Moche iconography from northern Peru, suggesting that women may have facilitated the transformation of sacrificial victims into offerings to the ancestral dead. She relates painted and modeled representations to archaeological evidence, arguing that ancestor veneration was a practice employed by elites to access origins and so validate their position in Moche society.

Hageman (chapter 9) identifies the creation of ancestors in imagery and changing burial patterns in Preclassic Maya farming villages. Referencing the large corpus of Maya art and epigraphy, Hageman traces the use of symbols by Classic Maya kings to appropriate ancestral powers and institutionalize and legitimize their rule through communication and physical contact with previous kings. Commoner subjects continued to revere ancestors absent a written record, but commoner ancestral symbols differed in meaning from their royal counterparts, a point with implications for our understanding of ancient Maya gender.

Acknowledgments

We thank our contributors first and foremost; without their patience and consideration, this book would not have been possible. We thank Patricia McAnany for writing the foreword. We were honored to have Tricia and Mary Helms participate in the original Society for American Archaeology (SAA) session that initiated this project. Miguel Astor-Aguilera generously shared his enthusiasm and insights on ancestors, which have informed our own work. We would also like to express our sincere appreciation to three anonymous reviewers, whose constructive recommendations strengthened the volume. Meredith Morris-Babb, former editor-in-chief John Byram, and the team at University Press of Florida have our thanks for supporting this project from the beginning and guiding us through every stage of production.

J. Hageman: Though not part of the SAA session, Charles Mather and Rod Campbell graciously agreed to represent Africa and China for this volume. Timothy Insoll kindly provided several offprints. I would also like to acknowledge the work of Patricia McAnany, which sparked my early interest in ancestors.

E. Hill: I thank Carla Antonaccio, Matthew Murray, and Estella Weiss-Krejci for their generosity and encouragement. Liz Kurtulik Mercuri, Art Resource, assisted with permissions for the cover image of "Twenty-One Ancestors." Many people kindly provided offprints or references, among them George Lau, Andy Jones, and Tim Pauketat. I am fortunate to work among such superb scholars and excellent colleagues. I am especially indebted to Jane Buikstra, who first introduced me to ancestors.

Note

1. Freedman's ethnographic work was conducted on materials from the provinces of Fujian (Fukien) and Guangdong (Kwangtung). Members of the lineages that he described identified themselves as descendants of the Tang Dynasty rather than as Han Chinese. In Guangdong, Tang is associated with Yue ethnicity and use of Cantonese.

Southeastern China experienced an influx of Han in the eighth and ninth centuries AD following the collapse of the Han dynasty and centuries of political unrest. The ongoing process of "sinicization" in the region has led to the integration of local ethnic traditions with those of the Han majority. In this chapter, we use "Chinese" in a very general sense to refer to the people in a number of different ethnic groups living in China, Taiwan, and Hong Kong.

References Cited

Ahern, Emily M.

1973 *The Cult of the Dead in a Chinese Village*. Stanford University Press, Stanford, California.

Bloch, Maurice

1968 Tombs and Conservatism among the Merina of Madagascar. *Man* 3(1):94–104.

1971 *Placing the Dead: Tombs, Ancestral Villages, and Kinship Organization in Madagascar*. Seminar Press, London.

1982 Death, Women and Power. In *Death and the Regeneration of Life*, edited by Maurice Bloch and Jonathan Parry, pp. 211–230. Cambridge University Press, Cambridge.

Bond, George C.

1987 Ancestors and Protestants: Religious Coexistence in the Social Field of a Zambian Community. *American Ethnologist* 14(1):55–72.

Brain, James

1973 Ancestors as Elders in Africa: Further Thoughts. *Africa* 43(2):122–133.

Calhoun, C. J.

1980 The Authority of Ancestors: A Sociological Reconsideration of Fortes's Tallensi in Response to Fortes's Critics. *Man* 15(2):304–319.

Clodd, Edward

1895 *Myths and Dreams*. Chatto and Windus, London.

Cohen, Myron L.

1969 Agnatic Kinship in South Taiwan. *Ethnology* 8(2):167–182.

1988 Souls and Salvation: Conflicting Themes in Chinese Popular Religion. In *Death Ritual in Late Imperial and Modern China*, edited by James L. Watson and Evelyn S. Rawski, pp. 180–202. University of California Press, Berkeley.

1990 Lineage Organization in North China. *Journal of Asian Studies* 49(3):509–534.

Cole, Jennifer, and Karen Middleton
2001 Rethinking Ancestors and Colonial Power in Madagascar. *Africa: Journal of the International African Institute* 71(1):1–37.
Drucker-Brown, Susan
1981 The Authority of Ancestors. *Man* 16(3):475–476.
Durkheim, Émile
1964 [1912] *The Elementary Forms of the Religious Life*. Translated by J. W. Swain. Allen & Unwin, London.
Feely-Harnik, Gillian
1991 *A Green Estate: Restoring Independence in Madagascar*. Smithsonian Institution Press, Washington, D.C.
Feuchtwang, Stephan
1974 Domestic and Communal Worship in Taiwan. In *Religion and Ritual in Chinese Society*, edited by Arthur P. Wolf, pp. 105–129. Stanford University Press, Stanford, California.
Fortes, Meyer
1945 *Dynamics of Clanship among the Tallensi*. Oxford University Press, London.
1949 *The Web of Kinship among the Tallensi*. Oxford University Press, London.
1959 *Oedipus and Job in West African Religion*. Cambridge University Press, Cambridge.
1961 Pietas in Ancestor Worship. *Journal of the Royal Anthropological Institute* 91(2):166–191.
1965 Some Reflections on Ancestor Worship in Africa. In *African Systems of Thought* edited by Meyer Fortes and Germaine Dieterlen, pp. 122–142. Oxford University Press for the International African Institute, London.
1976 An Introductory Commentary. In *Ancestors*, edited by William H. Newell, pp. 1–16. Mouton, The Hague.
1981 The Authority of Ancestors. *Man* 16(2):300–302.
Frazer, James G.
1913 *The Belief in Immortality and the Worship of the Dead*, vol. 1: *The Belief among the Aborigines of Australia, the Torres Straits Islands, New Guinea and Melanesia*. Macmillan, London.
1933 *The Fear of the Dead in Primitive Religion*. Macmillan, London.
1968 [1922] *The Belief in Immortality and the Worship of the Dead*, vol. 2: *The Belief among the Polynesians*. Dawsons, London.
1968 [1924] *The Belief in Immortality and the Worship of the Dead*, vol. 3: *The Belief among the Micronesians*. Dawsons, London.
Freedman, Maurice
1958 *Lineage Organization in Southeastern China*. Athlone, London.
1966 *Chinese Lineage and Society: Fukien and Kwantung*. Athlone, New York.
1967 Ancestor Worship: Two Facets of the Chinese Case. In *Social Organization: Essays Presented to Raymond Firth*, edited by Raymond Firth and Maurice Freedman, pp. 85–103. Aldine, Chicago.

1968 Geomancy. *Proceedings of the Royal Anthropological Institute of Great Britain and Ireland* 1968:5–15.

1979 [1970] Ritual Aspects of Chinese Kinship and Marriage. In *The Study of Chinese Society: Essays by Maurice Freedman*, edited by G. William Skinner, pp. 273–295. Stanford University Press, Stanford, California.

Freud, Sigmund

1918 *Totem and Taboo*. Translated by A. A. Brill. Moffat, Yard, New York.

Friedman, Jonathan

1975 Tribes, States, and Transformations. In *Marxist Analyses and Social Anthropology*, edited by Maurice Bloch, pp. 161–202. Malaby Press, London.

Friesen, Steven J. (editor)

2001 *Ancestors in Post-Contact Religion: Roots, Ruptures, and Modernity's Memory*. Harvard University Press for the Center for the Study of World Religions, Harvard Divinity School, Cambridge, Massachusetts.

Fustel de Coulanges, Numa Denis

1874 *The Ancient City: A Study on the Religion, Laws, and Institutions of Greece and Rome*. Translated by Willard Small. Lee and Shepard, Boston.

Glazier, Jack

1984 Mbeere Ancestors and the Domestication of Death. *Man* 19(1):133–147.

Gluckman[n], Max

1937 Mortuary Customs and the Belief in Survival after Death among the South-Eastern Bantu. *Bantu Studies* 11(2):117–136.

Goody, Jack

1962 *Death, Property and the Ancestors: A Study of the Mortuary Customs of the LoDagaa of West Africa*. Stanford University Press, Stanford, California.

Goossaert, Vincent, and David A. Palmer

2011 *The Religious Question in Modern China*. University of Chicago Press, Chicago.

Harrell, Stevan

1979 The Concept of Soul in Chinese Folk Religion. *Journal of Asian Studies* 38(3):519–528.

Helms, Mary W.

1998 *Access to Origins: Affines, Ancestors, and Aristocrats*. University of Texas Press, Austin.

Insoll, Timothy

2007 'Natural' or 'Human' Spaces? Tallensi Sacred Groves and Shrines and Their Potential Implications for Aspects of Northern European Prehistory and Phenomenological Interpretation. *Norwegian Archaeological Review* 40(2):138–158.

2008 Negotiating the Archaeology of Destiny: An Exploration of Interpretive Possibilities through Tallensi Shrines. *Journal of Social Archaeology* 8(3):380–404.

Janelli, Roger L., and Dawnhee Yim Janelli

1982 *Ancestor Worship and Korean Society*. Stanford University Press, Stanford, California.

Jevons, Frank Byron
1908 [1896] *An Introduction to the History of Religion*. Methuen, London.
Jordan, David K.
1999 *Gods, Ghosts, and Ancestors: Folk Religion in a Taiwanese Village*. 3rd ed. Department of Anthropology, University of California, San Diego. Electronic document, http://pages.ucsd.edu/~dkjordan, accessed 23 December 2014.
Keightley, David N.
2001 The "Science" of the Ancestors: Divination, Curing, and Bronze-Casting in Late Shang China. *Asia Major* 14(2):143–187.
2004 The Making of the Ancestors: Late Shang Religion and Its Legacy. In *Religion and Chinese Society*, vol. 1, *Ancient and Medieval China*, edited by John Lagerwey, pp. 3–64. Chinese University of Hong Kong, Hong Kong, and École Française d'Extrême-Orient, Paris.
Kendall, Laurel
1985 *Shamans, Housewives, and Other Restless Spirits: Women in Korean Ritual Life*. University of Hawaii Press. Honolulu.
Kendall, Laurel, and Griffin Dix (editors)
1987 *Religion and Ritual in Korean Society*. Institute of East Asian Studies, University of California, Berkeley.
Kopytoff, Igor
1971 Ancestors as Elders in Africa. *Africa: Journal of the International African Institute* 41(2):129–142.
1981 The Authority of Ancestors. *Man* 16(1):135–138.
1987 *The African Frontier: The Reproduction of Traditional African Societies*. Indiana University Press, Bloomington.
Kuba, Richard, and Carola Lentz
2002 Arrows and Earth Shrines: Towards a History of Dagara Expansion in Southern Burkina Faso. *Journal of African History* 43(3):377–406.
Kuper, Adam
1982 Lineage Theory: A Critical Retrospect. *Annual Review of Anthropology* 11:71–95.
Leach, Edmund
1954 *Political Systems of Highland Burma: A Study of Kachin Social Structures*. Beacon, Boston.
1966 Frazer and Malinowski: A CA Discussion. *Current Anthropology* 7(5):560–576.
Malinowski, Bronislaw
1916 *Baloma*: Spirits of the Dead in the Trobriand Islands. *Journal of the Royal Anthropological Institute of Great Britain and Ireland* 46:353–430.
Mather, Charles
2003 Shrines and the Domestication of Landscape. *Journal of Anthropological Research* 59(1):23–45.
McAnany, Patricia A.
1995 *Living with the Ancestors: Kinship and Kingship in Ancient Maya Society*. University of Texas Press, Austin.

McCall, John C.

1995 Rethinking Ancestors in Africa. *Africa* 65(2):256–270.

Meillassoux, Claude

1972 From Reproduction to Production: A Marxist Approach to Economic Anthropology. *Economy and Society* 1(1):93–105.

1981 *Maidens, Meal, and Money: Capitalism and the Domestic Economy*. Cambridge University Press, Cambridge.

Mendonsa, Eugene L.

1976 Elders, Office-Holders, and Ancestors among the Sisala of Northern Ghana. *Africa* 46(1):57–60.

Meyer, Birgit

1999 *Translating the Devil: Religion and Modernity among the Ewe in Ghana*. Edinburgh University Press for the International African Institute, Edinburgh.

Middleton, John

1960 *Lugbara Religion: Ritual and Authority among an East African People*. Oxford University Press for the International African Institute, London.

Morris, Ian

1991 The Archaeology of Ancestors: The Saxe/Goldstein Hypothesis Revisited. *Cambridge Archaeological Journal* 1(2):147–169.

Nadeau, Randall, and Chang Hsun

2003 Gods, Ghosts, and Ancestors: Religious Studies and the Question of "Taiwanese Identity." In *Religion in Modern Taiwan: Tradition and Innovation in a Changing Society*, edited by Philip Clart and Charles B. Jones, pp. 280–299. University of Hawai'i Press, Honolulu.

Naquin, Susan

1988 Funerals in North China: Uniformity and Variation. In *Death Ritual in Late Imperial and Modern China*, edited by James L. Watson and Evelyn S. Rawski, pp. 37–70. University of California Press, Berkeley.

Nelson, H.G.H.

1974 Ancestor Worship and Burial Practices. In *Religion and Ritual in Chinese Society*, edited by Arthur P. Wolf, pp. 251–277. Stanford University Press, Stanford, California.

Newell, William H. (editor)

1976a *Ancestors*. Mouton, The Hague.

1976b Good and Bad Ancestors. *In Ancestors*, edited by William H. Newell, pp. 17–29. The Hague: Mouton.

Otake, Emiko

1980 Two Categories of Chinese Ancestors as Determined by Their Malevolence. *Asian Folklore Studies* 39(1):21–31.

Pasternak, Burton

1973 Chinese Tale-Telling Tombs. *Ethnology* 12(3):259–273.

Potter, Jack M.

1970a Land and Lineage in Traditional China. In *Family and Kinship in Chinese Society*, edited by Ai-li S. Chin and Maurice Freedman, pp. 121–138. Stanford University Press, Stanford, California.

1970b Wind, Water, Bones, and Souls: The Religious World of the Cantonese Peasant. *Journal of Oriental Studies* (Hong Kong) 8(1):139–153.

Rasmussen, Susan J.

2000 Alms, Elders, and the Ancestors: The Spirit of the Gift among the Tuareg. *Ethnology* 39(1):15–38.

Smith, Robert J.

1974 *Ancestor Worship in Contemporary Japan*. Stanford University Press, Stanford, California.

Spencer, Herbert

1916 *The Principles of Sociology*, vol. 1. D. Appleton, New York.

Steadman, Lyle B., and Craig T. Palmer

1996 The Universality of Ancestor Worship. *Ethnology* 35(1):63–76.

Thompson, Stuart E.

1988 Death, Food, and Fertility. In *Death Ritual in Late Imperial and Modern China*, edited by James L. Watson and Evelyn S. Rawski, pp. 71–108. University of California Press, Berkeley.

Traphagan, John W.

2004 *The Practice of Concern: Ritual, Well-Being, and Aging in Rural Japan*. Carolina Academic Press, Durham, North Carolina.

Tsu, Timothy Y.

2000 Toothless Ancestors, Felicitous Descendants: The Rite of Secondary Burial in South Taiwan. *Asian Folklore Studies* 59(1):1–22.

Turner, Victor

1969 *The Ritual Process: Structure and Anti-Structure*. Aldine, Chicago.

1974 *Dramas, Fields, and Metaphors: Symbolic Action in Human Society*. Cornell University Press, Ithaca, New York.

Tylor, Edward B.

1958a [1871] *Primitive Culture: Researches into the Development of Mythology, Philosophy, Religion, Art, and Custom*, vol. 1: *The Origins of Culture*. Harper & Row, New York.

1958b [1871] *Primitive Culture: Researches into the Development of Mythology, Philosophy, Religion, Art, and Custom*, vol. 2: *Religion in Primitive Culture*. Harper & Row, New York.

Uchendu, Victor

1976 Ancestorcide! Are African Ancestors Dead? In *Ancestors*, edited by William H. Newell, pp. 283–304. Mouton, The Hague.

Watson, James L.

1982a Chinese Kinship Reconsidered: Anthropological Perspectives on Historical Research. *China Quarterly* 92:589–622.

1982b Of Flesh and Bones: The Management of Death Pollution in Cantonese Society. In *Death and the Regeneration of Life*, edited by Maurice Bloch and Jonathan Parry, pp. 155–186. Cambridge University Press, Cambridge.

1988a Funeral Specialists in Cantonese Society: Pollution, Performance, and Social Hierarchy. In *Death Ritual in Late Imperial and Modern China*, edited by James L. Watson and Evelyn S. Rawski, pp. 109–134. University of California Press, Berkeley.

1988b The Structure of Chinese Funerary Rites: Elementary Forms, Ritual Sequence, and the Primacy of Performance. In *Death Ritual in Late Imperial and Modern China*, edited by James L. Watson and Evelyn S. Rawski, pp. 3–19. University of California Press, Berkeley.

Watson, James L., and Evelyn S. Rawski (editors)

1988 *Death Ritual in Late Imperial and Modern China.* University of California Press, Berkeley.

Watson, Rubie S.

1981 Class Differences and Affinal Relations in South China. *Man* 16(4):593–615.

1982 The Creation of a Chinese Lineage: The Teng of Ha Tsuen, 1669–1751. *Modern Asian Studies* 16(1):69–100.

1988 Remembering the Dead: Graves and Politics in Southeastern China. In *Death Ritual in Late Imperial and Modern China*, edited by James L. Watson and Evelyn S. Rawski, pp. 203–227. University of California Press, Berkeley.

Whyte, Martin K.

1988 Death in the People's Republic of China. In *Death Ritual in Late Imperial and Modern China*, edited by James L. Watson and Evelyn S. Rawski, pp. 289–316. University of California Press, Berkeley.

Wolf, Arthur P.

1974 Gods, Ghosts, and Ancestors. In *Religion and Ritual in Chinese Society*, edited by Arthur P. Wolf, pp. 131–182. Stanford University Press, Stanford, California.

Zhou Daming

2002 The Lineage System of Fenghuang Village. *Chinese Sociology and Anthropology* 34(3):6–27.

2

The Archaeology of Ancestors

ERICA HILL AND JON B. HAGEMAN

General archaeological interest in ancestors is a relatively recent phenomenon, though the ancestral dead made an appearance as early as 1953, when Kathleen Kenyon identified Neolithic skulls from early Jericho as possibly those of venerated "tribal or family elders" whose personalities their descendants attempted to preserve through the creation of plastered likenesses (Kenyon 1954:108; Kenyon and Tushingham 1953:870). By the 1990s, ancient ancestors had undergone a veritable population explosion, prompting James Whitley to wonder whether there were simply "too many ancestors" in prehistories of the British Neolithic. Whitley (2002:124) highlighted the uncritical use of ancestors as explanations for a range of archaeological phenomena, writing that the imaginary ancestors of the past "can do anything—a spot of legitimation here, a touch of phenomenological meaning there."

Although Whitley's critique focused on ancestors in British prehistory, Americanist archaeologists have also employed ancestor veneration extensively in their reconstructions of the past. Ancestors form the foundation of corporate authority and territorial claims in contexts as varied as the Maya area (e.g., McAnany 1995), Peru (e.g., Bauer 2004; Isbell 1997), and the Eastern Woodlands (e.g., Brown 1990; Buikstra and Charles 1999; Charles and Buikstra 2002). Elsewhere, ancestors appear to represent new interpretive possibilities, as in the North American Southwest (e.g., Rakita 2009; Stinson 2005) and Teotihuacan (e.g., Headrick 2007; Manzanilla 2002).

Archaeology provides time depth to the study of ancestors—on the order of centuries or millennia—that is simply not available to ethnographers and shows how ancestor-oriented ritual and belief changed prior to the influence of Western colonialism. Archaeology can also illuminate the practices of those people left out of historical narratives, such as women and members of subaltern, rural, and lower-class groups. Ancestor-related ritual and belief may be identified in the same ways that archaeologists have proposed for the study of memory (Mills and Walker 2008; Van Dyke and Alcock 2003) and in reconstructing relationships with the dead more generally (Parker Pearson 1993). Nevertheless, "ancestors" and "the dead" are not equivalent terms.

As we see it, research on ancestors in archaeology has been plagued by two closely related problems. One is the expansive use of the term "ancestor" to include the dead in general, as opposed to a select subset of the deceased. The other is the failure to define terms. As discussed in chapter 1, who may become an ancestor varies cross-culturally. While we do not endorse a single, all-encompassing definition of "ancestor," we do advocate (1) the restricted use of the term to refer to a select category of deceased and (2) a definition or description of what constitutes an ancestor within the particular region or society under study.

In this chapter, we review the contributions of two landmark studies: *Living with the Ancestors* (McAnany 1995) and *Access to Origins* (Helms 1998). McAnany and Helms moved the study of ancestors beyond the processual insights of Saxe-Goldstein and laid the conceptual foundations for the more nuanced and ethnographically informed work of the twenty-first century. We then review the ways in which archaeologists have identified and studied ancient ancestors in China and Europe. Two other key world regions, Mesoamerica and the Andes, are dealt with elsewhere in this volume (i.e., Hageman, Hill). Finally, we outline the archaeological evidence that has been used to identify ancestors in the archaeological record and to reconstruct the roles of ancestors in past societies. These lines of evidence include funerary remains, archaeological features and landscapes, representational imagery, and documentary sources.

Critical Concepts in the Archaeology of Ancestors

As an archaeological concept, ancestors have their roots in the study of cemetery structure by processual archaeologists. Perhaps the most widely known reference linking the deceased with access to resources was the dissertation of Arthur Saxe (1970). Saxe evaluated eight cross-cultural hypotheses regarding the social implications of mortuary practices against ethnographic data from West Africa, New Guinea, and the Philippines. The eighth hypothesis is the one most relevant to the archaeology of ancestors. In Hypothesis 8, Saxe stated that, to the degree that crucial but restricted resources are accessible through lineal descent, social groups will maintain formal disposal areas (cemeteries, charnel houses, or mortuary structures) for their dead (1970:119). When a resource is scarce or access is competitive, the dead will be buried in cemeteries spatially associated with that resource. Thus burials, property, and inheritance are explicitly linked in Saxe's formulation.

Lynne Goldstein (1976, 1981) refined Saxe's hypothesis, suggesting that if a permanent bounded area for the dead exists, it likely represents a corporate group with rights to resources handed down lineally. The more formal and structured the disposal area, the greater the likelihood that the cemetery was linked to a corporate group (Goldstein 1976:60–61, 1981). The deceased members of the group were interred in formal, bounded areas maintained by their descendants, who were therefore indebted to them for access to land and other resources.

Building on the foundations established by Saxe and Goldstein, archaeologists in the 1990s began to explore ancestors as an explicit archaeological concept (e.g., Antonaccio 1995; McAnany 1995; Morris 1991). Carla Antonaccio sought the Greek origins of veneration of heroes and ancestors in Bronze and Iron Age cemeteries, where she documented reentry and reuse of tombs as well as evidence of feasting and libations. She argued that mythic heroes were a select subset of ancestors who were "remembered, respected, feared, and invoked" (Antonaccio 1995:1). Veneration occurred at altars, shrines, and tombs (see also de Polignac 1995:140–142; Whitley 2001:152–153). The Greek record, like that of Neolithic and Shang China, indicates that the form and frequency of interaction with ancestors were fluid phenomena that varied with social complexity, political organization, and ideological concerns.

Ian Morris (1991) focused on the ideological components of the manipulation of the dead in his application of the Saxe-Goldstein hypothesis to classical Greece and Rome. Citing Ahern (1973) and Glazier (1984), he found no consistent relationship among bounded disposal areas for the dead, ancestral rites, and land tenure. Instead, he argued that the dead were manipulated to resolve conflicts over power and property, with mortuary ritual providing an arena for negotiation (Morris 1991:156, 161–163). Morris concluded that the Saxe-Goldstein hypothesis, while broadly applicable, simplified the relationship between formal cemeteries and property, obscuring ideological motivations and political maneuvering. Links among corporate groups, the deceased, property, and ideology have been intensively explored in two landmark publications on ancestors: in Mesoamerica by Patricia McAnany (1995) and in comparative perspective by Mary Helms (1998).

Ancestors, Kinship, and Kingship

In *Living with the Ancestors*, McAnany (1995) examined the interrelated phenomena of ancestor veneration, lineage, and kingship among the Maya. Following Fortes, she distinguished ancestor veneration from a "cult of the dead," with ancestral spirits "standing for ritual validation of lineage ancestry and for mystical intervention in human affairs" (Fortes 1987:72 cited in McAnany 1995:11). Ancestors are defined as "a select subgroup of a population who were venerated by name because particular resource rights and obligations were inherited through them by their descendants" (McAnany 1995:161). McAnany argued that ancestors played key roles in the organization of society, rights to resources, and the development and institutionalization of social inequalities. Ancestors defined social group membership by descent and were linked to a specific locality through the creation of a "genealogy of place" (1995:99). Lineages formed the structural "glue" that held an intensive agricultural system together (1995:84–86, 91–96); the lineage leader ("he of the burden of the land") (1995:117) organized production and collected tribute. Patrilineal ancestors were of greatest importance in determining lineage membership, with matrilineal ancestors relevant only among the nobility (1995:24).

Regardless of socioeconomic status, ancestor veneration included feasting, domestic rituals, bloodletting and sacrifice, and the creation of material representations of progenitors. Among the nobility, texts and iconography on pottery, wood, and stone were used to record the ritual acts of ancestors and the genealogies of their descendants (McAnany 1995:31–49). Ancestors were buried either in residential contexts or in nonresidential structures, such as pyramids. Such parallel practices are reminiscent of Chinese veneration of ancestors in both the home and the ancestral hall (Freedman 1958:85, 1979 [1970]). These locations facilitated interaction between the Maya, their ancestors, and the cosmologically charged places in which the latter were interred (McAnany 1995:50–52).

The genesis of Maya ancestor veneration was among Formative or Preclassic (1000 BC–AD 250) agrarian commoners (McAnany 1995:53). At the site of K'axob, Belize, burial patterns shifted from extended to seated or flexed with preferential interment in low buildings that were reopened and renovated to deposit additional deceased, ornaments, and vessels. These building episodes and ritual practices represent the "progressive sacralization of place at K'axob" (1995:55). Refurbishing, repeated ritual use, interment of the bodies of the deceased, and deposition of votive objects are the "material residue of the intergenerational transmission of resource entitlements" (1995:99) that created physical links between the lineage and the land. Over time—centuries in some cases—lineage members established property rights to "exclusionary tracts with inherited entitlements" (1995:65). McAnany suggested that the Maya practice of remodeling residential complexes is indicative of descent rights and the process of inheritance, such that stratigraphic sequences of burial, structure renovation, and dedicatory deposits reflected genealogical sequences (1995:65–66, 161).

As in China, ancestors were the conceptual basis of social inequalities within and between lineages. The interment of ancestors expressed the principle of "first occupancy" and facilitated the development of large, powerful lineages that dominated high-quality land at the expense of smaller, weaker lineages (McAnany 1995:112–113). Inequalities within lineages are reflected in residential architecture and in burials—similar to the ways in which elaboration of ancestral halls and grave sites materialized differences between Chinese lineages.

McAnany argued that, from the Late Preclassic into the Classic (AD 250–900) period, ancestors were key to the transformation of the Lowland Maya from a relatively egalitarian, agrarian society to one dominated by divine kings. Ancestor veneration was appropriated by a few and sacralized, emplaced, and politicized in order to sanction elite power and authority. Evidence for this can be found in Classic Maya iconography and texts. Agrarian images of inheritance and regeneration, often featuring maize, appear in carved public monuments (Taube 2004:76). Classic texts describe elite bloodlines and marriages and often link the royal line with mythic creators (McAnany 1995:127–130). Royal lineages thus mobilized iconography and text, in addition to ritual practices in monumental public shrines, to establish authority. Image, genealogy, ritual, and place were all used to naturalize the relationship between ancestors and political office.

In sum, ancestors—both royal and commoner—figured prominently in the trajectory of ancient Maya society. This subset of the deceased linked descendants with rights to agricultural land through ritual action and the creation of sacred space. In so doing, inequalities within and between lineages emerged, as indicated by placement of the deceased, burial furniture marked with cosmologically significant imagery, and structure size and quality. Later, elites co-opted practices and beliefs surrounding ancestors to legitimize kingly power. They adapted agrarian imagery from commoner sources and structured domestic architecture and ritual practice in ways that differed profoundly from earlier forms. Kingship is therefore not "kinship writ large" (*sensu* Sanders and Webster 1988). Kings actually worked at cross-purposes to lineages to "establish hegemony over kinship" (McAnany 1995:143) by linking themselves to a divine moral order.

Ancestors, Affines, and Aristocrats

Mary Helms dealt with many of the same issues that McAnany considered—ancestors and elites, property and authority, lineage and legitimation—in an explicitly cross-cultural context. For Helms, ancestors, aristocrats, and affines are all ontological "others": aristocrats are "affinal outsiders" and living ancestors (Helms 1998:9). Each embodies cosmological origins, inherent inequalities, and the potential to establish hierarchies and institutionalize rights to labor and resources. Ancestors are either "rather distant beings related to the [social group] in a context of original or prior origins . . . or . . . specific named dead of the [social group] who are remembered as having achieved exceptional socially significant goals while still physically alive" (1998:35). Cross-culturally, what is considered to be "socially significant" varies. Helms (1998:36) cited ethnographic work in Africa and elsewhere in identifying necessary—but not sufficient—criteria for ancestorhood, such as successful parenthood, high moral standards, status as firstborn, experience of a "good" death, strength of character, and wisdom or esoteric knowledge.

Helms defined two types of ancestors: emergent and first principle. Emergent ancestors are "intangible beings associated with past time relative to the house" (i.e., lineage). They are emergent in the sense that they have "grown out" of the living membership of a lineage, a "temporal elaboration of the house" (Helms 1998:37–38). Emergent ancestors require service and obedience, and in return they provide good fortune and abundance for their descendants. Like some Chinese ancestors (Ahern 1973; Otake 1980; Wolf 1974), emergent ancestors can cause misfortune for their living descendants when ritual obligations are neglected. This paternalistic model of ancestor-descendant relations shares features with some of the classic African ethnographies on ancestors (e.g., Fortes 1959, 1965; Goody 1962).

The second form of ancestor refers to cosmological conditions of creation, or first principles. Similar to a founding ancestor (Kopytoff 1987; McCall 1995), first principle ancestors are associated with primordial origins; they may be immigrants from far away, like the "foreigners" described by Cole and Middleton (2001), or live in some distant cosmological locale. In some cases, places of origin may actually be located on the landscape and sacralized (Helms 1998:38–39); they are often salient features, such as rivers, mountains, caves, and lakes (1998:77–79). In contrast to emergent ancestors, who derive from lineage members, first-principle ancestors precede the lineage temporally. First-principle ancestors are also typically nurturing or bountiful, unlike the more capricious recently deceased (1998:42). Helms links first principle ancestors with the emergence of aristocracy; such ancestors provide aristocrats with privileged "access to origins" that legitimate their authority. By co-opting cosmological origins, aristocrats set themselves apart from commoners. As members of a superior social group that exists outside of and beyond the mundane, aristocrats are, in effect, living ancestors relative to the populace at large (Kopytoff 1971). In preindustrial societies, this model of social relations is predicated on the widespread belief that hierarchy and inequality are inherent in the structure of the cosmos (Helms 1998:95–99).

As cosmological others, aristocrats are distinguished by prescriptions and taboos that simultaneously deny their ordinariness while highlighting their qualitative superiority. These include freedom from manual labor, sexual and dietary restrictions, untouchability, and sumptuary laws (Helms 1998:109–120). As living ancestors, aristocrats stabilize their social and cosmological positions by representing themselves as part of the permanent order of the universe. They project "tangible durability" and the longevity of the lineage using heirlooms, skeletal remains, pelts, feathers, bones, and teeth of select animals, and potent minerals, shells, and metals. These items signify access to origins, and their accumulation enhances the tangibility of living "ancestorness" (1998:164–166).

Both McAnany (1995) and Helms (1998) viewed ancestors as powerful social, economic, and cosmological agents who legitimize hierarchy and link lineages to resources. McAnany focused on the relationship between ancestors and land claims, illustrating how ritual practice, caches, shrines, and pyramid construction sacralize space and materialize property claims. Among the nobility, human remains, texts, iconography, and monumental tombs placed lineage members within a divine social order that existed beyond the (mundane) bounds of kinship. Helms's comparative work complements McAnany's case study through an exploration of the mechanics of the divine social order upon which elites depend. In her view, elites construct themselves as "living ancestors" by establishing links to cosmological origins. Through the mobilization of durable markers of "otherness," elites claim divine sanction and stabilize emerging hierarchies. Helms's distinction between emergent and first principle ancestors highlights the versatile nature of the concept, which permits elites to mobilize lineage antecedents to serve multiple purposes. While McAnany's work outlined the historical particulars of Maya ancestor veneration, Helms describes some of the markers of ancestor/otherness that archaeologists worldwide may employ to identify ancestors or test hypotheses. For Helms, certain rituals and objects possess "tangible durability"; they "embody various mystical powers and, by their durability, keep these powers available, controlled, and harnessed" (1998:165). Below, we identify some of the artifacts, features, texts, and imagery that social groups have used to convey ideas about ancestors, origins, and the primordial past.

Ancient Ancestors in China and Europe

The Archaeology of Ancestors in China

Anthropologists and historians working in China have produced some of the most sophisticated studies of ancestor worship from any world region, providing diachronic perspectives and detailing the ways in which ritual practices vary across time and space (Rawson 1999; Thorp 1980). Archaeological evidence indicates that ancestor veneration in China developed over several thousand years, beginning as a collective ritual among egalitarian groups during the Neolithic circa 4500 BCE (Liu 2000; Yao 2013) and evolving into a highly institutionalized elite practice through the Late Shang (1200–1045 BCE) (Keightley 2004; Nelson 2003) and Zhou (1045–771 BCE) (Vogt 2012).

Liu Li analyzed burial patterns at several sites in the Yellow River valley, focusing on sacrificial activities near burials. Liu (2000:157) considered a general "cult of the dead" and formal ancestor veneration to be two forms of funerary ritual focused on ancestors rather than qualitatively different phenomena. At the site of Longgangsi (4500 BC), 168 burials were surrounded by 150 ash pits filled with carbonized organics, presumably the remains of sacrificial offerings. Liu (2000:138) interprets this as evidence that collective rites conducted by one or more lineages were dedicated both to individuals and to the deceased as a group. Collective secondary burial had developed by the fifth millennium BC in some regions, which Keightley (1998:780) sees as an extension of mortuary concerns beyond death and indicative of a "commemorative cult of the dead."

During the succeeding Shijia phase of the Yangshao culture (4300–4000 BCE), remains of males began to receive differential ritual elaboration, likely in association with patrilocal residence. As Liu notes (2000:144), women "were the first group to be alienated in mortuary practices through which the dead were transformed into ancestors." At the cemetery of Yangshan in Qingha (2600–2300 BCE), associated with the Majiayao culture, Liu identifies the veneration of selected dead based on the contents of three tombs and their spatial association with sacrificial pits. The men in these tombs were buried with drums—symbols of ritual authority—and were honored with offerings. At Yangshan, individuals, rather than groups, became the focus of veneration and, for the first time, "religious and political authority [became] intertwined with the ancestral cult" (Liu 2000:150).

Finally, the Chengzi cemetery (2500–2000 BC), associated with the Longshan culture, exhibits clear evidence of social stratification. The largest and most elaborate interments are fewest in number and spatially distinct; they contain adult males and are associated with pits containing burned pig bones, ceramic vessels, and stone and bone objects. The Chengzi burials link hierarchy with ancestor veneration, a pattern that became institutionalized during the Late Shang period (Liu 2000:152–157). At Chengzi, kin-based veneration of select prestigious ancestors

Figure 2.1. Bronze altar set of thirteen vessels used by Shang and Zhou elites to offer libations to ancestors. The set includes distinctive vessel forms, such as the tripodal *jue* (second from left, with spout) and the long-stemmed *gu* (center, at base of the altar). Used to warm and serve wine, the *jue* and *gu* are the most commonly encountered Shang ritual vessels. These vessels had ceramic counterparts that were used in the graves of those of lower status (Campbell, this volume). See Chengyuan (1980) and Thorp (1980) on bronze vessel forms. © Metropolitan Museum of Art (acc. no. 24.72.1–14), Munsey Fund, 1931.

is consistent with the model described by Fortes (1987) and McAnany (1995); however, in Liu's view (2000:157), Longshan-style ancestor worship represents a late and fully developed form of venerative ritual that originated as early as 4500 BC in the collective rites at Longgangsi.

By the Late Shang period, inscriptions on oracle bones and bronzes indicate that ancestor veneration had become a privileged practice and legitimation strategy used by royalty and other elites (figure 2.1). The elaborate rituals manifested elite efforts to avoid calamity and ensure prosperity; they validated a particular worldview and the place of the Shang within it (Allan 1991; Campbell, this volume; Keightley 2004:29; see also Helms 1998:109–120 for a comparative perspective). As Keightley (2001:186) has observed, the Shang were "craftsmen of ancestral order." Such order involved highly structured venerative and divinatory rituals that reinforced elite hierarchies and emerging bureaucratic institutions

(Keightley 1998). Shang rulers accessed selected ancestors as individuals through posthumous "temple names" (Chen 1996) and through offerings at tombs (Allan 1991), which included wine, food, and human sacrifices (Thorp 1980:56–57). Ancestorhood was achieved, as "certain dead were assigned jurisdictions on the basis of their generational, gender, and dynastic status" (Keightley 2004:27). These ancestors coexisted with an older, undifferentiated, and depersonalized assemblage of the dead who received offerings and appeals in a more general way.

The Chinese archaeological and historical evidence provide immense time depth to the study of ancestor veneration. When combined with recent ethnographic work, the record extends back some six millennia, to 4500 BCE, when rites conducted in cemeteries honored the collective dead (Keightley 1998; Liu 2000; Yao 2013). Through time, venerative rites were celebrated by ever smaller, more exclusive kin groups and were dedicated to fewer and fewer deceased until, during the Late Shang and Zhou, royalty devoted rites to a mere handful of named ancestors. The early history of Chinese ancestor worship bears similarities to the Maya trajectory, in which private domestic ritual shifted to public arenas, and small-scale rites became monumental performances (McAnany 1995). A similar long-term trend is evident in the Andes (DeLeonardis and Lau 2004; Hastorf 2003; Lau 2008; Mantha 2009). As with the Shang, Zhou, and Maya, ancestors and their veneration became resources that elites used to "embody the potency and authority of origins" and establish their "cosmological credentials" (Helms 1998:74). Chinese relations with the ancestral dead were diverse and dynamic; beginning in the Neolithic, they involved routine graveside sacrifices. During the Bronze Age, Shang and Zhou ancestor ritual expanded to include formalized divinatory appeals and bronze vessel displays in temple contexts as well as elaborate sacrificial offerings at elite tombs.

The Archaeology of Ancestors in Europe; or, Too Many Ancestors?

The Neolithic was a critical period for the development of ancient societies' interest in ancestors. Like Liu in China, archaeologists in the United Kingdom have suggested that the earliest ancestor-oriented rituals and beliefs emerged in tandem with Neolithic shifts in the treatment of the dead and engagement with the landscape beginning about 4000 BC. Since the mid-1980s, British archaeologists (e.g., Bradley 1984) have implicated ancestors in ritual practices, construction technologies, monuments and tombs, and the enculturation of landscapes. John Barrett's work (1988, 1990, 1994), in particular, has focused on how relationships between the living, the dead, and the ancestors shifted from the Neolithic to Bronze Age. During the Neolithic (4000–2500 BC), communion with ancestors occurred at megalithic tombs; reentry and manipulation of human skeletal remains created "heavily reworked symbolic residues" that expressed community values and materialized social distinctions (Barrett 1990:183). As corporate monuments, tombs provided places where the remains of ancestors could be used to structure and sanction relations among living descendants. These practices declined between the third and second millennium BC in favor of individual burial. Instead of ongoing venerative rites in which bodies were disarticulated and bones were arranged or removed, Bronze Age mourners ended their interactions with the deceased at interment (Barrett 1994).

Building upon Barrett's work, Julian Thomas (1988, 1996) situated Neolithic human remains within the performative context of the tomb. He suggested that identity, power, and authority were constituted through access to and enaction of rituals such as feasting, skeletal disarticulation, and body part circulation. Deposition and relocation of human remains represented control over the "symbolic universe" of the tomb (Thomas 1990:175). Physical closeness to the ancestors was transformed into social authority and legitimized emerging inequalities (Thomas 1988:556–557). The corpses themselves were critical to Neolithic ritual practice. Disarticulation and manipulation of remains dissolved the person and re-created him or her as an ancestor. These transformations entered bones into circulation as inalienable possessions; they were then moved, exchanged, and deposited across the landscape (Thomas 2000:662). Lucas (1996) developed some of these ideas, arguing that bones, bearing ancestral potency, were part of a gift-based ritual economy in Late Neolithic Yorkshire. Through the process of "ancestralisation," ties with the living were severed as the bodies of selected dead were disarticulated and processed within chambered tombs. The eventual removal of these bones from the tomb completed the transition of the deceased into an ancestor and integrated him or her into a new set of social relationships and obligations.

The shift to single, primary burial stopped this "flow" of human bodily substances, creating ancestors "fixed in space and time" (Thomas 2000:664–665). Thomas argues that the new burial practices highlighted specific ancestors in a Late Neolithic context in which personal identity was constituted less through group affiliation than through life history and descent. Abandonment of communal tombs and the end of the circulation of ancestors' bones reflected a new relationship with the dead. Descendants emphasized burial ritual, rather than ongoing veneration, and identified with a line of known ancestors who could be precisely located.

Many of the ideas developed by Barrett, Thomas, and others appeared in the burgeoning literature on the phenomenology of landscape in the 1990s. Neolithic and Bronze Age monuments, cemeteries, and landscapes were (re)interpreted in terms of "ancestral geographies" (Edmonds 1999). Stonehenge and Avebury, for example, figured as lithicized realms of the ancestral dead (Parker Pearson and Ramilisonina 1998). Materials such as stone were conceptualized in structural terms, as analogous to the bones of ancestors; structures, axes, and ceramic temper were thus imbued with "symbolic and ancestral significance" (Parker Pearson 2000:208). Mythic places where ancestors had emerged, imprinted themselves, or petrified dotted the Neolithic landscape (Tilley 1994; Tilley and Bennett 2001), prompting James Whitley to ask whether there were "too many ancestors" in British prehistory. He observed that "ancestors are everywhere, and everything is ancestral" (Whitley 2002:122), arguing that ancestors had become the default explanation for diverse phenomena without sufficient consideration of alternatives (cf. Whittle et al. 2007). He attributed the "obsession" with Neolithic ancestors (2002:121) in part to inappropriate and implicit African, Asian, and Malagasy analogies. In Whitley's view, appropriation and reuse of monuments—often associated with ancestor veneration—may be explained just as effectively through reference to beliefs about mythic beings, earlier races, gods, or heroes. His point was that "the universal ancestor has gone from being a suggestion to becoming an orthodoxy without [suffering] the indignity of being treated as a mere hypothesis" (2002:119). Whitley (2002:121–122) made three points critical to the study of ancient ancestors: (1) "ancestor" must be defined; (2) ancestorhood is an achieved status reserved for the select dead; and (3) burial and venerative rites are often both conceptually and spatially distinct. Therefore, rituals conducted at the site of interment may not represent ancestor worship.

Our review of the ethnographic literature in chapter 1 strongly supports Whitley's three assertions, as do the studies by McAnany (1995) and Helms (1998). Like Whitley, we advocate definition of the term "ancestor" and its restricted use, given the overwhelming evidence that who becomes an ancestor varies in time and space.

Archaeological Lines of Evidence for Ancestors

Archaeological evidence for ancestors generally involves materializing relations with selected dead through ritual and deployment of their physical remains. The bones and body parts of ancestors thus function as "natural symbols" (Douglas 1996) of the time depth and durability of lineage claims to land and resources. Among the Maya, as McAnany (1995) demonstrated, such durability was expressed through genealogies, iconography, ritual practice, monumental architecture, and spatial relationships. The intimate bond between ancestors and the land may be manifested in archaeological features, such as shrines or structured deposits, and in landscape modifications that naturalize and reify relationships between the living and the dead. Ancestors themselves may be represented on painted pottery, in rock art, or in sculptural form. Finally, ethnohistories, such as the reports of Spanish chroniclers, provide firsthand accounts of ancestors in action and the rituals that sustained them. Arguments for ancestors are most effective when multiple lines of evidence are employed. The forms of material culture that archaeologists have used to identify ancient ancestors include

1. mortuary remains, such as graves, burial furniture, bodies, and body parts;
2. shrines, features, and structured deposits;
3. architecture, monuments, and enculturated landscapes;
4. symbols, images, and essences;
5. and documentary sources, especially ethnohistories.

Below, we distinguish between categories of material culture and archaeological features for heuristic purposes; however, in practice, these categories overlap. For example, a feature, such as a human interment, may also be part of a monument and situated meaningfully upon the landscape.

Mortuary Remains

Preservation of the entire body through mummification, as among the Inca, creates an enduring ancestral presence and material focus for memorial practices at multiple scales. Individual body parts, especially skulls, may fulfill similar functions when recovered from primary burial contexts, curated, and displayed (Armit 2012; Arnold and Hastorf 2008; Chacon and Dye 2007; Duncan and Hofling 2011; Hill 2006; Houston et al. 2006; Needham 1976; Walter et al. 2004; Wright 1988). As mnemonic devices, bones may recall individual ancestors or, when deposited in ossuaries or other collective contexts, refer to lineage ancestors in more general and generic terms.

Evidence of curation and manipulation of the remains of the deceased is suggestive of ancestor-focused ritual referencing origins (Helms 1998:170–171), as is the practice of reopening or reentering tombs (Antonaccio 1995), what Isbell (1997:139) has termed the "open sepulcher." The provision of food offerings or libations following interment may also be indicative of ancestor ritual. However, such rites must be distinguished from funerary ritual itself. The mere provision of offerings is insufficient evidence of ancestor ritual, since the inclusion of food or beverages is a common practice cross-culturally when interring or disposing of the dead. Fortes's emphasis on "ritual service and tendance" (1965:124) is especially relevant, as this facet of ancestor worship involves ongoing patterned actions discernible archaeologically. Such service may be an exclusive practice associated with specific graves (Liu 2000) or be directed toward a larger subset of the deceased.

Rakita (2009:150) explored the curation of human bone at Casas Grandes, northern Mexico. He suggested that curation extends the liminal period between primary and secondary burial, enabling kin to develop and maintain their relationships with these powerful "others." Among elites, the remains of ancestors and their ritual manipulation provided powerful symbols of a connection with cosmological forces. Rakita's work highlighted the importance of liminality in ancestor ritual and, following Hertz (1960), suggested that the condition of the body and its parts reflect the condition of the soul and mourners (see also Rakita and Buikstra 2005).

Nineteenth-century funerals of Maori chiefs also involved the display of elite ancestors' bones that had been polished and kept in baskets as sacred relics (Fletcher 2000:24). Human bones are similarly potent among the Kwaio of the Solomons, where the skulls of some deceased men were exhumed several months after death, adorned with shell rings, and lashed with vines (Walter et al. 2004). The skulls are curated in ancestor shrines, the ancestral "skull house," or deposited in caves and fissures associated with specific kin groups (Keesing 1982:157, 175). Pig sacrifices take place at the shrines on altar-like "ovenstones." The arrangement of ovenstones constitutes a "physical map of the ancestral universe of a particular descent group" (1982:87). At a regional scale, "founding" shrines reify the establishment of territory; branch shrines mark subsequent settlements.

Although human bone is an especially potent material expression of ancestorhood, human remains themselves are neither necessary nor sufficient evidence of venerative beliefs and rituals. The Inca, for example, preferred to direct appeals and offerings to ancestors in the form of mummies; however, when the actual bodies of the deceased were unavailable, they employed proxy representations. Multiple cross-cultural examples of ancestors in lithified form (Lau 2008; MacCormack 1991:191–193) also demonstrate that absence of human remains is not necessarily absence of ancestors.

Shrines, Features, and Structured Deposits

Venerative rites, whether directed at the skeletal remains of an ancestor, an effigy, or some other object representing the deceased, may produce "structured deposits" (Bradley 2000; Hill 1995, 1996), like the spatially salient Kwaio shrines. Such deposits are patterned accumulations of ritual detritus of "service and tendance"; they are features usually associated with specific elements of the human skeleton or selected animal taxa, soils (e.g., Charles et al. 2004; Pauketat 2008), distinctive configurations of artifacts (e.g., Stahl 2008; Walter et al. 2004) representing offerings, or the residue of sacrifice, libations, or feasts (e.g., Dietler and Hayden 2001; Lau 2002; Nelson 2003). Such features may nevertheless be difficult to identify archaeologically for several reasons. First, the materials they contain may be indistinguishable from domestic refuse, as those species or artifacts used as offerings or to feast the ancestors may overlap with foods and objects in routine or daily use. Second, the remains of ritual acts, such as animal sacrifice, may be consumed or dispersed and so disappear from the record (Insoll 2007b). Third, deposits or features, such as shrines, may be located beyond the bounds of camps, settlements, or cemeteries and take apparently "natural" forms, such a fissures or groves.

Rather than attempting to define what a "shrine" is *a priori*, we advocate an emic perspective on what constitutes a shrine. Ethnographic accounts have shown that the venerative locus may be considered a place of ancestral residence and, at the same time, an instantiation of the ancestor. Shrines may mark the establishment of new territory (Keesing 1982) or embody the entire history of a lineage (Kuba and Lentz 2002). As Middleton (1960) has demonstrated for the Lugbara, shrine forms are highly diverse and may be dedicated to ancestors who are matrilineal, patrilineal, apical, or childless. Shrines may be pots, effigies, mounds, monumental edifices, or natural objects, such as trees, which do not fit comfortably within any single category of archaeological evidence (Mather, this volume). As Insoll (2007b:329) has observed among the Tallensi, shrines exist "in a bewildering range of configurations."

Shrines to different types of ancestors—matrilineal versus patrilineal, for example—may be distinguished by the sort of offerings provided and by location; they may be constructed under granaries, under verandas, or within the hedges of the family compound. Structurally, shrines may be domestic affairs incorporating the bones of the deceased (Hageman, this volume; McAnany 1995:100–101); small, "cocoon-like" structures or flat stones (Middleton 1960:52); wooden effigies eaten by termites (Goody 1962:389); or concentrations of specific objects, such a gun flints, beads, and python bones, beyond the bounds of habitation sites (Stahl 2008).

The Lugbara terms for shrines include the words for "house" or "territory" (Middleton 1960: 54). The idea of the shrine as house is a critical point since, as Helms notes (1998:15), "house" may refer simultaneously to a physical structure and, following Lévi-Strauss (1987), to a social entity or corporate group. The house is therefore both material and immaterial, perpetuated physically through land, structures, and objects and conceptually through inheritance of its name, wealth, and entitlements (Helms 1998:15). As discussed above, Fortes (1949:329, 1965:128–129, 1976:7) suggested that the "reincorporation" of the deceased into the social group as an ancestor was made tangible to the living through shrines, which symbolized the unity and corporate identity of lineage members (Fortes 1945:55). In other words, conceptualizing the shrine as a house conveys ideas about both kinship and genealogical and spatial proximity. Shrines and similar features are therefore highly salient in terms of their structure, location, and contents, though they may not be immediately recognizable as ritual loci.

For example, among the Tallensi, shrines may be landscape features, such as a grove of trees. Such trees appear to be "natural" spaces, but are actually cosmologically potent places sacralized through sacrifice, prayer, and offerings. Prohibitions regulate their use, making them analogous to anthropogenic forests. A Tallensi shrine may also be a small household feature, such as a pot containing artifacts associated with a deceased family member (Insoll 2007a:141). In one abandoned house, Insoll (2008:390) found a paternal shrine—a pot partially embedded in the mud platform of the building containing objects associated with the life of the deceased, including coins, cowry shells, blue plastic twine, a razor blade holder, a copper bell, bracelets, and a polished pebble. Such objects assist in the negotiation of a descendant's identity through the ancestors (2008:386) and demonstrate that the contents of structured deposits may be as varied as the form of the feature itself.

Animal remains, like human remains, are common components of structured deposits. They may be efficacious animal parts or represent sacrificial offerings or the remains of a feast. Assemblages may include salient wild taxa, such as python (Stahl 2008) or red deer (Sharples 2000), or domesticates familiar as foodstuffs. Fortes (1945:98) noted that "the selection of the [sacrificial] animal depends on a multiplicity of factors, such as the relative importance of the shrine at which it is offered, the importance of the occasion, the status of the suppliant, or the group offering the sacrifice." Distinctions between wild and domestic taxa appear to be similarly significant. Ancestors in Shang China (Liu 2000) and Oceania (Keesing 1970, 1982) preferred pigs, while Andean ancestors favored llamas (Lau 2002). Red deer, however, may have been the desired feast food in Neolithic Orkney, amid social transformations that fundamentally altered human engagement with animals and the landscape (Jones 1998; Jones and Richards 2003; Sharples 2000).

Finally, the disproportionate presence of specific vessel forms found in association with shrine or burial features is consistent with making offerings to or feasting ancestors. Hageman (2004), for example, found that middens associated with rural residences containing shrines in northwestern Belize had a dramatically higher frequency of food preparation and serving vessels than middens in non-shrine, domestic contexts. Dulanto (2002) found the highest counts of small decorated bottles amid offering and burial pits under patios at Pampa Chica, Peru. In the Central Andes, Lau (2002) argued that feasting of ancestors occurred in enclosures associated with decorated bowls, bone serving utensils, and camelid remains. Frequencies of these materials differed significantly from those in other contexts, indicating their celebratory function. Festal activities also served to reinforce group solidarity, as all who participate are ostensibly descended from or affinally related to those being honored.

In Neolithic China, pit features containing burned pig remains and objects made of stone and bone, in association with specific tombs, are indicative of routine tendance of select dead (Liu 2000). During the succeeding Shang and Zhou dynasties, offerings and consumption of food and drink produced deposits above the burial chamber as well as within it. As Keightley has noted, "The dead are notoriously thirsty" (1998:789–790); they prefer to drink from elaborate bronze vessels like the *jue* and *gu* (figure 2.1) (Allan 1991; Keightley 2001; Rawson 1999). Many distinctive vessel forms had earthenware counterparts and were in use for hundreds of years (Chengyuan 1980), indicating how durable ancestral rites were, despite the changing political and social landscapes of the Bronze Age.

As these examples have shown, shrines and other archaeological features exist within larger spatial and cosmological contexts. In Neolithic and Shang China, offering pits illustrate the importance of proximity to the remains of the dead. Elsewhere, access to ancestors may require specific architectural forms or monuments (Isbell 1997) or involve the creation or alteration of landscapes. Often these constructions house the dead and facilitate communication with them, but in some cases, the presence of ancestors on the landscape is metaphorical in nature.

Architecture, Monuments, and Enculturated Landscapes

Like the patterning associated with periodic ritual activities at shrines, the significance of the broader spatial context of ancestorhood has become implicit in the archaeological understanding of the phenomenon (Charles and Buikstra 2002; Parker Pearson 1993). The ancestral presence is highlighted through the erection of monumental tombs and manipulation of landscape features. Middleton (1960:67), for example, noted that some Lugbara shrines are actually "burial trees"—fig trees planted at the graves of important men and women with stones set beneath them. Over several generations, the trees accumulate and become "conspicuous landmarks; their distribution on the open Lugbara landscape shows the past of the lineages dispersed across it and gives a visible sign of a single tradition of development from the founders to the present members" (1960:67).

Mounds, too, may serve to mark territories and establish the antiquity of lineages. For example, work by Arnold (2002) and Murray (1995, this volume) has documented a network of spatial relationships at Iron Age sites in Germany where La Tène people appropriated earlier Hallstatt burial mounds. They buried their dead within Hallstatt tumuli and constructed rectangular enclosures for corporate feasting nearby. Through these practices, La Tène situated themselves amid a "landscape of ancestors" and accessed the cosmological power that resided within it (for additional examples, see Fontijn 1996; Roymans 1995; Roymans and Kortland 1999). As Weiss-Krejci (this volume) demonstrates, the creation of fictive ancestral kinship-by-association with mounds or monuments is an enduring sociopolitical strategy.

The monumental tombs of the Merina of Madagascar are perhaps the best ethnographic example of the use of architecture in tandem with human remains to communicate corporate property rights. Bloch's classic work (1971) describes the *famadihana* ritual, in which a monumental tomb is reopened and the corpses within are manipulated and rearranged. The ritual dramatizes the transition of the deceased from individuals into an ancestral collective, while the tomb and its contents represent the ideal of descent-group unity. Crossland's (2001) work in the Andratsay region of Madagascar links Bloch's insights to the archaeological record; she argues that the tombs and their locations on the landscape materialize a network of beliefs and practices through which social identity is constructed and maintained. The tombs themselves create an impression of permanence and continuity; their altitudinal relationships convey information about social hierarchies. The oldest and "most senior" tombs (i.e., those of the most powerful lineages) are located on the highest hilltops (Crossland 2001:833). Crossland suggests that in the nineteenth century, these ancestral landscapes—including tomb locations—were manipulated to establish the legitimacy of the emerging Merina state.

Collective tombs in Madagascar have served as analogs for the interpretation of Neolithic monuments in Britain where, it has been suggested, the intimate "co-presence of stones and ancestors [is] a structuring principle" (Parker Pearson and Ramilisonina 1998:310). Barrett (1990:182) cited the Merina tombs in his interpretation of megaliths. He argued that the construction of monuments was critical to the creation of Neolithic society. The tombs and their use in venerative and burial rites established membership in social groups and distinguished members from "others" (*sensu* Helms 1998). Emphasis was on exclusivity since, as Turner (1974:185) has observed, ancestral cults "tend to represent crucial power divisions and classificatory distinctions within and among politically discrete groups." In Barrett's view (1990), Neolithic societies in Britain employed monumentality and landscape to build a spatial focus for the community, an arena in which the living and the ancestors interacted.

Relationships among ancestors, monuments, and landscape have also been explored in the Americas; interpretations often parallel those advanced for the British Neolithic. The stone *chullpas* of the Andean region, for example, were highly visible sites of interment and veneration that simultaneously materialized social and territorial boundaries (Isbell 1997; Mantha 2009; Nielsen 2008). Hopewell and Mississippian mounds and henges may have played similarly complex roles in North American societies, where their location, construction, and deposition commemorated the ancestral dead and "sedimented" memory (Pauketat 2008:77; see also Buikstra and Charles 1999; Charles and Buikstra 2002; Pauketat and Alt 2003).

Symbols, Images, and Essences

Ancestors may be represented in two- or three-dimensional form; symbolized by some class of artifact, such as a pot or tablet; or embodied by a technological process. The distinction between an object *as* ancestor and an object *representing* an ancestor may be fluid or nonexistent. Some ancestor "objects" were in fact ontological subjects, possessing agency and personhood, animacy and generative capacity (Lau 2008). Given these complex issues, we make no clear distinctions here among those forms of material culture that are understood to *be* ancestors, those that *represent* or embody ancestors, and those that contain some fundamental essence *of* the ancestor. Examples of ancestors as subjects and objects illustrate this categorical complexity.

As discussed above, bodies and body parts, especially the skull, may be understood to be ancestors, as among the Inca, where mummies of rulers were conceptual subjects capable of communicating, celebrating, and consuming. Not all ancestors existed in human form. Fortes observed that "every Tallensi knows that these crocodiles are the incarnation of important clan ancestors. . . . To kill one of these is like killing a person" (Fortes 1987:249 [1973]). Perhaps more accurately, it is not *like* killing a person, it *is* killing a person—a person in crocodile form. The idea that ancestors exist as animals (Jones and Richards 2003) begs a reexamination of thousands of animal burials worldwide; we suspect that many animals buried "like" humans were actually considered to be persons themselves (Hill 2013); some of them may have been ancestors.

More commonly, ancestors are represented by some two-dimensional image or three-dimensional object. Ancestor or "spirit" tablets are perhaps the best known material embodiment of ancestors (figure 2.2). Such tablets have been used in China (Addison 1924; Hsu 1948; Watson and Rawski 1988), Japan (Smith 1974), and Korea (Janelli and Janelli 1982; Kyu 1984). They were usually made of wood or paper and contained the name of the deceased. As objects of veneration, they were erected in shrines within the home or ancestral hall. Within the last fifty years, photographs have begun to replace the more traditional tablets (Suzuki 2013).

Among the Nayar of the Malabar coast of India, representations of ancestors made of wood or stone are erected in the inner courtyard of the house (Raman Manon 1920). The Dagara (i.e., LoDagaa) of Ghana carved bamboo rods in anthropomorphic form (Goody 1962:224–225, plate 213), similar to the wooden shrine figurines of the Moba of Ghana and Togo (Kreamer 1987). On Irian Jaya, Indonesia, Kamoro anthropomorphic ancestor boards, or *yamate*, were made of carved wood. They honored recently deceased individuals and were sometimes used to adorn the prows of boats (Kjellgren 2007:37; Smidt 2003; Zee 2009). A final example of ancestors in material form are the carved and painted posts, panels, and lintels found in Maori meetinghouses in New Zealand (Neich 2001; Salmond 1976). Through construction and use of the house, descent groups "symbolize their unity and . . . distinction from other subtribes" (Meijl 1993:205). The meetinghouses themselves are named after famous ancestors, and their structure reproduces the ancestral body. Progression through the house is likened to movement through time from the earliest ancestor at the back, along the walls where his descendants are carved, to the front, where the recently deceased are represented (Meijl 1993).

Perhaps the best archaeological evidence for ancestors as objects in North America comes in the form of anthropomorphic stone statuary from Mississippian sites (figure 2.3). Dozens of such sculptures have been identified, representing men and women in stylized kneeling poses (Smith and Miller 2009). Following Waring (1968:62) and Brown (1985), Knight (1986) has suggested that the statuary functioned as *sacra* in a cult of "aristocratic" ancestors. Veneration of the ancestors underpinned

Figure 2.2. Twenty-one ancestors with spirit tablet. The inscription reads, "The ancestral tablet of the honorable Madame Wu, the first wife." The tablet is visible to the left of the central figure. Qing Dynasty (1644–1911). Ink on paper; artist unknown. © Metropolitan Museum of Art (acc. no. 69.100); gift of Mrs. F. L. Hough, 1969.

Figure 2.3. Mississippian sandstone sculpture, probably representing a chiefly ancestor. This is one of a male and female pair recovered in 1895 from the Duck River region, Tennessee; 67 × 36 × 27 cm. See Smith and Miller (2009) for discussion of Mississippian ancestors. © Metropolitan Museum of Art (acc. no. 1979.206.476); Michael C. Rockefeller Memorial Collection. Bequest of Nelson A. Rockefeller.

chiefly power, possibly by facilitating exclusive claims to ancestry (Brown 1997:467; see also Emerson 1997:233–241). Another possibility is that the sculptures actually *were* the ancestors or were imbued with their essence. Brown (1985:105) notes that they were cared for scrupulously, in some cases interred in their own chests or graves. Contemporary accounts indicate that their destruction was a desecratory practice in warfare.

George Lau (2008) has described several material forms of ancestors in the Andes, most notably in his study of anthropomorphic Recuay sculpture that, like other effigies, facilitated physical interaction between the living and the dead. At the site of Chinchawas, Lau (2002:297) documented stone monoliths depicting anthropomorphs in "conventionalized poses reminiscent of mummy bundles and positions." The sculptures were associated with tombs that had evidence of reentry and postmortem venerative ritual. Their purpose, he suggests, was to "create sacred spaces in which esteemed lithified individuals were incorporated permanently as observers and participants" (Lau 2008:1035).

Mabry (2003), in a thorough discussion of Near Eastern ancestors, suggests that Neolithic figurines were used in household venerative rituals to underscore spatial and temporal continuity, reference origins, and highlight more distant social ties as communities grew. Mabry's study is notable for a number of reasons, including his attention to context, diachronic patterns, and recognition that multiple categories of ancestors may have been represented by figurines. He argues that while public rituals may have affirmed common ancestry and integrated multiple lineages, ceramic figurines used in female-focused household rites operated at the scale of the lineage on a more routine basis.

Representations of ancestors, such as female figurines (Mabry 2003) or Recuay monoliths (Lau 2002), often take anthropomorphic form; however, ancestors may also appear as objects or processes that bear no obvious similarity to the human body. As Mather (this volume) illustrates, shrines often blur the line between signifier and signified; that is, the shrine erected to an ancestor may also be understood to *be* the ancestor. Similarly, ancestral essences may be implicated in productive or reproductive activities. Among the Fipa of western Tanzania, the iron smelting process involves the transformation of the furnace into a fecund woman through the use of certain tree species—associated with ancestors—as fuel (Schmidt 2009:277–278). The successful transformation of an inert object into an agential subject within the female body of the furnace indicates the approval of the ancestors and ensures economic and reproductive prosperity. Mike Parker Pearson (2002:156) also sees the involvement of ancestors in transformative processes, suggesting that metaphorical shifts from wood to stone on the Neolithic landscape paralleled the transition of the corpse from flesh to bone. In his view, stone circles represented the permanency and durability of an ancestral social order; the subsequent technological shift to metalworking and single burial thus represented a change in Neolithic ideas about death, being, and time.

Metaphorical ancestors may be present in clay, chalk, or stone, often considered conceptually equivalent to bone (Boivin 2004:7), or embodied in wood, ceramic, or lithic form. In societies with relational ontologies, in which things are invested with animacy, sentience, or personhood, stone sculptures—such as the Recuay andesite monoliths or Mississippian statues—may be ancestors themselves. In the Andes (Dean 2010) and in Aboriginal Australia (Taçon 1991), stone outcroppings and other landscape features were—and still are—considered to be the remains of ancient people or mythic ancestors. In these cases, as Parker Pearson (2004; Parker Pearson and Ramilisonina 1998) has argued for the British Neolithic, the medium is meaningful. While stone conveys ideas about durability, permanence, and antiquity, more mobile, plastic, or transitory forms, such as the wooden figures consumed by termites used by the Dagara (Goody 1962:389), indicate that the revered dead could also be impermanent entities, lasting only as long as their physical form.

Documentary Sources

Ethnohistoric documents represent a final line of evidence for ancestor beliefs and veneration in the past. Such documents are best used in tandem with contextual and artifactual evidence and recognition of the usual caveats that pertain to sources written by Western observers.

Bishop Diego de Landa's sixteenth-century *Relación de las Cosas de Yucatán* provides one of the most complete accounts of contact era Maya religion as practiced in Mexico. Landa noted the emphasis the Maya placed on knowing their family origins, observing that genealogy was "one of their sciences." Further, the Maya "were proud of the men who have been distinguished in their families" (Tozzer 1941:98). While such observations are general in nature, they provide context for accounts of Maya funerary practices, several of which have archaeological referents. Among the more prominent Maya, leaders of lineages were afforded special burial treatment. A portion of the body was burned, and the ashes were placed inside the head of a wooden statue. Skin from the back of the head was placed on the back of the statue. Along with other "idols," the statue was placed in the *oratorio* (shrine) of the house (McAnany 1995; Hageman, this volume) and the body interred within (Tozzer 1941:131). These idols were held in "very great reverence and respect." On festival days, they received offerings of food (Tozzer 1941:131). A 1562 account described "idols" discovered in a cave near Maní, Yucatán, along with decorated human skulls (Farriss 1984:290–291; Scholes and Adams 1938:24–31; Scholes and Roys

1938:585–620). Such "idols" were reportedly worshipped "so that it would rain and that [the idols] would give them much corn and so that they would kill many deer" (Clendinnen 1987:73).

Among the best known ethnohistoric accounts of ancestors in the Americas are those of Spanish chroniclers describing Inca beliefs and rituals. Bernabe Cobo (1979:31), for example, reported that the Inca "show more concern for the place they were to be put after death than for the dwelling in which they lived." He also described the preservation of the deceased Inca ruler, noting that "the body was handed down to the most prominent members of the family" (1979:111). In the same document, Cobo noted that images of the deceased were venerated and that some ancestors were believed to have turned to stone. As in the Maya region, accounts by Spanish officials charged with extirpating idolatry described many beliefs and practices related to ancestor veneration. The *Huarochirí Manuscript*, for example, written around 1600 in Quechua, records the veneration of proxy figurines in place of mummies (Salomon and Urioste 1991:§319). The same source identifies social groups with specific locations of the dead and describes the dancing and feasting of masks representing ancestors (1991:§155, §321–323). Such accounts suggest that Andean ancestors were manifest in multiple forms, only some of which were recognizable as human remains.

Conclusions

Some of the most convincing arguments for the existence of ancient ancestors are those that effectively mobilize multiple lines of evidence. Lau (2002), for example, employed ceramic, faunal, iconographic, burial, and architectural evidence in his analysis of Recuay materials at Chinchawas. Similarly, Thomas (2000) integrated tomb architecture, human remains, and spatial evidence to suggest that Neolithic monuments functioned as arenas for ancestor-focused ritual.

While the conceptual depth and spatial breadth that currently exist in the archaeological study of ancestors provided a plethora of approaches and examples, the failure to define terms remains a problem. Using "ancestors" as a synonym for the dead in general is both imprecise and confusing, doing little to advance the study of either. Contributors to this volume define ancestors in multiple ways and employ multiple lines of evidence to argue for their existence. The mutable nature of ancestors—their flexible adaptation to the demands of time and place—make them valuable tools to address issues of authority, land tenure, descent, and identity in complex societies. This mutability explains both their persistence through time and their broad distribution across the world.

Archaeologists have yet to thoroughly explore the origins of ancestors; role(s) that ancestors play in small-scale and semi-sedentary societies; how ancestorhood is gendered; the division of labor in ancestor veneration; and the differential scale and distribution of ancestor veneration in hierarchical societies. These questions suggest that the archaeological study of ancestors has a very productive future.

References Cited

Addison, James Thayer

1924 The Modern Chinese Cult of Ancestors. *Journal of Religion* 4(5):492–503.

Ahern, Emily M.

1973 *The Cult of the Dead in a Chinese Village*. Stanford University Press, Stanford, California.

Allan, Sarah

1991 *The Shape of the Turtle: Myth, Art, and Cosmos in Early China*. State University of New York Press, Albany, New York.

Antonaccio, Carla M.

1995 *An Archaeology of Ancestors: Tomb Cult and Hero Cult in Early Greece*. Rowman and Littlefield, Lanham, Maryland.

Armit, Ian

2012 *Headhunting and the Body in Iron Age Europe*. Cambridge University Press, Cambridge.

Arnold, Bettina

2002 A Landscape of Ancestors: The Space and Place of Death in Iron Age West-Central Europe. In *The Space and Place of Death*, edited by Helaine Silverman, pp. 129–143. Archeological Papers no. 11. American Anthropological Association, Arlington, Virginia.

Arnold, Denise Y., and Christine A. Hastorf

2008 *Heads of State: Icons, Power, and Politics in the Ancient and Modern Andes*. Left Coast Press, Walnut Creek, California.

Barrett, John C.

1988 The Living, the Dead, and the Ancestors: Neolithic and Early Bronze Age Mortuary Practices. In *The Archaeology of Context in the Neolithic and Bronze Age: Recent Trends*, edited by John C. Barrett and Ian A. Kinnes, pp. 30–41. Department of Archaeology, University of Sheffield, Sheffield.

1990 The Monumentality of Death: The Character of Early Bronze Age Mortuary Mounds in Southern Britain. *World Archaeology* 22(2):179–189.

1994 *Fragments from Antiquity: An Archaeology of Social Life in Britain, 2900–1200 BC.* Blackwell, Cambridge, Massachusetts.

Bauer, Brian S.

2004 *Ancient Cuzco: Heartland of the Inca.* University of Texas Press, Austin.

Bloch, Maurice

1971 *Placing the Dead: Tombs, Ancestral Villages, and Kinship Organization in Madagascar.* Seminar Press, London.

Boivin, Nicole

2004 From Veneration to Exploitation: Human Engagement with the Mineral World. In *Soils, Stones, and Symbols: Cultural Perceptions of the Mineral World,* edited by Nicole Boivin and Mary Ann Owoc, pp. 1–29. University College London Press, London.

Bradley, Richard

1984 *The Social Foundations of Prehistoric Britain: Themes and Variations in the Archaeology of Power.* Longman, London.

2000 *An Archaeology of Natural Places.* Routledge, London.

Brown, James A.

1985 The Mississippian Period. In *Ancient Art of the American Woodland Indians,* edited by David S. Brose, James A. Brown, and David W. Penney, pp. 93–145. H. N. Abrams and Detroit Institute of Arts, New York.

1990 Archaeology Confronts History at the Natchez Temple. *Southeastern Archaeology* 9(1):1–10.

1997 The Archaeology of Ancient Religion in the Eastern Woodlands. *Annual Review of Anthropology* 26:465–485.

Buikstra, Jane E., and Douglas K. Charles

1999 Centering the Ancestors: Cemeteries, Mounds, and Sacred Landscapes of the Ancient North American Midcontinent. In *Archaeologies of Landscape: Contemporary Perspectives,* edited by Wendy Ashmore and A. Bernard Knapp, pp. 201–228. Wiley-Blackwell, Malden, Massachusetts.

Chacon, Richard J., and David H. Dye (editors)

2007 *The Taking and Displaying of Human Body Parts as Trophies by Amerindians.* Springer, New York.

Charles, Douglas K., and Jane E. Buikstra

2002 Siting, Sighting, and Citing the Dead. In *The Place and Space of Death,* edited by Helaine Silverman and David B. Small, pp. 13–25. Archeological Papers of the American Anthropological Association no. 11, Arlington, Virginia.

Charles, Douglas K., Julieann Van Nest, and Jane E. Buikstra

2004 From the Earth: Minerals and Meaning in the Hopewellian World. In *Soils, Stones, and Symbols: Cultural Perceptions of the Mineral World,* edited by Nicole Boivin and Mary Ann Owoc, pp. 43–70. University College London Press, London.

Chen Lie

1996 The Ancestor Cult in Ancient China. In *Mysteries of Ancient China: New Dis-*

coveries from the Early Dynasties, edited by Jessica Rawson, pp. 269–272. George Braziller, New York.

Chengyuan, Ma

1980 The Splendor of Ancient Chinese Bronzes. In *The Great Bronze Age of China: An Exhibition from the People's Republic of China*, edited by Wen Fong, pp. 1–19. Metropolitan Museum of Art, New York.

Clendinnen, Inga

1987 *Ambivalent Conquests: Maya and Spaniard in Yucatan, 1517–1570*. Cambridge University Press, Cambridge.

Cobo, Bernabe

1979 *History of the Inca Empire*. Translated by Roland Hamilton. University of Texas Press, Austin.

Cole, Jennifer, and Karen Middleton

2001 Rethinking Ancestors and Colonial Power in Madagascar. *Africa: Journal of the International African Institute* 71(1):1–37.

Crossland, Zoë

2001 Time and the Ancestors: Landscape Survey in the Andrantsay Region of Madagascar. *Antiquity* 75:825–836.

de Polignac, François

1995 *Cults, Territory, and the Origins of the Greek City-State*. Translated by Janet Lloyd. University of Chicago Press, Chicago.

Dean, Carolyn

2010 *A Culture of Stone: Inka Perspectives on Rock*. Duke University Press, Durham, North Carolina.

DeLeonardis, Lisa, and George F. Lau

2004 Life, Death, and Ancestors. In *Andean Archaeology*, edited by Helaine Silverman, pp. 77–115. Blackwell, Oxford.

Dietler, Michael, and Brian Hayden (editors)

2001 *Feasts: Archaeological and Ethnographic Perspectives on Food, Politics, and Power*. Smithsonian Institution Press, Washington, D.C.

Douglas, Mary

1996 *Natural Symbols: Explorations in Cosmology*, revised ed. Routledge, London.

Dulanto, Jalh

2002 The Archaeological Study of Ancestor Cult Practices: The Case of Pampa Chica, a Late Initial Period and Early Horizon Site on the Central Coast of Peru. In *The Space and Place of Death*, edited by Helaine Silverman, pp. 97–117. Archeological Papers of the American Anthropological Association, Arlington, Virginia.

Duncan, William N., and Charles Andrew Hofling

2011 Why the Head? Cranial Modification as Protection and Ensoulment among the Maya. *Ancient Mesoamerica* 22(1):199–210.

Edmonds, Mark Roland

1999 *Ancestral Geographies: Landscape Monuments and Memory*. Routledge, London.

Emerson, Thomas E.

1997 *Cahokia and the Archaeology of Power*. University of Alabama Press, Tuscaloosa.

Farriss, Nancy
1984 *Maya Society under Colonial Rule: The Collective Enterprise of Survival*. Princeton University Press, Princeton, New Jersey.
Fletcher, Adele L.
2000 *Religion, Gender, and Rank in Maori Society: A Study of Ritual and Social Practice in Eighteenth and Nineteenth-Century Documentary Sources*. Unpublished PhD dissertation, Maori and Indigenous Studies, University of Canterbury, Christchurch, New Zealand.
Fontijn, David
1996 Socializing Landscapes: Second Thoughts about the Cultural Biography of Urnfields. *Archaeological Dialogues* 3:77–87.
Fortes, Meyer
1945 *Dynamics of Clanship among the Tallensi*. Oxford University Press, London.
1949 *The Web of Kinship among the Tallensi*. Oxford University Press, London.
1959 *Oedipus and Job in West African Religion*. Cambridge University Press, Cambridge.
1965 Some Reflections on Ancestor Worship in Africa. In *African Systems of Thought*, edited by Meyer Fortes and Germaine Dieterlen, pp. 122–142. Oxford University Press for the International African Institute, London.
1976 An Introductory Commentary. In *Ancestors*, edited by William H. Newell, pp. 1–16. Mouton, The Hague.
1987 *Religion, Morality, and the Person: Essays on Tallensi Religion*. Cambridge University Press, Cambridge.
1987 [1973] The Concept of the Person. In *Religion, Morality, and the Person: Essays on Tallensi Religion*, edited by Jack Goody, pp. 247–286. Cambridge University Press, Cambridge.
Freedman, Maurice
1958 *Lineage Organization in Southeastern China*. Athlone Press, London.
1979 [1970] Ritual Aspects of Chinese Kinship and Marriage. In *The Study of Chinese Society: Essays by Maurice Freedman*, edited by G. William Skinner, pp. 273–295. Stanford University Press, Stanford, California.
Glazier, Mark
1984 Mbeere Ancestors and the Domestication of Death. *Man* 19(1):133–147.
Goldstein, Lynne G.
1976 *Spatial Structure and Social Organization: Regional Manifestations of Mississippian Society*. PhD dissertation, Department of Anthropology, Northwestern University, Evanston.
1981 One-Dimensional Archaeology and Multi-dimensional People: Spatial Organization and Mortuary Analysis. In *The Archaeology of Death*, edited by Robert Chapman, Ian Kinnes, and Klavs Randsborg, pp. 53–69. Cambridge University Press, Cambridge.
Goody, Jack
1962 *Death, Property, and the Ancestors: A Study of the Mortuary Customs of the LoDagaa of West Africa*. Stanford University Press, Stanford, California.

Hageman, Jon B.

2004 The Lineage Model and Archaeological Data in Late Classic Northwestern Belize. *Ancient Mesoamerica* 15(1):63–74.

Hastorf, Christine A.

2003 Community with the Ancestors: Ceremonies and Social Memory in the Middle Formative at Chiripa, Bolivia. *Journal of Anthropological Archaeology* 22:305–332.

Headrick, Annabeth

2007 *The Teotihuacan Trinity: The Sociopolitical Structure of an Ancient Mesoamerican City*. University of Texas Press, Austin.

Helms, Mary W.

1998 *Access to Origins: Affines, Ancestors, and Aristocrats*. University of Texas Press, Austin.

Hertz, Robert

1960 A Contribution to the Study of the Collective Representation of Death. In *Death and the Right Hand*, pp. 27–86. Translated by Rodney Needham and Claudia Needham. Free Press, Glencoe, Illinois.

Hill, Erica

2006 Moche Skulls in Cross-Cultural Perspective. In *Skull Collection, Modification, and Decoration*, edited by Michelle Bonogofsky, pp. 91–100. BAR International Series 1539. Archaeopress, Oxford.

2013 Archaeology and Animal Persons: Towards a Prehistory of Human-Animal Relations. *Environment and Society: Advances in Research* 4:117–136.

Hill, J. D.

1995 *Ritual and Rubbish in the Iron Age of Wessex: A Study on the Formation of a Specific Archaeological Record*. BAR British Series 242. Tempus Reparatum, Oxford.

1996 The Identification of Ritual Deposits of Animals. In *Ritual Treatment of Human and Animal Remains*, edited by Sue Anderson and Katherine Boyle, pp. 17–32. Proceedings of the first meeting of the Osteoarchaeological Research Group. Oxbow Books, Oxford.

Houston, Stephen D., David Stuart, and Karl A. Taube

2006 *The Memory of Bones: Body, Being, and Experience among the Classic Maya*. University of Texas Press, Austin.

Hsu, Francis L. K.

1948 *Under the Ancestors' Shadow: Chinese Culture and Personality*. Columbia University Press, New York.

Insoll, Timothy

2007a "Natural" or "Human" Spaces? Tallensi Sacred Groves and Shrines and Their Potential Implications for Aspects of Northern European Prehistory and Phenomenological Interpretation. *Norwegian Archaeological Review* 40(2):138–158.

2007b "Totems," "Ancestors," and "Animism": The Archaeology of Ritual, Shrines, and Sacrifice amongst the Tallensi of Northern Ghana. In *Cult in Context: Reconsidering Ritual in Archaeology*, edited by David A. Barrowclough and Caroline Malone, pp. 328–335. Oxbow Books, Oxford.

2008 Negotiating the Archaeology of Destiny: An Exploration of Interpretive Possibilities through Tallensi Shrines. *Journal of Social Archaeology* 8(3):380–404.

Isbell, William H.

1997 *Mummies and Mortuary Monuments: A Postprocessual Prehistory of Central Andean Social Organization.* University of Texas Press, Austin.

Janelli, Roger L., and Dawnhee Yim Janelli

1982 *Ancestor Worship and Korean Society.* Stanford University Press, Stanford, California.

Jones, Andrew

1998 Where Eagles Dare: Landscape, Animals, and the Neolithic of Orkney. *Journal of Material Culture* 3(3):301–324.

Jones, Andrew, and Colin Richards

2003 Animals into Ancestors: Domestication, Food, and Identity in Late Neolithic Orkney. In *Food, Culture, and Identity in the Neolithic and Early Bronze Age*, edited by Mike Parker Pearson, pp. 45–51. BAR International Series 1117. Archaeopress, Oxford.

Keesing, Roger M.

1970 Shrines, Ancestors, and Cognatic Descent: The Kwaio and Tallensi. *American Anthropologist* 72(4):755–775.

1982 *Kwaio Religion: The Living and the Dead in a Solomon Island Society.* Columbia University Press, New York.

Keightley, David N.

1998 Shamanism, Death, and the Ancestors: Religious Mediation in Neolithic and Shang China (ca. 5000–1000 BC). *Asiatische Studien / Études Asiatiques* 52(3):763–831.

2001 The "Science" of the Ancestors: Divination, Curing, and Bronze-Casting in Late Shang China. *Asia Major* 14(2):143–187.

2004 The Making of the Ancestors: Late Shang Religion and Its Legacy. In *Religion and Chinese Society*, vol. 1, *Ancient and Medieval China*, edited by John Lagerwey, pp. 3–64. Chinese University of Hong Kong and the École Française d'Extrême-Orient, Hong Kong.

Kenyon, Kathleen M.

1954 Excavations at Jericho. *Journal of the Royal Anthropological Institute* 84(1–2):103–110.

Kenyon, Kathleen, and A. Douglas Tushingham

1953 Jericho Gives Up Its Secrets. *National Geographic* 104(6):853–870.

Kjellgren, Eric

2007 *Oceania: Art of the Pacific Islands in the Metropolitan Museum of Art.* Metropolitan Museum of Art, New York.

Knight, Vernon James

1986 The Institutional Organization of Mississippian Religion. *American Antiquity* 51(4):675–687.

Kopytoff, Igor

1971 Ancestors as Elders in Africa. *Africa: Journal of the International African Institute* 41(2):129–142.

1987 *The African Frontier: The Reproduction of Traditional African Societies*. Indiana University Press, Bloomington.

Kreamer, Christine Mullen

1987 Moba Shrine Figures. *African Arts* 20(2):52–55, 82–83.

Kuba, Richard, and Carola Lentz

2002 Arrows and Earth Shrines: Towards a History of Dagara Expansion in Southern Burkina Faso. *Journal of African History* 43(3):377–406.

Kyu, Lee Kwang

1984 The Concept of Ancestors and Ancestor Worship in Korea. *Asian Folklore Studies* 43(2):199–214.

Lau, George F.

2002 Feasting and Ancestor Veneration at Chinchawas, North Highlands of Ancash, Peru. *Latin American Antiquity* 13(3):279–304.

2008 Ancestor Images in the Andes. In *Handbook of South American Archaeology*, edited by Helaine Silverman and William H. Isbell, pp. 1027–1045. Springer, New York.

Lévi-Strauss, Claude

1987 *Anthropology and Myth: Lectures 1951–1982*. Translated by Roy Willis. Blackwell, Oxford.

Liu Li

2000 Ancestor Worship: An Archaeological Investigation of Ritual Activities in Neolithic North China. *Journal of East Asian Archaeology* 2(1–2):129–164.

Lucas, Gavin M.

1996 Of Death and Debt: A History of the Body in Neolithic and Early Bronze Age Yorkshire. *Journal of European Archaeology* 4(1):99–118.

Mabry, Jonathan B.

2003 The Birth of the Ancestors: The Meanings of Human Figurines in Near Eastern Neolithic Villages. In *The Near East in the Southwest: Essays in Honor of William G. Dever*, edited by Beth Alpert Nakhai, pp. 85–116. American Schools of Oriental Research, Boston.

MacCormack, Sabine

1991 *Religion in the Andes: Vision and Imagination in Early Colonial Peru*. Princeton University Press, Princeton, New Jersey.

Mantha, Alexis

2009 Territoriality, Social Boundaries, and Ancestor Veneration in the Central Andes of Peru. *Journal of Anthropological Archaeology* 28(2):158–176.

Manzanilla, Linda

2002 Houses and Ancestors, Altars and Relics: Mortuary Patterns at Teotihuacan, Central Mexico. In *The Place and Space of Death*, edited by Helaine Silverman and David B. Small, pp. 55–65. Archeological Papers of the American Anthropological Association, no. 11, Arlington, Virginia.

McAnany, Patricia A.
1995 *Living with the Ancestors: Kinship and Kingship in Ancient Maya Society*. University of Texas Press, Austin.
McCall, John C.
1995 Rethinking Ancestors in Africa. *Africa* 65(2):256–270.
Meijl, Toon van
1993 Maori Meeting-Houses in and over Time. In *Inside Austronesian Houses: Perspectives on Domestic Designs for Living*, edited by James J. Fox, pp. 201–224. Department of Anthropology, Australian National University, Canberra.
Middleton, John
1960 *Lugbara Religion: Ritual and Authority among an East African People*. Oxford University Press for the International African Institute, London.
Mills, Barbara J., and William H. Walker
2008 Memory, Materiality, and Depositional Practice. In *Memory Work: Archaeologies of Material Practices*, edited by Barbara J. Mills and William H. Walker, pp. 3–23. School for Advanced Research Press, Santa Fe.
Morris, Ian
1991 The Archaeology of Ancestors: The Saxe/Goldstein Hypothesis Revisited. *Cambridge Archaeological Journal* 1(2):147–169.
Murray, Matthew L.
1995 Viereckschanzen and Feasting: Socio-Political Ritual in Iron-Age Central Europe. *Journal of European Archaeology* 3(2):125–151.
Needham, Rodney
1976 Skulls and Causality. *Man* 11:71–88.
Neich, Roger
2001 *Carved Histories: Rotorua Ngāti Tarawhai Woodcarving*. Auckland University Press, Auckland, New Zealand.
Nelson, Sarah Milledge
2003 Feasting the Ancestors in Early China. In *The Archaeology and Politics of Food and Feasting in Early States and Empires*, edited by Tamara L. Bray, pp. 65–89. Kluwer Academic/Plenum, New York.
Nielsen, Axel E.
2008 The Materiality of Ancestors: *Chullpas* and Social Memory in the Late Prehispanic History of the South Andes. In *Memory Work: Archaeologies of Material Practices*, edited by Barbara J. Mills and William H. Walker, pp. 207–231. School for Advanced Research Press, Santa Fe.
Otake, Emiko
1980 Two Categories of Chinese Ancestors as Determined by Their Malevolence. *Asian Folklore Studies* 39(1):21–31.
Parker Pearson, Mike
1993 The Powerful Dead: Archaeological Relationships between the Living and the Dead. *Cambridge Archaeological Journal* 3(2):203–229.
2000 Ancestors, Bones, and Stones in Neolithic and Early Bronze Age Britain and

Ireland. In *Neolithic Orkney in Its European Context*, edited by Anna Ritchie, pp. 203–214. McDonald Institute for Archaeological Research, Cambridge.

2002 Placing the Physical and the Incorporeal Dead: Stonehenge and the Changing Concepts of Ancestral Space in Neolithic Britain. In *The Space and Place of Death*, edited by Helaine Silverman and David B. Small, pp. 145–160. Archeological Papers of the American Anthropological Association, no. 11, Arlington, Virginia.

2004 Earth, Wood, and Fire: Materiality and Stonehenge. In *Soils, Stones, and Symbols: Cultural Perceptions of the Mineral World*, edited by Nicole Boivin and Mary Ann Owoc, pp. 71–89. University College London Press, London.

Parker Pearson, Mike, and Ramilisonina

1998 Stonehenge for the Ancestors: The Stones Pass on the Message. *Antiquity* 72(308):308–326.

Pauketat, Timothy R.

2008 Founders' Cults and the Archaeology of *Wa-kan-da*. In *Memory Work: Archaeologies of Material Practices*, edited by Barbara J. Mills and William H. Walker, pp. 61–79. School for Advanced Research Press, Santa Fe.

Pauketat, Timothy R., and Susan M. Alt

2003 Mounds, Memory, and Contested Mississippian History. In *Archaeologies of Memory*, edited by Ruth M. Van Dyke and Susan E. Alcock, pp. 151–179. Blackwell, Malden, Massachusetts.

Rakita, Gordon F. M.

2009 *Ancestors and Elites: Emergent Complexity and Ritual Practices in the Casas Grandes Polity*. Altamira Press, Lanham, Maryland.

Rakita, Gordon F. M., and Jane E. Buikstra

2005 Corrupting Flesh: Reexamining Hertz's Perspective on Mummification and Cremation. In *Interacting with the Dead: Perspectives on Mortuary Archaeology for the New Millennium*, edited by Gordon F. M. Rakita, Jane E. Buikstra, Lane A. Beck, and Sloan R. Williams, pp. 97–106. University Press of Florida, Gainesville.

Raman Manon, V. K.

1920 Ancestor Worship among the Nayars. *Man* 20(3):42–43.

Rawson, Jessica

1999 Ancient Chinese Ritual as Seen in the Material Record. In *State and Court Ritual in China*, edited by Joseph P. McDermott, pp. 20–49. Cambridge University Press, Cambridge.

Roymans, Nico

1995 The Cultural Biography of Urnfields and the Long-Term History of a Mythical Landscape. *Archaeological Dialogues* 2(1):2–24.

Roymans, Nico, and Fokko Kortland

1999 Urnfield Symbolism, Ancestors, and the Land in the Lower Rhine Region. In *Land and Ancestors: Cultural Dynamics in the Urnfield Period and the Middle Ages in the Southern Netherlands*, edited by Frans Theuws and Nico Roymans, pp. 33–58. Amsterdam University Press, Amsterdam.

Salmond, Anne

1976 *Hui: A Study of Maori Ceremonial Gatherings*. A. H. and A. W. Reed, Wellington, New Zealand.

Salomon, Frank, and George L. Urioste (editors)

1991 *The Huarochirí Manuscript: A Testament of Ancient and Colonial Andean Religion*. University of Texas Press, Austin.

Sanders, William T., and David Webster

1988 The Mesoamerican Urban Tradition. *American Anthropologist* 90(3):521–546.

Saxe, Arthur A.

1970 *Social Dimensions of Mortuary Practices*. Department of Anthropology, University of Michigan, Ann Arbor.

Schmidt, Peter

2009 Tropes, Materiality, and Ritual Embodiment of African Iron Smelting Furnaces as Human Figurines. *Journal of Archaeological Method and Theory* 16:262–282.

Scholes, France V., and Eleanor B. Adams (editors)

1938 *Don Diego de Quijada, Alcalde Mayor de Yucatán, 1561–1565*. Editorial Porrua, México.

Scholes, France V., and Ralph L. Roys

1938 *Fray Diego de Landa and the Problem of Idolatry in Yucatan*. Carnegie Institution, Washington, D.C.

Sharples, Niall

2000 Antlers and Orcadian Rituals: An Ambiguous Role for Red Deer in the Neolithic. In *Neolithic Orkney in Its European Context*, edited by Anna Ritchie, pp. 107–116. McDonald Institute for Archaeological Research, Cambridge.

Smidt, Dirk (editor)

2003 *Kamoro Art: Tradition and Innovation in a New Guinea Culture*. KIT, Amsterdam.

Smith, Kevin E., and James V. Miller

2009 *Speaking with the Ancestors: Mississippian Stone Statuary of the Tennessee-Cumberland Region*. University of Alabama Press, Tuscaloosa.

Smith, Robert J.

1974 *Ancestor Worship in Contemporary Japan*. Stanford University Press, Stanford, California.

Stahl, Ann B.

2008 Dogs, Pythons, Pots, and Beads: The Dynamics of Shrines and Sacrificial Practices in Banda, Ghana, 1400–1900 CE. In *Memory Work: Archaeologies of Material Practices*, edited by Barbara J. Mills and William H. Walker, pp. 159–186. School for Advanced Research Press, Santa Fe.

Stinson, Susan L.

2005 Remembering the Ancestors: Ceramic Figurines from Las Capas and Los Pozos. In *Material Cultures and Lifeways of Early Agricultural Communities in Southern Arizona*, edited by R. Jane Sliva, pp. 207–216. Center for Desert Archaeology, Tucson.

Suzuki, Iwayumi

2013 Beyond Ancestor Worship: Continued Relationship with Significant Others. In *Death and Dying in Contemporary Japan*, edited by Hikaru Suzuki, pp. 141–156. Routledge, Abingdon, UK.

Taçon, Paul S. C.

1991 The Power of Stone: Symbolic Aspects of Stone Use and Tool Development in Western Arnhem Land, Australia. *Antiquity* 65(247):192–207.

Taube, Karl

2004 Flower Mountain: Concepts of Life, Beauty, and Paradise among the Classic Maya. *RES: Anthropology and Aesthetics* 45:69–98.

Thomas, Julian

1988 The Social Significance of Cotswold-Severn Burial Practices. *Man* 23(3):540–559.

1990 Monuments from the Inside: The Case of the Irish Megalithic Tombs. *World Archaeology* 22(2):168–178.

1996 *Time, Culture, and Identity: An Interpretive Archaeology*. Routledge, New York.

2000 Death, Identity, and the Body in Neolithic Britain. *Journal of the Royal Anthropological Institute* 6(4):653–668.

Thorp, Robert L.

1980 Burial Practices of Bronze Age China. In *The Great Bronze Age of China: An Exhibition from the People's Republic of China*, edited by Wen Fong, pp. 51–64. Metropolitan Museum of Art, New York.

Tilley, Christopher

1994 *A Phenomenology of Landscape: Places, Paths, and Monuments*. Berg, Providence, Rhode Island.

Tilley, Christopher, and Wayne Bennett

2001 An Archaeology of Supernatural Places: The Case of West Penwith. *Journal of the Royal Anthropological Institute* 7(2):335–362.

Tozzer, Alfred M.

1941 *Landa's Relación de las Cosas de Yucatán*. Papers of the Peabody Museum of American Archaeology and Ethnology, no. 18. Peabody Museum, Harvard University, Cambridge, Massachusetts.

Turner, Victor

1974 *Dramas, Fields, and Metaphors: Symbolic Action in Human Society*. Cornell University Press, Ithaca.

Van Dyke, Ruth M., and Susan E. Alcock

2003 Archaeologies of Memory: An Introduction. In *Archaeologies of Memory*, edited by Ruth M. Van Dyke and Susan E. Alcock, pp. 1–13. Blackwell, Malden, Massachusetts.

Vogt, Paul N.

2012 *Between Kin and King: Social Aspects of Western Zhou Ritual*. Unpublished PhD dissertation, East Asian Languages and Cultures, Columbia University, New York.

Walter, Richard, Tim Thomas, and Peter Sheppard
2004 Cult Assemblages and Ritual Practice in Roviana Lagoon, Solomon Islands. *World Archaeology* 36(1):142–157.

Waring, Antonio J.
1968 The Southern Cult and Muskhogean Ceremonial. In *The Waring Papers: The Collected Works of Antonio J. Waring Jr.*, edited by Stephen Williams, pp. 30–69. Peabody Museum, Harvard University, Cambridge, Massachusetts.

Watson, James L., and Evelyn S. Rawski (editors)
1988 *Death Ritual in Late Imperial and Modern China*. University of California Press, Berkeley.

Whitley, James
2002 Too Many Ancestors. *Antiquity* 76(291):119–126.

Whitley, Richard
2001 *The Archaeology of Ancient Greece*. Cambridge University Press, Cambridge.

Whittle, Alasdair, Alistair Barclay, Alex Bayliss, Lesley McFadyen, Rick Schulting, and Michael Wysocki
2007 Building for the Dead: Events, Processes, and Changing Worldviews from the Thirty-Eighth to the Thirty-Fourth Centuries cal. BC in Southern Britain. *Cambridge Archaeological Journal* 17(supp):123–147.

Wolf, Arthur P.
1974 Gods, Ghosts, and Ancestors. In *Religion and Ritual in Chinese Society*, edited by Arthur P. Wolf, pp. 131–182. Stanford University Press, Stanford, California.

Wright, G.R.H.
1988 The Severed Head in Earliest Neolithic Times. *Journal of Prehistoric Religion* 2:51–56.

Yao, Alice
2013 Engendering Ancestors through Death Ritual in Ancient China. In *The Oxford Handbook of the Archaeology of Death and Burial*, edited by Sarah Tarlow and Liv Nilsson Stutz, pp. 581–596. Oxford University Press, Oxford.

Zee, Pauline van der
2009 *Art as Contact with the Ancestors: The Visual Arts of the Kamoro and Asmat of Western Papua*. KIT, Amsterdam.

3

Memory, Power, and Death in Chinese History and Prehistory

RODERICK CAMPBELL

What is an ancestor? In archaeology, but especially Chinese archaeology, ancestors seem to be everywhere. Indeed, China is arguably the paradigmatic source of case studies concerning ancestor veneration. Could it be possible, then, that early China has "too many ancestors" and that they contribute to both an essentialist discourse about ancient China and an undermotivated functionalist-evolutionist historical paradigm? In what follows I argue for just this scenario. A strict definition of ancestors tied to biological kinship, or functionally to specific institutions, cannot capture the polysemy of ancestors in the Chinese context. On the other hand, without practical and discursive context, "ancestors" are at best a category without explanatory utility and at worst a projection of essential Chineseness onto earlier and non-Han situations. Instead, I will argue for a soft definition of ancestors in the Chinese tradition as a nexus of genealogical, commemorative, political, and religious practice and belief of great promiscuity and mutable historical meaning. Ancestors, or 祖先 *zuxian*, have been, since at least the Shang, a select group of dead progenitors or, perhaps more accurately, a desired state of relations between the living and certain dead (Puett 2014). On the other hand, ancestor veneration has provided a general idiom for Chinese practices and beliefs concerning life, death, and the afterlife that extends beyond the bounds of biological kinship.

Chinese Ancestors

A number of scholars have observed that ancestors were and are very important in China (Ebrey and Watson 1986; Jordan 1999; Liu 1999; Watson and Rawski 1988). Indeed, one could make the case that China is the original source of the concept of "ancestor worship" in the Western imagination. I would argue, however, that despite some striking continuities, the referent and meaning of "ancestors," even within the traditions of China, changed over time and from context to context. As putatively key sites of social practice and discursive formation as early as the Neolithic (Liu 1999), ancestors have shifted in meaning and use with changed circumstances. In China and elsewhere, the answer to the question of what an ancestor is must be sought within local entanglements of kinship, power, memory, identity, place, death, and life.

In order to map out something of the diverse practical and discursive territory covered by the term "ancestors" in Chinese history, I present four cases drawn from the work of ethnographers, religious scholars, and historians. These are the role of ancestors and the dead in early Daoism and Buddhism; the strategic use of genealogy and lineage in Ming dynasty Fujian province; the rebuilding of a temple to Confucius in post–cultural revolution North China by his putative descendants; and the construction and use of Mao's mausoleum. I will then move to Shang archaeology and epigraphy in order to show what can be said about Shang ancestors from primary sources. In placing the historical case studies first, my goal is paradoxically ethnographic: to problematize and defamiliarize the concept of ancestors for a Western audience. Armed with a broadened notion of the discursive range of ancestors in Chinese history and the importance of a historical contextual perspective, we will be better placed to read the Shang archaeological evidence on something closer to its own terms. The point, of course, is not simply to obtain a better understanding of Shang ancestors but to underline the necessity of a deep and wide contextualization of what is ultimately an extremely complex nexus of relations and institutions.

The first point that I wish to make concerning ancestors in China is the importance of taking into consideration concepts of death and the dead. If there is a generic sense that ancestors are benevolent in the literature within and beyond China, in part encouraged by elite ideals of filial piety and well-ordered relations, it is important to realize that from early times in China the dead were also considered a source of contagion and ill fortune. Of medieval China (third through seventh centuries CE), Strickmann (2002:71) writes:

> Though elite upper-class accounts of Chinese culture would have us believe that the only attitude ever manifested toward one's own dead was solemn respect, the evidence leads us to a quite different conclusion. The terminology itself should provoke a closer look at the scope afforded to the dead, since there is no basic terminological distinction between them and demons.

Indeed, although the dead (and especially the recent dead) had been seen as sources of illness and misfortune since at least the Bronze Age, the relationship between the living and dead was increasingly troubled in early medieval times (Bokenkamp 2007). In the apocalyptic post-Han world (third to fourth centuries CE) of plague, war, and political turmoil, death, ghosts, and demons gained particular salience. It is perhaps not surprising that early Daoism essentially set itself up in opposition to cults of the ancestors: "the celestial Tao against the ill-omened, unhallowed dead and everything connected with them" (Strickmann 2002:4). Notions of spectral lawsuits and of intergenerational group responsibility—in heaven as it was on earth—meant that the deeds of one's ancestors could come back to haunt living descendants, usually in the form of sickness and death. Even more troubling for people in medieval China, and for the notion that ancestor veneration concerns only descendants, is the fact that potentially destructive spirits might not even be those of one's own dead. Indeed, one of the chief targets of Daoist polemic was the shrines of "false gods": "the hero-cults dedicated to dead warriors" (Strickmann 2002:52). What the worship of gods, ghosts, and ancestors in medieval China had in common was a general logic of service to the dead, who were potential sources of both blessing and calamity structured and imagined through the refracting lens of local and translocal dynamic realities.

Even the increasing popularity of Buddhism in the fourth to seventh centuries with its emphasis on personal (as opposed to group) responsibility and rebirth, hells, and postmortem suffering could not dislodge practices of offering to the dead or their underlying (and contradictory) visions of ghosts and an otherworldly bureaucracy (Bokenkamp 2007). Instead, Buddhist monks (in addition to Daoist priests and local religious specialists) came to play major roles in funerals where they would burn petitions and chant "sutras and penances in order to transfer merit to the soul of the deceased" (Naquin 1988:59), fulfilling filial obligation to reduce the suffering of a dead relative in the afterlife as well as mitigate the potential for baleful influence from beyond the grave.

For a study of "ancestor worship," a couple of important points emerge from the early medieval Chinese case. First, "ancestors" are embedded in a larger complex of techniques and ideas concerning relations between the living and the dead. Second, while rituals involving one's own dead relatives occupied a central practical and discursive place, they are scarcely intelligible without reference to wider beliefs about death, ghosts, and contagion and to related institutions such as hero-cults, rites of healing/exorcism, and religious organizations. The larger point is that the wider religious and political milieu must figure in any account of what ultimately is but one element of a constellation of interrelated practices, beliefs, and institutions. Without situation in their local historical contexts, "ancestors" lose all specificity and, I would argue, comparative utility.

The importance of historical and political particularity in contextualizing the contested ground of ancestors can be further elaborated with Szonyi's (2002) work on kinship strategies in Ming dynasty (1368–1644) Fujian province. In that work, Szonyi shows how genealogies were manipulated—even fabricated—and lineage halls proliferated in creative negotiations of status and ethnic identity and in response to an array of changing conditions and state administrative and extractive policies. To give just one example, descendants of households that had been designated "military households" at the beginning of the dynasty and thus had to supply an adult male to the imperial armies in perpetuity found it necessary to organize in order to select one of their number for military service, to raise funds to maintain that delegate, and to construct genealogical records either to demonstrate the fulfillment of state obligations or to evade that responsibility. In short, military households found it expedient to construct lineages where none had existed before (Szonyi 2002:69; see Weiss-Krejci, this volume, for a European example of lineage construction).

The creation of lineages and lineage halls was also impacted by the institution of the *lijia* system at the beginning of the Ming, whereby the population was divided into groups of households that rotated annually in supplying the state with labor and other services. Over time these originally single family households became extended kin groups, many of which found it expedient to organize on the basis of kinship in order to meet state extractions. The *lijia* system, moreover, was tied to an early

Ming attempt to integrate local religion into a state hierarchy whereby each *li* group of one hundred households was to maintain altars and sacrifices to two cults: one directed toward the spirits of the soil and grain, the other toward the hungry ghosts not receiving ancestral cults (Szonyi 2002:175). In practice, however, many illicit cults, often to deceased generals or deified historical figures, became attached to these *lijia* units, which in turn became increasingly lineage-based over time.

> The Ming system tied local popular religion to the lijia system and hence to the lineage. . . . Kinship then came to define issues such as temple affiliation and to shape the ritual practices associated with the temple and its gods [Szonyi 2002:195].

In a sense, then, popular religious cults (frequently directed toward deified but unrelated dead) in sharing social, physical, and conceptual space with lineage-based ancestral ritual proper became "ancestralized." Indeed, despite the variety of religious activities that occurred in the ancestral halls of Ming Fujian, "the descriptions of the rituals in the sources invariably attempt, with varying degrees of success, to cast them in terms of a single, unified, national standard of orthodoxy, Zhu Xi's *Family Rituals*" (Szonyi 2002:205). In other words, these rituals were presented as neo-Confucian orthodoxy expressed in an idiom of ancestor veneration.

The lesson that could be drawn from this example is that kinship and concomitant ancestor veneration were not stable entities so much as variably practiced strategies: kinship and ancestors were (and are) good to think and act with in China. This very utility or promiscuity makes the sociopolitical contextualization of ancestors all the more important as an element of practical kinship.

The contested meaning of ancestors and their potential role in the production of collective memory and place is also highly relevant and poignantly portrayed in Jing's (1996) ethnography of the Kong lineage and their reconstruction of a temple to Confucius in the wake of persecution, relocation, and the destruction of the original temple.

Sharing a surname with and tracing their descent from Confucius, the Kongs came to Dachuan, Gansu, in the late nineteenth century and founded a large ancestral cult there (Jing 1996:8). Singled out for persecution in anti-Confucian campaigns, the Kongs suffered physical and psychological trauma and closure of their ancestral temple in 1958 and finally its destruction in 1974. In the post-Mao era, however, the Kongs were able to rebuild their temple, resuscitate their ancestral ritual, and organize a regional Confucius cult.

Simultaneously site and symbol of collective trauma and rejuvenation, the reborn Confucius temple became both a location of lineage-based ancestor veneration and, through religious innovation, a public cult (Jing 1996:175). By installing a votive statue of Confucius and two separate tables for the ancestral tablets of the Dachuan Kongs' founding ancestors on the one hand and for Confucius and his main disciples on the other, Confucius could be simultaneously worshipped as an ancestor by the Kongs and as a deity by non-Kongs, a distinction not always clearly made in Chinese popular religion anyway (Jordan 1999). Claimants to a 2,500-year-old genealogy, the Kongs of Dachuan turned their revolutionary stigma into a post-Mao locus of social capital and an alternative to central government constructions of local memory (Jing 1996:171).

In terms of an archaeology of ancestors, the Confucius temple at Dachuan illustrates the fact that ancestor veneration often serves as the site of contested memory and that archaeologically visible places of potential ancestor worship such as lineage temples and tombs are also often key sites in highly charged emotional and political topographies. From a prescriptive biological perspective, if we ask, "Is the Dachuan Confucius temple the site of ancestor veneration?" we can only respond affirmatively if we believe the accuracy of a 2,500-year-old genealogy. Nevertheless, in a very real sense, what is relevant in the Kongs' case, inscribed in the terms of their three decades of persecution and their newfound status, is the fact that their claims to descent from Confucius have been taken seriously. Moreover, although the public festivals venerating Confucius organized around the temple stretch the definition of ancestor veneration beyond even fictitious descent, these practices cannot be understood apart from the idiom of ancestral ritual and services to the dead.

From ancient times to the present, the group-forming yet hierarchy-enacting potential of ancestor veneration, and thus its utility as political religion, was realized by a variety of political formations in China. The cult of emperors could be taken as a paradigmatic case of Chinese political ritual as well as the paradox of its simultaneous public and private nature: public in the sense that it portrayed itself as an essential link between humanity and divinity, private in the sense that it was also the cult of one privileged lineage (Rawski 1988).

The Qing emperors (1644–1911), for instance, played the roles of both exemplars of filial piety and leaders of state ritual. The intensely political nature of imperial ancestor veneration and its role in legitimating succession meant that, unlike ordinary ancestor temples, the Qing Temple of Ancestors (Taimiao) in Beijing contained only the direct line of emperors, excluding all collaterals (Rawski 1988:232). Moreover, inclusion in or exclusion from the Temple of Ancestors or the imperial cemetery depended as much on the results of political struggles as genealogy. Imperial death ritual also deviated from the norm in that mourning requirements were universal rather than governed by the five grades of relations (1988:240). Dead emperors, then, were figured both as universal ancestors and as unique sites of conflict and legitimacy. With this in mind, let us now consider the case of Mao's mausoleum presented in Wakeman (1988).

Upon his death in 1976, Mao's physical and discursive body became the site of intense political struggle culminating in its interment under glass in a public mausoleum in spite of his orders, his family's wishes, and the official party policy of cremating the leaders of the revolution. Referencing imperial mausoleums and the cult of imperial ancestors, Mao's mausoleum, like those of Chiang Kai-shek and Sun Yat-sen, became a public shrine for the cult of nation and party. Indeed, Wakeman (1988:263) notes the displacement of Mao's family at the actual funeral by Mao's political affines: "Mao as a person, with family and friends, was displaced by Mao as a transcendent revolutionary leader without a private domain of his own." If the imperial cult can be seen as a politico-religious extension of family-based ancestor ritual, Mao's example can be seen as a further extension of the political to the point that kinship is completely subsumed.

Despite not strictly falling under the common sense, kinship-based remit for ancestors, Wakeman's (1988) analysis of Mao's mausoleum refers to imperial traditions as well as more general Chinese practices of death ritual and ancestor veneration, yet at the same time demonstrates the importance of understanding political context. In communist China, Mao's mausoleum and cult of personality could draw on powerful pre-revolution historical traditions, but in the discourse of leadership at the time, there was no political place for traditional lineage ritual—Mao instead became an apotheosized ancestor of the party.

The above cases illustrate the polysemy of ancestors, the plasticity of their local deployments, and multiple engagements with wider social, political, and religious visions and structures. Ultimately they argue for the necessity of soft definitions and sensitive hermeneutics: ancestral practices and beliefs blend into other formations and local understandings, and it is only with reference to these wider contexts that a study of ancestors can move beyond empty generalizations.

Archaeology of Ancestors

If "ancestors" are at once discursively promiscuous, historically protean, and inextricably intertwined with social, political, and religious features of a long and historically complex tradition, how are we to approach the study of ancestors comparatively? The study of such a potentially rich topic must take account of history in both geographic and temporal terms. It is only within local webs of meaning and logics of practice that we can hope to avoid the empty platitudes and ahistorical generalizations rightly decried by those who argue that there are too many ancestors (Whitley 2002; Hill and Hageman, this volume). Relocated within their constellations of concerns and accretions of tradition and innovation, the topic of ancestors might serve as a fertile ground of comparison—not of isolated socioreligious features and their putative functions, but of networked discursive and practical operators.

Archaeologically speaking, operationalizing a study of ancestors necessitates a broad, nuanced, and integrative approach. An archaeology of ancestors is potentially an archaeology of memory, death, ritual, kinship, identity, and power. These intangibles are difficult to study archaeologically, but in keeping with recent work (e.g., Ingold 2007; Latour 2005; Webmoor and Whitmore 2008), I would argue that the supposed straightforward concreteness of "tangibles" is founded on a blindness to the social life of things and the materiality of the social. In support of this position I offer the example of ancestors in the context of Late Shang Anyang.

Late Shang Ancestors (c. 1250–1050 BCE)

At the outset it should be said that the sources for the study of ancestors at Anyang are rich. Excavated with only brief interruptions for more than eighty years, Late Shang Anyang (figure 3.1), traditionally named Yinxu (the ruins of Yin), covers over 30 km^2 and has yielded thousands of sacrificial pits, large rammed earth "palace-temple" structures, a royal burial ground, over 10,000 burials, and numerous workshops, middens, and residences (Bagley 1999; Campbell 2007, 2014; Chang 1980; Li 1977;

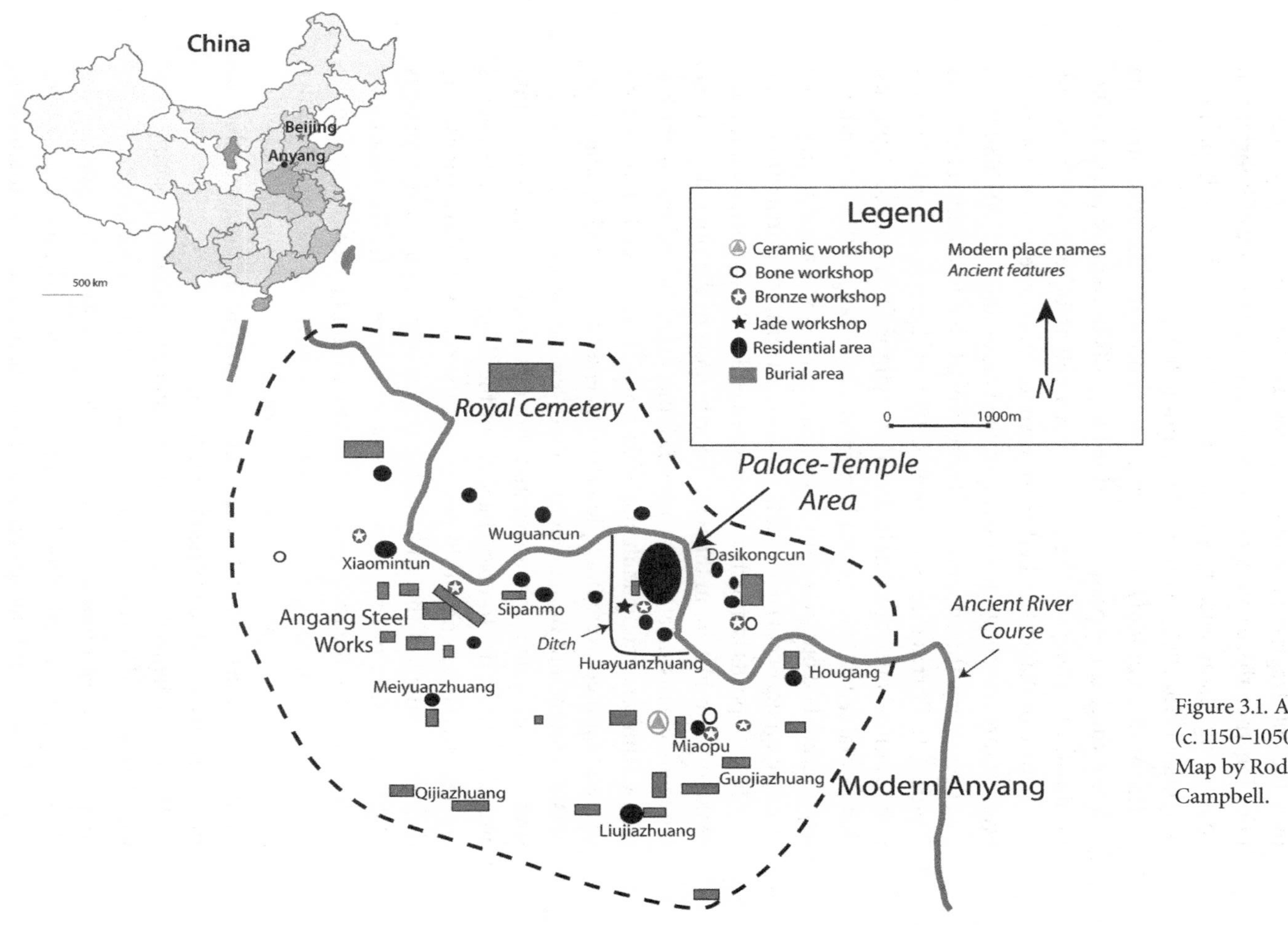

Figure 3.1. Anyang (c. 1150–1050 BCE). Map by Roderick Campbell.

Tang 2004; Thorp 2006). In addition, epigraphic sources include scattered examples of jades and other artifacts, dozens of bronze vessels, and over 100,000 fragments of oracle bones used in (mostly) royal divination. Together, these sources prove to be a rich repository of information concerning Shang ancestors (Campbell 2007; Itō and Takashima 1996; Keightley 1999, 2000; Schwartz 2013; Smith 2008).

The most commonly used indicator of ancestor veneration in China and elsewhere is the presence of ritual deposits in cemeteries (Liu 1999). Minimally, this suggests the presence of a cult associated with the dead. The nature of that cult, whether we wish to call it ancestral or not, however, requires elucidation. Looking at the Late Shang (c. 1250–1050 BCE) royal cemetery, the ritual deposits are remarkable in a number of ways (figure 3.2). First is their scale: over 2,500 have been found, and in addition to animal offerings that included everything from dogs to elephants, they contained at least 12,000 human victims (Tang 2005). Second, the deposits are laid out in orderly rows that occasionally overlap, suggesting multiple events occurring at different times. Third, the distribution of the sacrificial deposits is mostly in the eastern end of the cemetery while most of the royal tombs are in the west. Fourth, most of the ritual deposits do not seem to be associated with any one tomb. Fifth, the majority of the human victims are young adult and adult males. Taken together, these facts suggest that there were multiple sacrificial episodes involving large numbers of animal and human victims that were not directly related to the royal burials, which were associated with additional victims both within and adjacent to the tombs. The scale of the deposits and the resources terminated there signal the importance of the rituals for those sponsoring them, while the fact that most of the victims were military-age males is highly suggestive of captive sacrifice on a massive scale. The location of these remains in the royal cemetery as well as similar deposits within the tombs themselves suggests the continuation of rituals for the dead after burial. If this is so, the location of the ritual events suggests that either contiguity to the tomb of the ritual recipient was unimportant or that the rites were dedicated to the dead collectively.

The tombs themselves are of monumental size and, extrapolating from what has escaped looting and analogies drawn from smaller, intact tombs, they would have housed astronomical concentrations of resources derived from specialized labor (Campbell 2007). Clearly, the death rituals of royalty were of intense concern to the Shang. The royal tombs were

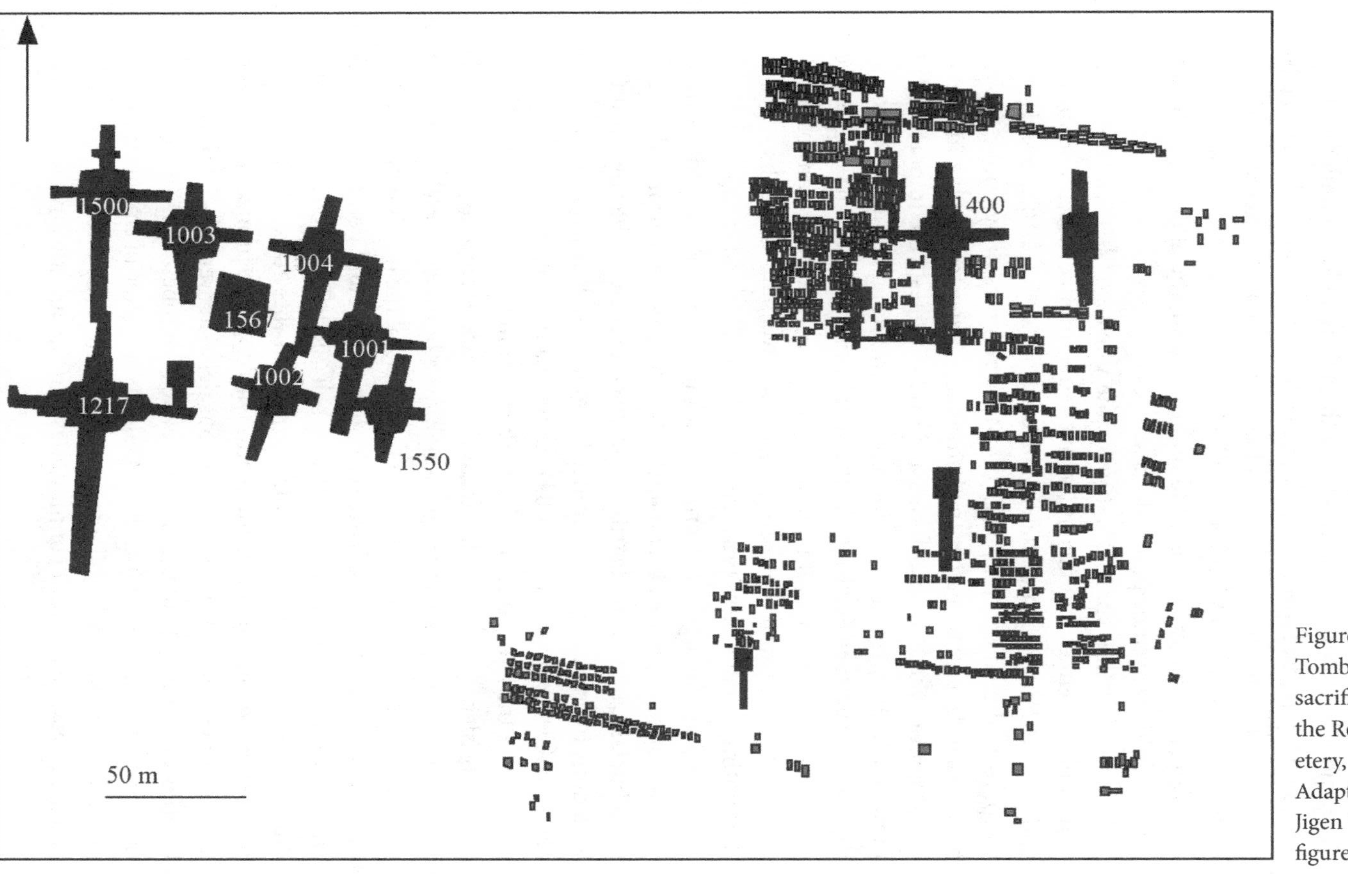

Figure 3.2. Tombs and sacrificial pits in the Royal Cemetery, Anyang. Adapted from Jigen Tang 2004, figure 7.5.

subterranean, and thus their monumentality would have been experienced by the living only during the mortuary rites before the sealing of the tomb. The nature of the tombs, with their wooden chambers, death attendants, guards, food offerings, bronze feasting vessels, chimes, bells, weapons, and jade artifacts of ritual and ornament, further suggest notions of a chthonic royal afterlife. What is more, if the sacrificial pits are full of dynastic enemies offered to the royal dead, the afterlives of Shang kings would seem to be political ones.

If we look at the specific nature of the grave goods themselves, the enormous resources and ingenuity invested in bronze vessels and bronze and jade weapons is immediately apparent. Indeed, feasting vessels and weapons had held central places in elite economies of symbolic capital for thousands of years before the Late Shang. Nevertheless, the immense investment in these artifact forms at Anyang suggests the importance of the activities they signify: feasting and war. In this light, the livestock and captives in the sacrificial pits of the royal cemetery become suggestive of a continued commensal relationship between the living and the dead. Further, the inclusion of feasting vessels and weapons in tombs suggests the continuation of these practices among the deceased.

Other Late Shang burial grounds scattered around Anyang show a similar concern for death ritual. Dubbed lineage cemeteries, the nonroyal burial grounds are distributed in discrete clusters sharing common variations in assemblage and bronze insignia as well as associations with clusters of settlements (Tang 2004). These features suggest discrete communities of the living and the dead. These communities, moreover, were internally hierarchical, ranging from elite, ramped tombs associated with chariot burials to pits just large enough for a body with few or no grave goods. The most common category of tomb is not the nearly empty pit but rather a small grave with a basic ceramic vessel set and perhaps a bronze weapon or small jade ornament (Campbell 2007; Tang 2004). These ordinary tombs share structural homologies with elite graves, including the replacement of human death attendants with dogs and bronze vessels with ceramic ones. Moreover, these analogous deposits were placed in similar locations in elite and common tombs alike (Campbell 2007). From these facts, it would appear that death ritual was a matter of importance to a broad spectrum of society, it was practiced with vastly unequal resources, and it was associated with communities who apparently envisioned their dead as having communal afterlives and requiring continued service, as suggested by sacrificial pits in some non-royal cemeteries.

From the connections between groups of living and dead and the huge investment in death ritual, the dead seem to have played a central role in Shang life. Given the vast disparity between the resources devoted to the royal tombs and sacrifices compared with those of ordinary folk, Shang mortuary ritual seems to have been hierarchy-enacting and, to some degree, ordered by sumptuary rules (Campbell 2007; Tang 2004). It was also community forming, bringing together groups of living with their dead, and based on the evidence of captive sacrifice, it was political. If we can draw the further conclusion that these hierarchical communities of the living and dead were kin-based, then the Late Shang sociopolitical landscape was fundamentally an ancestral one (Keightley 2000).

Inscriptions

While the material record at Anyang can tell us certain things about Shang relations between the living and the dead, contemporaneous oracle-bone and bronze inscriptions can tell us even more. The oracle-bone inscriptions as records of (mostly) the king's divination are, perhaps not surprisingly, good sources for studying the king's relations with the unseen forces of the world, including the dead. What is surprising is the degree to which ancestors or, more literally, deceased "fathers," "brothers," "mothers," "grandfathers,"[1] "grandmothers," and even more remote individuals figured in the king's divinations. As in later Chinese traditions, Shang ancestors were thought to be responsible for illness and misfortune as well as good fortune and success. As such, they were frequent recipients of sacrificial rituals focused on "reporting," "hosting," and even "exorcising" malevolent ancestral influences.

As sources of illness, as in medieval China, more recently deceased Shang royal ancestors appear to have been the most dangerous, as the following divinations suggest (Keightley 2000: 103):

1. Tested: [As for] the sick tooth, it is [due to] Father Yi's curse (*heji* 13649).
2. Tested: [As for] the sick tooth, perform an exorcism ritual against Father Yi (*heji* 13652).

3. Exorcise Father Yi [offering] three specially reared sheep (*heji* 2195 reverse).

In these inscriptions we can see both the ambivalent relationship between the living and the dead and the manner in which that relationship was structured: like the spirits of the mountains, rivers, earth, and winds, the dead required sacrifice. For dead kings and their consorts, the scale of those offerings could be large indeed as the following example shows.

4. Tested: Perform an exorcism from Tang [to] Da Jia, [to] Ancestor Yi using one hundred qiang-captives, one hundred specially reared sheep (*heji* 300).

This example shows not only the scale of some thirteenth-century BCE ancestral exorcisms but also their group nature. As suggested by the positioning of sacrificial pits in the royal cemetery, one could offer sacrifices to royal ancestors collectively. From other inscriptions we know that the ancestors were sometimes addressed in terms of "the upper and lower altars" or the remoter ancestors as simply "high ancestors." Shang royal ancestors, then, could be both collectively and individually invoked, suggesting that the line between individualized and collective ancestors drawn by some authors (Whitley 2002) (with the latter being supposedly rare and therefore an inappropriate analogy for prehistoric cases) may be too simplistic.

A more positive relationship with the dead can be seen in the "hosting" rituals, whereby the king or other high elites "hosted" (*bin* 賓) royal ancestors with sacrificial offerings, possibly followed by feasting, as in these examples.

5. Cracked on Jiayan day, Yin tested: The king should host Da Jia performing a *rong* ritual [and if he does] there will be no fault (*heji* 22723).
6. Tested: Da [Jia] hosts with Di (*heji* 1402).

In this pair of examples we can see not only the king hosting his ancestor but also a high ancestor hosting (or perhaps being hosted by) the high god Di. Di is apparently never sacrificed to directly by the living, only indirectly receiving cult through a generational hierarchy of ritual intercession (Keightley 2000:100). Though mirroring later imperial Chinese notions of an afterlife organized in a celestial bureaucracy with petitions passing up through hierarchically organized departments, the Shang postmortem hierarchy reflects a politics based on genealogical seniority, a community of the living and the dead, and a world structured in terms of kinship.

This last point is powerfully instantiated in an ancestralizing tendency over the course of Late Shang ritual (Itō and Takashima 1996). In the middle of the Late Shang period, sweeping changes took place across a number of practices, including divination and sacrifice as well as burial ritual, and reflected wider sociopolitical changes (Campbell 2007; Jiang 2012). In terms of sacrifice, formerly ad hoc royal ritual was replaced with a system of cyclical sacrifice, with each ancestor receiving cult on the day of the ten-day weekly cycle for which they were named (Chang 1987). Where in this cycle then do nonancestors fit, for example, spirits of mountains and rivers without day names? It is likely that they too were somehow integrated with the rhythm of the royal sacrifice and, indeed, with the sixty-day cycle tied to the king's ancestral cult. In one sense it could not have been otherwise: time itself came to be told in terms of royal ancestral ritual, as this inscription on the bronze of an official indicates.

> 7. On Dingsi day the King inspected Nao X [a place]. The King presented Minor Retainer Yu with Nao cowry shells. It was during the King's coming to campaign against the Ren Fang. It was the King's fifteenth ritual cycle on the day of the *rong*-ritual (The Minor Retainer Yu Zun).

Just as the high ancestors had always mirrored the powers of the nature spirits (e.g., to bring rain or sun, strong winds or calm, and to control the weather in general), by the end of the Late Shang period the powers of the land had begun to be assimilated to "high ancestral" status, as the following example suggests.

> 8. Xinwei day, tested: We should pray for good harvest to the high ancestor River and on Xinsi day perform *you* [cutting?] and *liao* [burning?] rituals (*heji* 32028).

In a sense, then, the Late Shang world was fundamentally mediated by the king's ancestral ritual practices.

If the king presided over a world-ordering complex of ancestral ritual fed with war captives and livestock from near and far, he was not alone in his preoccupation with ancestors. Inscriptions on bronze feasting vessels of the period reveal the context of their creation in their records of reward and ancestral dedication.

> The King awarded lesser retainer Yue[?] five years of the yields of Yu. Yue thereupon made this vessel for offerings in Eldest son Yi's family ritual. X [common Shang clan insignia] Father Yi (Xiaochen Yue *fangding*).

In this example we can see not only a record of royal reward and thus merit but also the vessel's raison d'être framed in terms of dedication to the dead and their continued ritual service. The fact that it is a deceased son who is the "ancestor" in this dedication again raises the point that "ancestor ritual" in Late Shang China is embedded within larger concerns about ritually mediating relations with the dead and is not restricted to deceased relatives ancestral to the ritual officiant.

Returning to Late Shang burial assemblages and the importance of bronze vessel sets, the immense social investment in the casting of bronze vessels, and the homologous role of ceramic forms in smaller, poorer tombs, an important point emerges: offerings to ancestors played a central role in the lives of elites and non-elites alike. Indeed, it seems that king and commoner shared important principles of ancestral ritual, as the examples of six jade "handle-shaped" objects found in Hougang 91M3 (ZSKY 2005:21–26) suggest (figure 3.3). These artifacts each bear, in the same format as royal ancestor designations, the day name of an ancestor, indicating that ancestor veneration was practiced even among non-royal lineages. Indeed, in light of the broad participation in ancestor veneration and the cosmology, seen in the royal inscriptions, of a generational hierarchy of living and dead, the discrete clusters of residences and tombs revealed by recent work at Anyang take on a new significance: a basic ordering of Shang society in terms of hierarchical kinship communities of the living and the dead.

To summarize the evidence concerning ancestors at Late Shang Anyang: there is most conspicuously the enormous social energy directed toward monumental tombs, episodes of large-scale sacrifice independent of burial events but nonetheless spatially associated with them, bronze ritual feasting vessels and highly refined osteomantic divinatory practices. The corpus of written materials, whether inscriptions on bronze vessels or records of oracle-bone divination, largely revolves around ancestors: ancestral curses, ancestral ritual, ancestral approval, and ancestor dedications.

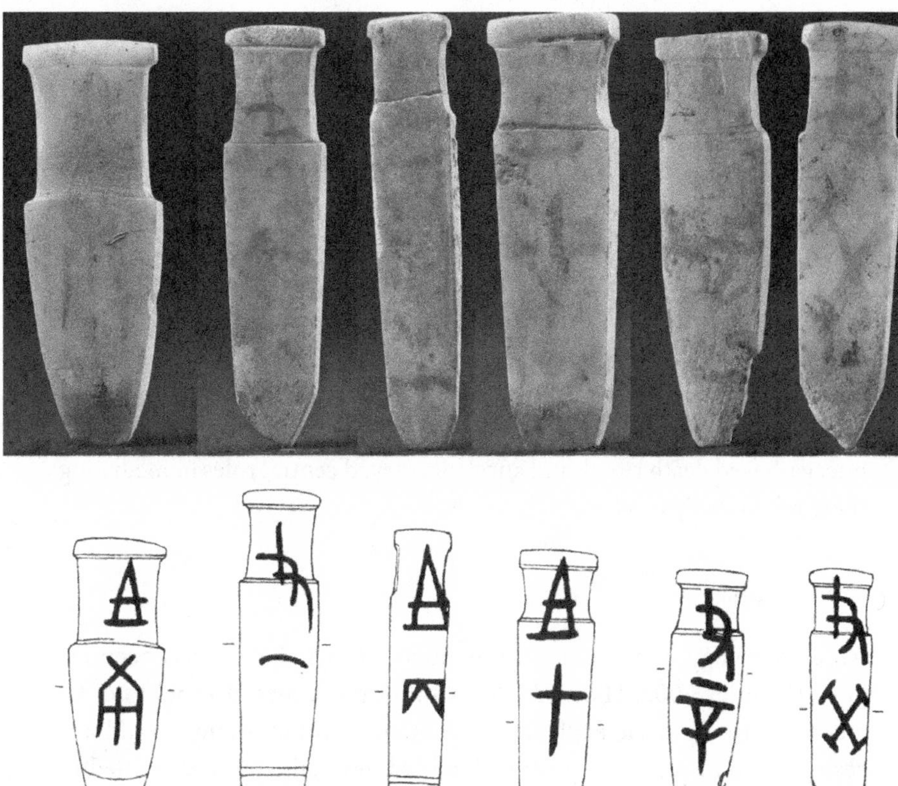

Figure 3.3. Jade "handle-shaped" objects from Hougang 91M3. From left to right they read, Ancestor Geng, Father X, Ancestor Bin, Ancestor Jia, Father Xin, and Father Gui. Adapted from Jigen Tang 2008, 157.

The ritual bronze vessels—based on their shapes, the inscriptions they bear, their prominence in tombs, and the references to hosting ancestors found on the oracle-bones—were focal participants in sacrifice and feasting events that linked the living and the dead in common communities. Non-royal burial and sacrificial practices also bear witness to similar phenomena on a smaller scale and the division of residential and burial areas into discrete but internally hierarchical clusters further suggests a basic division in terms of kin groups centered around the worship of common apical ancestors.

Late Shang ancestors were embedded in collective ideas about and engagements with the world for king and lineage member alike. The line between baleful specter and beneficent ancestor was not a categorical one for Shang people but rather contingent and ambiguous. For the residents of Anyang, the dead mediated the misty borders between the domains of nature, civilization, and supernature. Put another way, if hierarchical kinship was the organizing principle of Shang collectives, ancestral ritual at once instantiated the hope that the unseen dangers of the world could be tamed, tempered with the fear that they could not (Puett 2002). At the same time, rites of burial and sacrifice were sites for the negotiation of genealogy, memory, and, above all, status. If royal and imperial ancestor veneration were always political in China, the stakes were never higher than for the Late Shang kings. Political power, religious authority, and social status were all linked through common hierarchical practices of lineage-based death ritual, and ancestors played central roles in mediating these relationships.

Conclusion

An archaeology of ancestors can be many things. But, as has been argued (Whitley 2002; Hill and Hageman, this volume), it should not be a content-free generic explanation. Neither, I would argue, should ancestors become a narrowly defined, reified, nomothetic category tied to cross-cultural functionalist explanatory modes. Comparison needs both a common ground and a sensitivity to local meanings, practices, and being-in-the-world. Ancestors, for instance, are dead and therefore embedded in complexes of death ritual and ideas concerning death and the afterlife. Death, moreover, though universal, is locally figured in discourse and intersubjectively experienced as a relationship between the departed and those who remain behind. Ancestors, then, are instantiations of relational discourses on life, death, and memory, however diffracted through lenses of affect, tradition, and power. Ancestors are also nominally predicated on kinship, but it should be clear from the examples above that kinship is also a flexible and variable set of relations, metaphorically extendible and often, from an objective genealogical point of view, fictional. Nevertheless, fictional or metaphoric kin relations are no less socially real and, from the standpoint of practical kinship, may be more relevant than actual biological descent. If kinship is a frequently fuzzy and promiscuous category, then how much more so its projection across the variably construed alterities of death.

The cases I have provided from China illustrate that ancestors in practice and discourse vary over time and from place to place: from ordering principle of the world to increasingly abstract national metaphor; from site of prestige to site of trauma and back again. They are impacted by specific notions of death and the dead from early Daoist curative practices, to Buddhist ideas of salvation/damnation, to modern discourses of science and reason. Chinese ancestors were also variable elements of micro- and macro-political strategies, good to think and act with, constituents of memory and identity, place and meaning in life as much as in death. Archaeologies of ancestors, then, are necessarily metaphorically excavations of large and complex sites. Indeed, it is the very power of institutions such as ancestors that makes them the foci of contested meaning and provides the motives for appropriation. The more powerful a concept, the more protean its instantiations and the more important its historical contextualization.

Note

1. The kinship term for two generations prior to ego and earlier is *zu*, so what I have translated as "grandfathers" could also be translated as "ancestors."

References Cited

Bagley, Robert

1999 Shang Archaeology. In *Cambridge History of Ancient China*, edited by Michael Loewe and Edward Shaughnessy, pp. 124–231. Cambridge University Press, Cambridge.

Bokenkamp, Stephen R.

2007 *Ancestors and Anxiety: Daoism and the Birth of Rebirth in China.* University of California Press, Berkeley.

Campbell, Roderick

2007 Blood, Flesh, and Bones: Kinship and Violence in the Social Economy of the Late Shang. PhD dissertation, Departments of Anthropology and East Asian Languages and Civilizations, Harvard University, Cambridge, Massachusetts.

2014 *Archaeology of the Chinese Bronze Age: From Erlitou to Anyang.* Cotsen Institute of Archaeology, University of California, Los Angeles.

Chang, K. C.

1980 *Shang Civilization.* Yale University Press, New Haven, Connecticut.

Chang, Yuzhi

1987 *Shangdai zhouji zhidu.* Zhongguo shehuikexue chubanshe, Beijing.

Ebrey, Patricia B., and James L. Watson (editors)
1986 *Kinship Organization in Late Imperial China, 1000–1940*. University of California Press, Berkeley.

Ingold, Tim
2007 Materials against Materiality. *Archaeological Dialogues* 14(1):1–16.

Itō, Michiharu, and Ken-ichi Takashima
1996 *Studies in Early Chinese Civilization: Religion, Society, Language, and Paleography*. Kansai Gaidan University Press, Osaka.

Jiang Yude (Roderick Campbell)
2012 Guo zhi da shi: Shangdai wanqi zhong de lizhi gailiang (The Great Affairs of the State: The Late Shang Ritual Reforms). In *Yinxu kexuefajue 80 nian xueshu jinianhui*, edited by Tang Jigen, pp. 267–276. Science Press, Beijing.

Jing Jun
1996 *The Temple of Memories: History, Power, and Morality in a Chinese Village*. Stanford University Press, Stanford, California.

Jordan, David K.
1999 *Gods, Ghosts, and Ancestors: Folk Religion in a Taiwanese Village*. 3rd ed. Department of Anthropology, University of California, San Diego.

Keightley, David
1999 The Shang: China's First Historical Dynasty. In *Cambridge History of Ancient China*, edited by Michael Loewe and Edward Shaughnessy, pp. 232–291. Cambridge University Press, Cambridge.
2000 *The Ancestral Landscape: Time, Space, and Community in Late Shang China (ca. 1200–1045 BC)*. Institute of East Asian Studies, University of California, Berkeley.

Latour, Bruno
2005 *Reassembling the Social: An Introduction to Actor-Network Theory*. Oxford University Press, Oxford.

Li Chi
1977 *Anyang*. University of Washington Press, Seattle.

Liu Li
1999 Who Were the Ancestors? The Origins of Chinese Ancestral Cult and Racial Myths. *Antiquity* 73: 603–613.

Naquin, Susan
1988 Funerals in North China: Uniformity and Variation. In *Death Ritual in Late Imperial and Modern China*, edited by James L. Watson and Evelyn S. Rawski, pp. 37–70. University of California Press, Berkeley.

Puett, Michael
2002 *To Become a God: Cosmology, Sacrifice, and Self-Divinization in Early China*. Harvard University Press, Cambridge, Massachusetts.
2014 Ritual Disjunctions: Ghosts, Philosophy, and Anthropology. In *The Ground Between: Anthropologists Engage Philosophy*, edited by Veena Das, Michael Jackson, Arthur Kleinman, and Bhrigupati Singh, pp. 218–232. Duke University Press, Durham, North Carolina.

Rawski, Evelyn S.

1988 The Imperial Way of Death: Ming and Ch'ing Emperors and Death Ritual. In *Death Ritual in Late Imperial and Modern China*, edited by James L. Watson and Evelyn S. Rawski, pp. 228–253. University of California Press, Berkeley.

Schwartz, Adam

2013 Huayuanzhuang East I: An Annotated Translation of the Oracle-Bone Inscriptions. PhD dissertation, East Asian Languages and Civilization, University of Chicago, Chicago.

Smith, Adam

2008 Writing at Anyang: The Role of the Divination Record in the Emergence of Chinese Literacy. PhD dissertation, Archaeology, University of California, Los Angeles.

Strickmann, Michel

2002 *Chinese Magical Medicine*. Edited by Bernard Faure. Stanford University Press, Stanford, California.

Szonyi, Michael

2002 *Practicing Kinship: Lineage and Descent in Late Imperial China*. Stanford University Press, Stanford, California.

Tang, Jigen

2004 The Social Organization of Late Shang China: A Mortuary Perspective. PhD dissertation, Institute of Archaeology, University of London.

2005 The True Face of Antiquity: Anyang Yinxu Sacrificial Pits and the Dark Side of "Three Dynasties Civilization." Unpublished manuscript in possession of the author.

2008 *Yinxu: yige wangchao de beijing / Yinxu: The Background of a Royal Dynasty*. Kexue chubanshe, Beijing.

Thorp, Robert

2006 *China in the Early Bronze Age: Shang Civilization*. University of Pennsylvania Press, Philadelphia.

Wakeman, Frederic

1988 Mao's Remains. In *Death Ritual in Late Imperial and Modern China*, edited by James L. Watson and Evelyn S. Rawski, pp. 254–288. University of California Press, Berkeley.

Watson, James L., and Evelyn S. Rawski (editors)

1988 *Death Ritual in Late Imperial and Modern China*. University of California Press, Berkeley.

Webmoor, Timothy, and Christopher Whitmore

2008 Things Are Us! A Commentary on Human/Things Relations under the Banner of a "Social" Archaeology. *Norwegian Archaeological Review* 41(1):53–70.

Whitley, James

2002 Too Many Ancestors. *Antiquity* 76(291):119–26.

ZSKY (Zhongguo Shehuikexueyuan, Kaogu Yanjiusuo)

2005 *Anyang Yinxu chutu yuqi / Jades from Yinxu*. Kexue chubanshe, Beijing.

4

Achieving Ancestorhood in Ancient Greece

CARLA ANTONACCIO

Though the Greeks of the Classical period (fifth century BC) were cognizant of social standing, privilege, and citizen rights as determined by birth, they did not practice anything like the cult of the dead or of ancestors such as that known from other cultures in the ethnographic and archaeological literature (cf. Humphreys 1980). Says James Whitley (2002:124): "There is little . . . to suggest that ancestors played a major role in the imagination of Archaic Greeks—whereas there is much to suggest that gods, heroes, and other races did." Whitley draws a clear distinction between ancestors and other figures who are, as he elsewhere has it, "aliens; they had no genealogical or genetic relations with the present inhabitants." This statement begs a definition of the term "ancestor." Whitley quotes that of Maurice Bloch: "The term ancestor is used in anthropology to designate those forebears who are remembered" (Whitley 2002:122; see also Bloch 2002 [1996] on ancestor worship more generally). This minimal definition has the virtue of being simple, allowing for the varieties of what a given culture may deem a "forebear." Whitley's own "minimal definition" of an ancestor is "someone who has procreated, died but has descendants who remember him/her" (2002:121). Both scholars stress remembrance, which in the ethnographic and archaeological literature usually takes the form of worship of ancestors, or ancestor cult, sometimes quite developed, and celebrated in societies such as those of China or Madagascar or in antiquity among, say, the Romans.

Whitley, however, takes the notion of "ancestor" as one that requires actual descent in a biological sense; he does not recognize that Greek heroes are essentially fictive or idealized ancestors. This is a key factor in his critique of the tendency to find ancestors everywhere in European prehistory. The other factor is his own insistence on continuity of memory.

The veneration of ancestors as a feature of Greek religion is downplayed not only by Whitley. But all students of ancient Greece, including archaeologists, accept that the heroes provided a point of reference for membership in civic, clan, and regional groups articulated through interlocking systems of shared descent for communities and ethnic groups in Greek territory (e.g., the Dorians, Ionians, Achaeans, Aeolians; cf. Hall 1999, 2002). They are a category of persons whose parentage is both human *and* divine, yet who are mortal despite their semi-divine origins. Violent death at a young age is the most common fate for a Greek hero, who was not, therefore, a god. In compensation for their deaths, however, heroes had undying glory (in Greek, *kleos aphthiton*)—glory that was passed down in song, in the traditional forms of epic poetry.

Greek heroes are entirely human in that they suffer, and they are neither immortal nor invincible. They die, and though they may have a continuing existence in an afterlife, the price for undying glory is still death. As Achilles himself said, speaking to his fellow warrior Odysseus, who had journeyed to the underworld in a classic and archetypal heroic quest: "I would rather live in service to another man, a man without possessions, than rule over all the wasted dead" (*Odyssey*, book 11, lines 489–491; Schmiel 1987). Heroes were (and are) appealing precisely because they are not gods—not, by nature, immortal and all-powerful. Indeed, the warrior example of Greek heroes and their compensatory *kleos* was invoked as worthy of emulation in the ancient Greek present, providing a hortatory example for archaic and classical warriors risking their lives in the kind of close combat that epic heroes also undertook. (It should be noted that women, such as Odysseus's wife, Penelope, could also obtain *kleos*, as discussed by Katz 1991.)

Family ancestors in the immediate kin group also had their place in Greek society. Descent defined property rights, legitimated citizenship, and so forth, but the heroes of myth functioned in a different way. Though not divine, they had supernatural powers and articulated larger notions of belonging and relating that linked territories, cities, and human lineages that claimed descent from them. Moreover, while Greek heroes originated in particular regions or communities, and were often claimed by later inhabitants of the places where they were born, had died, or had accomplished something of note, their significance was often more than local, and more than one locality could appeal to them.

Thus something that is no longer really operative in our own popular notions about heroes and heroism is that heroes in Greek society also functioned as ancestors. Among their deeds Greek heroes procreated—even the young and unmarried ones, such as Achilles, managed to father children who carried on their lineages. Individual Greeks, families, and communities might invoke heroic ancestors as their founders. Taking one step further, they might share in the divine parentage that heroes claimed, since they themselves were the offspring of a divinity and a mortal. The purported graves and physical relics of heroes were powerful. By the eighth century BC, the practice of hero cult—ritual practices intended to honor these collective and mythical ancestors—had been established in several places, and these ancestors had become the ultimate referents for communal and regional identity and affinity (see essays in Albersmeier and Anderson 2009).

As already mentioned, a particular family's *remembered* forebears were also important to personal as well as civic identity and privilege. Moreover, there is evidence for the remembrance or acknowledgment of a group of ancestors whose names had been lost or forgotten—distinct from any group of heroes. This is a somewhat shadowy collectivity called the Tritopatreis or Tritopatores—anonymous ancestors beyond the boundaries of human memory. Thus in the Archaic and Early Classical periods (seventh to fifth centuries BC), there are several categories of ancestors: named, often epic heroes discussed above; the recent, family dead, those whom the present generation knew and whose graves they made and could visit; and the Tritopatreis and other anonymous figures (on the recent dead, see Johnston 1999).

In this chapter I will outline the ancient Greeks' views on their own past through their relationships with different categories of ancestors. This requires understanding what we might mean by "ancestors" in Greek antiquity. I propose a definition that is somewhat different than those advanced by Bloch and Whitley. I hope to show that the Greeks had several categories of ancestors and views of the past. Rather than see these domains in need of reconciliation, I suggest that they serve different social, political, and ritual purposes. It is also important to understanding the function of different categories of ancestors and their relationships with the living—not just in terms of the features of the landscape that might be attributed to them.

Archaeologies of Ancestors

The 1970s, 1980s, and 1990s saw a great deal of attention to heroes, in particular the archaeology of the origins of Greek heroes and their veneration (Antonaccio 1995). These investigations frequently began with Greek epic poetry, in tandem with new archaeological discoveries at the sites of heroic cults and a new interest in the period during which Homeric epic was circulated: the Greek Iron Age, ca. 1100 to 700 BC. At the same time, archaeologists working in Europe and elsewhere, especially in prehistory, invoked a cognizance of ancestors in antiquity to explain a variety of features, such as monumental tombs (and their reuse and renovation sometimes over long periods of time) and the manipulation of the remains of the dead, as well as social exclusion and inequality, territorial boundaries, and access to resources. Something that explains everything comes to explain nothing, and so the classical archaeologist James Whitley, who himself contributed to this discourse about the importance of the past and of ancestors, especially heroes and the heroic dead in Greek antiquity, eventually came to the following conclusion: "There are too many ancestors in contemporary archaeological interpretation, and they are being asked to do too much" (Whitley 2002:119). Ancestors had become what could be called a totalizing phenomenon, invoked as a "legitimizing strategy" upon which claims of power were founded and used to explain every interaction of societies with the remains of the past, such as burials or monuments from former times.

Referring to the "specter" of the "omnipresent ancestor" in the study of British prehistory, Whitley observed how this shadow came to haunt other pasts studied by British scholars like himself. He attributed this to a "theoretical unconscious" in 1970s and 1980s archaeology dealing with the Neolithic, one that was extrapolated to the study of Greek prehistory (Whitley 2002:120)—for example, the Minoans of Crete (figure 4.1). Such an unconscious, then, also characterized approaches to the Greek Iron Age. Scholars frequently used Homer to explain early Greek society and culture and invoked the influence of Homeric poetry, focused on heroic narratives, to account for the spread of the veneration of heroes in the period during which Homer's poetry was thought to have first

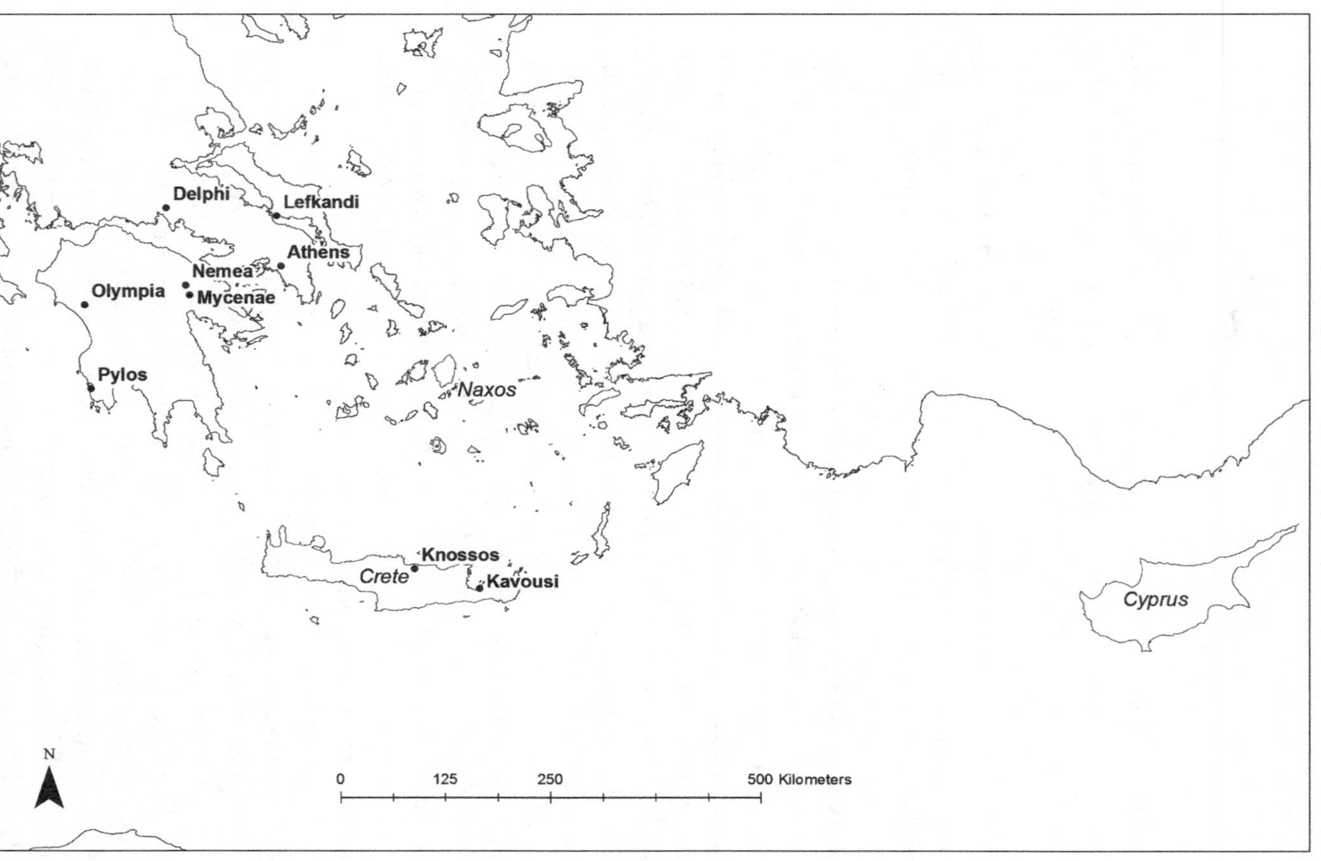

Figure 4.1. Map of Greece with sites mentioned in the text. Map by Timothy Shea.

been performed (the eighth century BC as proposed by Coldstream 1976). While this approach no longer dominates Classical archaeology today, its influence is still detectable.

Whitley decried what he called the "flattening of the landscape" of the Greek past through the constant invocation of ancestors by modern scholars, a tendency that ignores other narratives and strategies by which the ancient Greeks explicated their own past: Greek mythology and folktales are concerned with generations of divinities, among whom Whitley would count the heroes, but not ancestors as he defines them. The claim, however, that an ancestral panacea is nothing more than a nifty work-around for "the tedious business of undertaking contextual analysis or testing specific models against the available evidence" (Whitley 2002:120) is not one supported by a reading of other scholars' work. Indeed, Whitley's brief reference to my own work ignores the contextual analysis that I undertook and only referred to part of my conclusions. Nor does Whitley make much use of the work on the archaeology of Greek ritual practices in the Iron Age and Archaic periods, preferring to turn to the narratives of the nineteenth-century Greeks or medieval Irish to emphasize the disconnection of later generations with the past visible in the landscape.

As often happens, much disagreement turns on the definition of terms. Having examined the idea of the hero, I come back to the term "ancestor." As noted above, Whitley's own "minimal definition" of an ancestor is "someone who has procreated, died but has descendants who remember him/her" (2002:121). He also quotes with approval Bloch's definition of the term "ancestor" (Bloch 2002:66 [1996]). Whitley (2002:122) elaborates on the minimal definition in a way that I propose to adopt:

> Ancestorhood is an achieved status. . . . Ancestors are the elect of the dead, those whom later generations regard as important. . . . Rites of burial and rites of "ancestor worship" are ritually and often spatially distinct. Ancestors are frequently revered in places which bear no obvious relation to the place of burial.

The notion that ancestorhood is an achieved status is an important refinement of Bloch's basic definition as applied to the ancient Greek case. A key question, then, is how this status is achieved, how the accomplishments or demonstrated qualities of individual actors lead them to attain a given status. Thus for Whitley, "ancestor" is a term that embraces not all forebears, stretching back to some indefinite origin, but only those with descendants who "remember" them through, one assumes, stories, rituals, custody, and curation of their remains.

In expounding on his definition, Whitley stresses specificities of status, place, and ritual: properly speaking, ancestors are not a collectivity but individuals whose descendants deem them significant. It is a kind of postmortem achievement of status, but the criteria for remembering are, at least in the early period of Greek history, achievements of some form—for example, fighting gloriously, amassing wealth that attracts followers, being able to feast such followers, or having access to and distributing prestige goods. Such a definition implies, moreover, a continuity of memory. This insistence on continuity is the crux of Whitley's dispute with scholarly ancestral conspirators: he criticizes the idea that every reuse of an ancient monument in the past is an ancestralizing strategy—that is, one that seeks to enlist powerful ancestors in support of descendants (or claimants to status) in the present, perhaps by people with no direct descent from those to whom they appeal for legitimacy. Whitley attributes the lack of interest in ancestors to discontinuities in Greek history, especially between the Bronze Age and later periods. Thus a brief overview of the Greek Bronze Age (3300–1200 BC) helps set the stage for the rest of this discussion, since the period following the Bronze Age is crucial.

The Antiquity of the Greek Past

The last centuries of the Bronze Age (1600–1200 BC) on the Greek mainland featured a strong chiefdom or even state-level society, a literate bureaucracy, a highly developed redistributive economy with long-distance trade relations, impressive monumental architecture, and elaborate rituals. At Mycenae, the mainland type site that gives its name to both the culture and time period, elite family tombs, the so-called shaft graves, marked the beginning of the Late Bronze Age. These are the burials of Grave Circle A (ca. 1600–1500 BC) discovered by Heinrich Schliemann, the pioneer excavator of Mycenae and Troy who sought to prove the truth of Homer's poems (Gere 2006). A second circle of shaft graves was discovered in the 1950s, a short distance away from the tombs found by Schliemann. These discoveries helped to establish the importance and even the existence of the preclassical Greek past. The incredibly rich burials of the first circle, loaded with gold objects, elaborate ceremonial weapons, and imported objects from as far away as Egypt and the steppes, were marked with stone

Figure 4.2. Mycenaean tholos tomb, so-called Treasury of Agamemnon, Mycenae. Photo by C. Antonaccio.

stelai. The other circle was outside the defensive walls, part of a cemetery that continued in use into the Iron Age.

The Late Bronze Age saw the construction of monumental defensive walls and of monumental dynastic tombs at several sites (figure 4.2). Stone-built, corbelled collective burial chambers developed out of communal collective tombs on the island of Crete, and they coexisted with chamber tomb cemeteries, which were also used for multiple burials, though for deceased of lesser status. In both types of tomb, collective burial is presumed to be based on kinship. Shaft Grave Circle A, out of use for centuries, was reserved inside a walled precinct within the city walls of Mycenae, right next to the main gate of the citadel (figure 4.3). This enclosure of Circle A suggests a cognizance of the past and of the earlier tombs even in the Late Bronze Age. The use of some of these tombs for several generations suggests a short time depth for the lineages using them, however.

Figure 4.3. Grave Circle A, Mycenae (1600–1500 BC). Photo by C. Antonaccio.

To complement this archaeological picture, we have a few fragmentary written records from the end of the period, especially from Pylos, a site in the far southwest of the Greek peninsula. In a very archaic form of Greek, these record offerings to deities among the transactions taking place in the regional centralized redistributive economy. The names famously include some of the later Greek gods, including one called *ti-ri-se-ro-e*. This would be rendered in classical Greek as "triple hero." At Pylos, this figure seems to be connected with the individual at the top of the social and economic hierarchy, a ruler called *wanax* (a title, not a personal name). The *tiriseroe* is likely related to the later entity called the Tritopater (plural: Tritopatreis, Tritopatores) or "Triple Father(s)." The Tritopatores have garbled mythological narratives, but they are conceptualized in the sixth century BC as a kind of ancestral collective: undifferentiated ancestors who represent the dead beyond some three generations in the past (figure 4.4). It is notable that the term "hero" appears already in this Late Bronze Age document, whereas no names of epic heroes have so far been identified in contemporary Linear B texts (Antonaccio 2006).

Bronze Age Greek society collapsed in a poorly understood series of events around 1200 BC that destroyed most of its main centers. Among what survived to emerge again in the historical period around 750 BC were the Greek language, some of the Greek gods, and the form of heroic poetry called epic—the poetry of Homer and of Hesiod. Among other things, the use of writing and monumental construction, especially using stone, was lost. Burial, both elite and non-elite, ceased to be collective, a development often taken as a strong sign of social and settlement disruption and discontinuity.

Continuity or discontinuity on either side of this collapse is a key issue in considering Greek ancestors, for it is beyond dispute that a major rupture occurred with the collapse of the Bronze Age. Indeed, both the causes of this collapse and the completeness of the attendant discontinuity in Greek history and culture have long been debated. Greek myth itself describes cycles of time, and speaks of a "return" of descendants of Herakles who, having been exiled from their rightful homeland in the Peloponnese, claim the Mycenaean heartland three generations after the Trojan War; this is generally known as the "Dorian Invasion." Among historians and archaeologists up to a generation ago, the historical collapse was attributed to everything from climate change, trade disruption, social unrest, and invasion (from the north by the Dorians or from the

Figure 4.4. Tritopatreion *horos* (boundary marker), Athens. Photo by C. Antonaccio.

eastern Mediterranean by the same groups that harassed the Egyptians in this period). The period after 1200 BC was held to be an impoverished, illiterate, and isolated Dark Age, a time of conflict, mass migration, insecurity, and even the end of a settled way of life; farming, it was claimed, gave way to a transhumant pastoral existence. While the causes remain somewhat obscure, the view of the post-collapse period recently has been revised, along with terminology: rather than a Dark Age, it is now usually referred to as the Iron Age. Invasion and climate have both been downplayed as key causes. Multiple variables were undoubtedly in play, and greater continuity between the Bronze Age and the ensuing Iron Age has been admitted.

It was always recognized that some continuity had to have been the case: the Greek language and many of the Greek gods made it over the gap, as likely did the tradition of epic poetry. Some settlements continued to be inhabited, for example, Athens and Lefkandi. Bronze Age cemeteries were often abandoned when the population centers were, though not always; in Athens, for example, burials continued to be made in some areas until the expansion of habitation in the seventh and sixth centuries put the old burial grounds out of use. Yet it is clear that even without speaking of continuity or discontinuity, Greek culture and society were transformed after 1200 BC and again during the course of the seventh century BC, a time that ushers in the fully historical period of Greek history and sees the spread of the alphabet, borrowed and adapted from the Phoenicians, overseas settlement, and investment in sanctuaries, among other phenomena. The Greek Bronze Age, moreover, supplied a past that Greeks of later periods could draw upon, whether through the performance of epic poetry, heroic narratives in other forms, or directly interacting with the remains of the past: the citadels, tombs, and other visible signs of earlier generations on the landscape. Such remains were also the subject of competing or multiple claims to the legitimacy that the past and its ancestors conferred.

Narrating the Past

We have some narratives about the Bronze Age to draw on in understanding how later Greeks viewed their past. Hesiod, an epic poet who was roughly contemporary with Homer, offers a view of the past from the vantage point of the late historical Iron Age in his poem "Works and Days" (lines 109–201). He sings of five ages (sometimes translated as "races," a term that has misleading connotations; the word is *genos*, which usually means a breed, type, or family). Four are named after metals in a descending order of value: Golden, Silver, Bronze, and Iron. Within this metallic order, a Heroic age is interpolated between the Bronze and Iron. Hesiod identifies his own time with the Iron Age, and he identifies the preceding Heroic age as that of the Trojan War. All the ages were made by the gods, usually by Zeus himself, the god who established the present order. The trajectory is one of decline; each multigenerational *genos* ends and is covered by the earth.

The Heroic age is an exception and may have been inserted into an earlier scheme of metals, which is clearly related to Near Eastern versions of this system. Concerning the inhabitants of these ages Whitley (2002:124) says: "These beings were not ancestors, but aliens; they had no genealogical or genetic relations with the present inhabitants." But this statement does not recognize Hesiod's location of himself in the age of iron, which is the fifth of the ages, nor that these "races" are even human. But they are human, though some are wondrous in their physiognomies and abilities, and they are mortal. The last two generations of the Heroic age are certainly conceived of as historic in the sense that its heroes are the progenitors of Hesiod's own Iron age. The generations or ages are cycles of time and thus are related by descent but not in a linear fashion. The system is structured in a way that situates the present generation, Hesiod's own, as both connected to and cut off from previous generations (Antonaccio 1994; cf. Morris 1997). Hesiod's narrative shows us one view of the past in a form not discernable from the archaeological evidence alone, though the evidence for a serious crisis and disruption after 1200 BC and some continuity (in religion and language, at least) is discernable in Hesiod's placement of his own generation in the age of iron. It remains to examine how the historical period called the Iron Age made ritual use of the past and how it engaged with the past generations, who thereby achieved the status of ancestors.

In Iron Age burial grounds (after 1100 BC), despite the adoption of individual burial and the introduction of cremation instead of the earlier rite of inhumation, strategies to relate the dead to one another in time and space were deployed. For example, groups of individual tombs were created with boundary walls or by using tumuli for multiple burials, by opening earlier tombs to introduce new burials, or by overlapping and

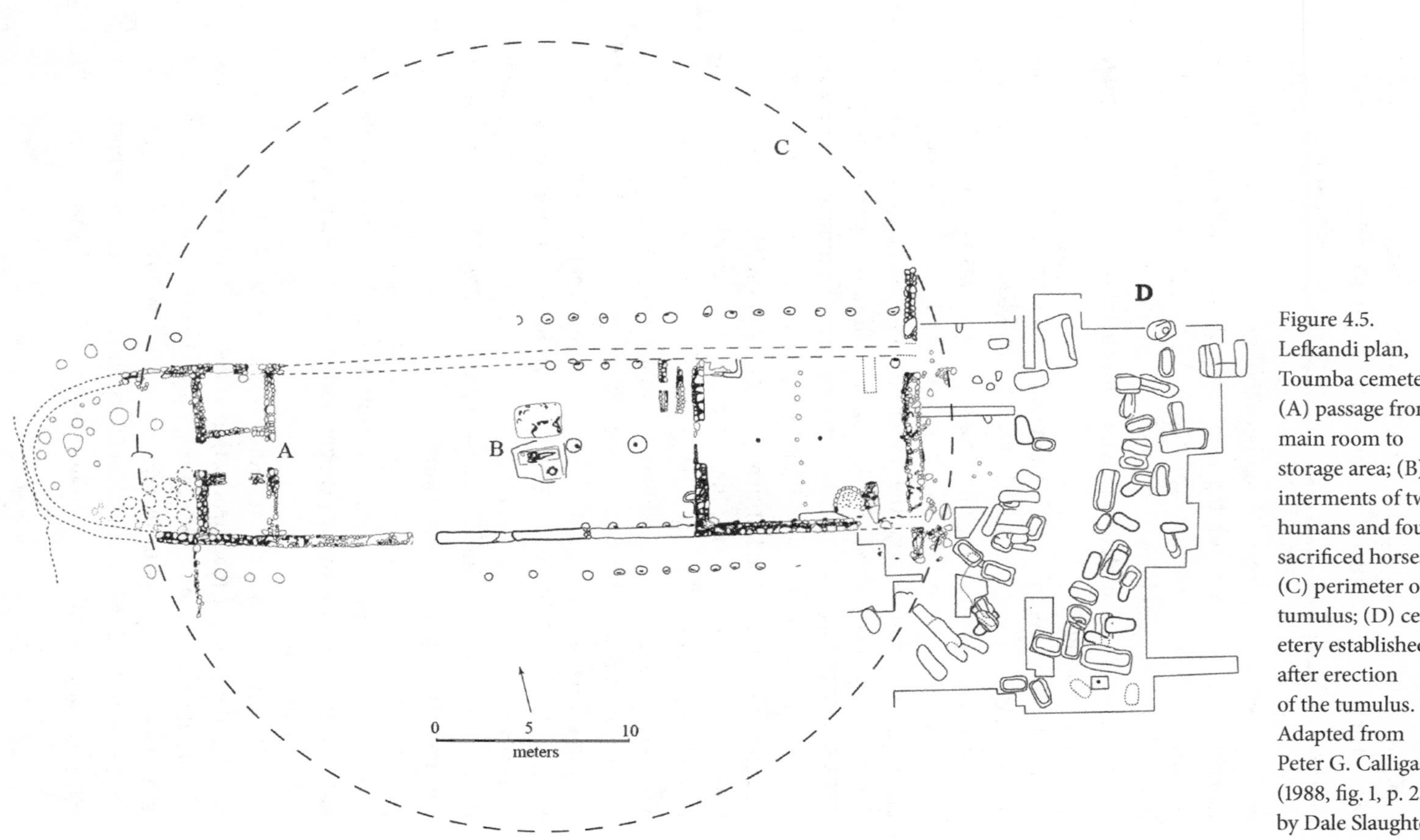

Figure 4.5. Lefkandi plan, Toumba cemetery. (A) passage from main room to storage area; (B) interments of two humans and four sacrificed horses; (C) perimeter of tumulus; (D) cemetery established after erection of the tumulus. Adapted from Peter G. Calligas (1988, fig. 1, p. 231) by Dale Slaughter.

crosscutting earlier burials. Such groupings may have functioned to establish new lineages and to elevate particular individuals to an achieved ancestorhood, as defined by Whitley. One site, Lefkandi on the island of Euboia, is an unusually clear example of this strategy in the Early Iron Age (figure 4.5). Around 950 BC, a pair of elite burials (cremated male, inhumed female), unusual for having only metalwork as offerings and no ceramics, were made in a deep shaft sunk into the bedrock. A second shaft held four sacrificed horses. Subsequently, a very large building of mudbrick and thatch was erected, the largest of its time ever discovered (about 48 m in length), only to have been deliberately destroyed shortly after its completion—within a generation or less. A tumulus was created atop this building and a cemetery established around it, the first burials cutting into the margins of the tumulus.

Among the many interesting features of the original pair of burials, as well as the ensuing burials in the cemetery, is the deposition of antique and exotic metalwork from Cyprus (bronze vessels for the male) and as far afield as Mesopotamia (gold jewelry for the female). The inclusion of old and exotic objects is a practice that can be identified on other sites in the Early Iron Age as well: a similar pattern can be discerned on Crete, at the North Cemetery near the old palatial site of Knossos (summarized in Antonaccio 1995, 2006; Lemos 2007). Thus the new lineage cemetery at Lefkandi, if that is what it is, located away from other burials and at a distance from the settlement, may have been used to establish legitimacy and links with a distant and heroic past through the prestige invoked by old and strange objects, out of place and time at their moment of deposition.

It is interesting that prestige and legitimacy seem to be conferred by exotic antique or heirloom objects, especially of metal (Nightingale 2007), since such objects seem to be among the most desirable described in Greek epic in which such items come with their own lineages, their own biographies. One such object, a silver bowl made by the smith god Hephaistos, was given as a gift to Telemachus, son of Odysseus, by Menelaus, king of Sparta, who had received it himself as a gift from the king of Sidon in Phoenicia. This marvelous and high-status object had its origins and previous exchange history recited when the gift was mentioned (*Odyssey* book 15, lines 111–121). Though mythical, such objects, whose lineages were proclaimed when they changed hands, may have expressed the values of past ages for those listening to epic poetry in early Greek history. By deploying exotic, prestigious objects from other places and times in the

Greek Iron Age, the past was mystified in various ways that would benefit those whose interests were at stake—those holding or trying to gain power and prestige. It is consonant with evidence that a few individuals in the Early or Middle Iron Age (tenth and ninth centuries BC) still had access, possibly through gift exchange, to such objects, which originated overseas, most likely through Cyprus (Nightingale 2007). On the other hand, Bronze Age ancestors and their monuments were mostly ignored until late in the period, despite epic poetry's backward-looking view and traditional form and despite the Early Iron Age deployment of pedigreed objects.

I have suggested elsewhere (Antonaccio 2002) that in the earlier Iron Age (tenth and ninth centuries), high-status individuals with this kind of access functioned as what Mary Helms calls "living ancestors." As she says, "When elites are accepted as legitimate aristocrats, it is because commoners regard and accept them as *qualitatively different types of beings* from themselves, and vice versa" (Helms 1998:5). She continues:

> The qualities of seniority or of being "first" . . . relate aristocrats as a group to ancestral founders and creators of social order and customs, and this association with cosmological origins legitimizes their primacy and their aristocratic positions. Yet it is insufficient to recognize a close association of aristocrats with ancestors. Aristocrats must be understood as qualitatively ancestral themselves . . . to be literally imbued with ancestral qualities and to be distinguished as a social collectivity by *living* ancestorship that places them in a qualitatively different state or condition of being relative to commoners [Helms 1998:6].

Further, such living ancestors, though existing in present time and space, "reach beyond the immediate and ordinary to be contained within the more distant or more encompassing realms of the cosmological there-and-then" (Helms 1998:6). Finally, "Cosmological contacts can be achieved by many means, including formal ceremony, artistic creativity, long-distance acquisitional trade, hunting, and physical and spiritual travel" (1998:8). Tangible expressions of durability, especially heirlooms and restricted items acquired through long-distance trade, are key aspects. "Human life and the life of the house of the polity are inherently fragile especially in low-technology societies, but durable goods and, by extension, the values and qualities they embody are more lasting" (1998:173). In this pivotal time between the Bronze Age collapse and the literate and expansive period in the eighth century, certain individuals used such strategies to achieve living ancestorhood. Helms's notions may be compared with those of Kopytoff, writing about African kinship systems in which the authority of elders is predicated on their closeness to ancestors. Kopytoff observed, "African kin-groups are often described as communities of both the living and the dead" (1971:129), and he noted that different categories of ancestors had different functions for the living.

Strategies changed as the Iron Age ebbed—around the time of Hesiod and Homer. Then, when Bronze Age tombs were more intensively frequented, late in the eighth century BC, and there is sometimes written evidence for the intentions of actors in the form of inscriptions on objects, it seems that such tombs were not identified as those of epic heroes. This is the case even though the stories that epic tells (e.g., the Trojan War sagas) are situated in the historical Bronze Age, the "Heroic age" of Hesiod. Rather, these tombs receive offerings appropriate to the recent dead, especially ceramics and small pieces of metalwork. They sometimes receive additional burials—a feature that seems to point to attempts to link the much earlier dead with the family dead of centuries later. This practice requires knowledge of the location of such tombs. In the case of chamber tombs, excavated into hillsides out of natural rock, this entailed finding the passageway into the chamber and removing part of the wall blocking the chamber itself to introduce a burial. Reuse of tumuli required nothing more than adding a new interment to the mound, but it had to be acceptable practice to do so. With this practice, the exotica and heirlooms nearly vanish from burial contexts as well. We can trace this frequenting and occasional reuse of Late Bronze Age tombs widely across Greece; it is not limited to a few sites as was the case in the tenth century. And as we have seen, this co-option of earlier tombs is itself a legacy of the Late Bronze Age.

Connections between this eighth-century veneration and reuse of Bronze Age tombs with practices in contemporary cemeteries provide ritual contexts that give reason to consider these practices an ancestralizing pattern that is not reflected in the written sources (Antonaccio 1995). Not every practice of the past in literate societies is documented in words that survive to us. For example, low circular stone-built platforms connected with funerary feasting appear in Late Iron Age cemeteries in the mid-eighth century BC, as well as in the building at Lefkandi, discussed above, from two centuries earlier, connected again with contemporary burials (Antonaccio 1994). These platforms hold a fraction of burned material and broken pottery that were left as token deposits to mark the occasion of the feast or to dedicate a portion to the ancestors. Such a platform was introduced into a Mycenaean chamber tomb at the site of Mycenae itself. Clearly intended to co-opt the Mycenaean dead as family ancestors and implying not a single visit but a feature designed for multiple uses, its surface was renewed at least once. Thus the varied attitudes toward earlier tombs is demonstrated in the evidence from the tombs themselves and clarified by context. From the dates of the objects offered and the physical evidence of more than one entry, we know that some tombs were entered once, some multiple times, and a few received burials together with offerings. While the particulars might vary from region to region and site to site, these practices were widespread, from the islands (e.g., Naxos) to the mainland. They can be said to form a ritual pattern and one that differs from strategies of elite display and investment at the nascent sanctuaries of Olympia, Delphi, Nemea, and elsewhere. They may also indicate a struggle over the meaning of the past and a multiplicity of strategies and claims on the dead as Greek society diversified and became more complex over time (Antonaccio 1995).

It must be stressed that the phenomena described above occur at tombs that had gone out of use centuries before, and therefore indicate an intervening period of social and historical discontinuity, or at least of disregard. None of the later offerings introduced into Bronze Age tombs are inscribed, so we cannot say for certain what motivated this activity. But while it could not be directed at anyone Whitley would define as an ancestor, I see these cases as the creation—even fabrication—of ancestors, though this suggests that something illegitimate or inauthentic is happening. Rather, these earlier dead are ancestors in the sense that they achieve ancestorhood because of those who later seek them out and claim them as such. We may be encouraged in such a view precisely because of contextual analysis. In several cases, early in the Iron Age, burials were introduced into abandoned settlements, such as at Naxos in the Aegean (Lambrinoudakis 1988) and Kavousi on Crete (Gesell and Day 2009). This strategy seems designed to preserve or extend a link between the living who had moved away and the place where they had lived for generations. The later burials in Bronze Age tombs—which were, like the settlements, abandoned at the time they were reutilized for burials—seem likely to be a related phenomenon.

The gap in time between the Bronze Age and the later Iron Age encompasses and engenders a crisis of legitimacy in the social and political dimensions of Greek society. But this discontinuity is precisely the point: with no continuously venerated ancestors to call upon, and with widespread shifts in patterns of habitation, subsistence, trade, and ritual, ancestors had to be sought, invented, claimed, recovered. Increased population and the fissioning of lineages may have put pressure on resources—some of the factors that the Saxe-Goldstein hypothesis suggests create a need for ancestors on whom to predicate claims to resources (Morris 1991; see also Whitley 2002), but this is surely only one. A number of strategies were employed: burials in old habitation areas; new, elite cemeteries that drew upon exotic antiques (rather than local heirlooms), a strategy that seems intended to control both time and distance as legitimating devices and to create new lineage ancestors; and only late in the game, at the end of the Iron Age, the reuse and veneration of Bronze Age tombs in an effort to directly connect the ancient dead with the recently deceased.

By the sixth and fifth centuries BC, ritual practices directed at or referencing heroes were well developed, such as the athletic contests whose foundations the Greeks traced to funeral games in honor of particular heroes at the occasion of their burial, as well as sacrifices ordained in ritual calendars on a regular basis. Heroes could also be invoked in times of crisis, such as invasion, famine, or plague. There was also a strategy to recover "heroic" relics in the form of bones to secure the favor of a given hero for a particular city. The founders of new cities were given heroic honors. The family dead were subject to a fairly well defined, if locally and socially variable, set of practices including laying out and mourning at home, a procession to the place of burial, interment of the remains with burial gifts, and subsequent visits to the tomb for prescribed periods of time with further offerings—a cult of the dead, if not exactly one of ancestors. The Tritopatores existed in several communities, expressing an ancestral consciousness of a different order. As the fifth century neared its end, heroic honors were extended to the recent dead, eliding the categories (Jones 2010).

Conclusion: The Multiplicity of the Past

There is no space here to consider Greek concepts of history, the development of a historical consciousness, and the place of written discourse in a society with limited literacy. Nor is this the place to consider the scholarship on epic poetry and its origins, evolution, and function (Bertolín Cebrián 2006; Carter 1995). But the multiplicity of the past is something that Bloch has considered as well. Bloch deconstructs the idea that narratives actually construct reality and that ways of cognizing differ. Drawing on his work in Madagascar and discussing a range of narratives and other cultural practices concerned with narrative, Bloch (1998:110) states that

> because of the multiplicity of these types of narratives it is not legitimate to assume that any can be equated with the Zafimaniry cognition of the past and of the passage of time. . . . Concepts of duration, causality, or person are neither constructed nor contained in any one type of narrative. Instead narratives are used to present a certain representation of a world which must be known in a way neither constructed nor transparently or completely reflected by narratives.

While the Zafimaniry may not present a case directly comparable to that of early Greece, the point here is that different discourses, serving different social and cultural purposes, can coexist in a given society and that none is definitive.

Thus multiple concepts of ancestors served a multiplicity of functions for the Greeks, some of which are revealed by context. The written accounts that Whitley calls upon to provide other mythic narratives, as for example to record stories such as that of the monstrous Cyclopes (divine, or semi-divine, but not themselves heroes) who built the walls of Mycenae, suggest still other versions of the past. These stories, too, are varied: Poseidon, for example, is said to have built the walls of Troy, and Poseidon fathered heroes with mortal mothers—and fathered the Cyclopes encountered by Odysseus in his journeying after Troy. Whitley invokes Irish folk stories in connection with Hesiod's five ages, but Hesiod's account cannot be compared very easily with such tales, nor does Hesiod, to my way of thinking, "emphasize discontinuity."

But even if the Greek equivalent of fairies was said to have built all the old Bronze Age citadels, the importance of human ancestors could still be defended. Stories of supernatural beings from a distant past constructing the walls of Troy (Poseidon, Apollo) and Mycenae (Cyclopes) are a way of imbuing these visible, surviving structures with supernatural power. Gods and Cyclopes would have been a kind of exotic distancing even from a heroic past—which parallels the genealogies of selected objects in the epic poems, with their exotic origins, age, and superior workmanship.

In conclusion, we should reject Whitley's contention that discontinuity in the use or veneration of a grave or lack of continuous memory of individual named ancestors cannot accommodate an "interest in ancestors" (Whitley 2002:124 quoting Antonaccio 1995:250) on the part of those who lived many centuries later. Whitley remarks, "Veneration of ancestors—real, identifiable ones that is—requires continuity, at least of memory if not of cult. . . . The only ancestors who could have been the recipients of such cults would be imaginary ones" (2002:124), which is precisely my point. The Greeks of the Middle and Late Bronze Age found ancestors good to think with. Having experienced a discontinuity with their Bronze Age past after 1200 BC, Greeks in the Iron Age, when descent became a metaphor for all kinds of group identity and the basis for citizenship as well, forged a different kind of connection with ancestors than Whitley envisions. Only by excluding heroes from ancestors can Whitley (2002:124) assert,

> There is . . . little to suggest that ancestors played a major role in the imagination of Archaic Greeks—whereas there is much to suggest that gods, heroes, and other races did. The ruined landscape of Archaic and Classical Greece was not peopled by ancestors, but by other races and other powerful presences.

The heroes *were* ancestors, but other ancestors in the Greek imaginary cannot be denied. Nor can multiple pasts.

References Cited

Albersmeier, Sabine, and Michael J. Anderson (editors)

2009 *Heroes: Mortals and Myths in Ancient Greece.* Johns Hopkins University Press, Baltimore.

Antonaccio, Carla

1994 Contesting the Past: Hero Cult, Tomb Cult, and Epic in Early Greece. *American Journal of Archaeology* 98:389–410.

1995 *An Archaeology of Ancestors: Tomb Cult and Hero Cult in Early Greece.* Rowman and Littlefield, Lanham, Maryland.

2002 Warriors, Traders, and Ancestors: The Heroes of Lefkandi. In *Images of Ancestors*, edited by J. M. Højte, pp. 13–42. Aarhus University Press, Aarhus.

2006 Religion, Basileis, and Heroes. In *Ancient Greece: From the Mycenaean Palaces to the Age of Homer*, edited by Sigrid Deger-Jalkotzy and Irene S. Lemos, pp. 381–395. University of Edinburgh Press, Edinburgh.

Bertolín Cebrián, Reyes

2006 *Singing the Dead: A Model for Epic Evolution.* Peter Lang, New York.

Bloch, Maurice

1998 *How We Think They Think: Anthropological Approaches to Cognition, Memory, and Literacy.* Westview, Boulder, Colorado.

2002 [1996] Ancestors. In *Encyclopedia of Social and Cultural Anthropology*, edited by Alan Barnard and Jonathan Spencer, pp. 66–67. Routledge, London.

Calligas, Peter G.

1988 Hero-Cult in Early Iron Age Greece. In *Early Greek Cult Practice*, edited by Robin Hägg, Nanno Marinatos, and Gullög Nordquist, pp. 229–234. Swedish Institute at Athens, Stockholm.

Carter, Jane

1995 Ancestor Cult and the Occasion of Homeric Performance. In *The Ages of Homer: A Tribute to Emily Townsend Vermeule*, edited by Jane B. Carter and Sarah P. Morris, pp. 285–312. University of Texas Press, Austin.

Coldstream, Nicholas

1976 Hero-Cults in the Age of Homer. *Journal of Hellenic Studies* 96: 8–17.

Gere, Cathy

2006 *The Tomb of Agamemnon.* Harvard University Press, Cambridge Massachusetts.

Gesell, Geraldine, and Leslie P. Day

2009 *Kavousi IIA: The Late Minoan IIIC Settlement at Vronda. The Buildings on the Summit.* INSTAP Academic Press, Philadelphia.

Hall, Jonathan

1999 *Ethnic Identity in Greek Antiquity.* Cambridge University Press, Cambridge.

2002 *Hellenicity: Between Ethnicity and Culture.* University of Chicago Press, Chicago.

Helms, Mary

1998 *Access to Origins: Affines, Ancestors, and Aristocrats.* University of Texas Press, Austin.

Humphreys, Sarah

1980 Family Tombs and Tomb Cult in Ancient Athens: Tradition or Traditionalism? *Journal of Hellenic Studies* 100:96–126.

Johnston, Sarah Iles

1999 *Restless Dead: Encounters between the Living and the Dead in Ancient Greece.* University of California Press, Berkeley.

Jones, Christopher

2010 *New Heroes in Antiquity: From Achilles to Antinoos.* Harvard University Press, Cambridge, Massachusetts.

Katz, Marilyn

1991 *Penelope's Renown: Meaning and Indeterminacy in the Odyssey.* Princeton University Press, Princeton, New Jersey.

Kopytoff, Igor

1971 Ancestors as Elders in Africa. *Africa: Journal of the International African Institute* 41(2):129–142.

Lambrinoudakis, Vassilis

1988 Veneration of Ancestors in Geometric Naxos. In *Early Greek Cult Practice*, edited by R. Hägg, N. Marinatos, and G. C. Nordquist, pp. 235–245. Svenska Institutet i Athen, Stockholm.

Lemos, Irene

2007 Homeric Reflections in Early Iron Age Elite Burials. In *Keimelion: Elitenbildung und elitärer Konsum von der mykenischen Palastzeit bis zur homerischen Epoche*, edited by E. Alram-Stern and G. Nightingale, pp. 275–284. Österreichischen Akademie der Wissenschaften, Vienna.

Morris, Ian

1991 The Archaeology of Ancestors: The Saxe/Goldstein Hypothesis Revisited. *Cambridge Archaeological Journal* 1(2):147–169.

1997 Periodization and the Heroes: Inventing a Dark Age. In *Inventing Ancient Culture? Historicism, Periodization, and the "New Classics,"* edited by Mark Golden and Peter Toohey, pp. 96–131. Routledge, New York.

Nightingale, George

2007 Lefkandi: An Important Node in the International Exchange Network of Jewelry and Personal Adornment. *Aegaeum* 27:421–429.

Schmiel, Robert

1987 Achilles in Hades. *Classical Philology* 82:35–37.

Whitley, James

2002 Too Many Ancestors. *Antiquity* 76(291):119–126.

5

The Ethnoarchaeology of West African Ancestors

Kusasi Shrines and Domestic Space

CHARLES MATHER

The goal of this chapter is to refine our use of the ancestor concept and show that ancestors are a factor in the creation and use of some forms of material culture that are likely to survive in the archaeological record. Beliefs about and actions toward the ancestors are expressed in a host of material remains, especially assemblages and sites related to religion and death (e.g., shrines, monuments, tombs, graves).

The focus of this discussion is ethnoarchaeological observations among the Kusasi of northern Ghana. Beliefs and actions associated with ancestors are recorded in domestic architecture and the distribution of shrines within Kusasi compounds. Ancestors and their accompanying shrines are reference points in both social and spatial organization. When it comes to the physical layout of the compound and the structure of the social order, ancestors are pervasive. The results presented here are relevant to archaeology because they demonstrate that patterns in material culture reflect the centrality of ancestors in Kusasi society.

Background

A major purpose of this chapter is to demonstrate how the ancestor concept can be linked to empirical observations of material remains. The starting point for this endeavor is defining what an ancestor is and overcoming the unwillingness to distinguish between different types of ancestors. Ethnoarchaeological observations may be used to differentiate between ancestors and thereby isolate principles of spatial organization that are evident in material culture. Archaeologists may find such principles of use when interpreting patterns in archaeological data sets.

The ethnoarchaeological observations discussed here come from nine months of field research on shrines among the Kusasi of the Upper East Region, Ghana, West Africa (Mather 2000, 2003, 2005, 2007). Shrines occur in a variety of settings and take many forms. I am concerned with ancestor shrines as they appear in domestic contexts, namely, in and around compounds. The distribution of shrines and compound layout embody the fundamental organizational principles of Kusasi society, in which ancestors play a prominent role.

The Kusasi are one of many linguistically and historically related groups that occupy the Volta basin of northern Ghana and southern Burkina Faso. The traditional homeland of the Kusasi lies between the Red Volta River and the Togo–Ghana border, extending north into southwestern Burkina Faso and south as far as the Gambaga escarpment (figure 5.1). Traditional Kusasi society was patrilineal, patrilocal, and polygynous. Although many people maintain traditional practices, bilaterality, monogamy, and nuclear families are increasing. The Kusasi speak Kusal (Spratt and Spratt 1968, 1972), which is mutually intelligible with the other languages of the Gur family, distributed throughout northern Ghana and Burkina Faso (Naden 1988). Historical research suggests that the Kusasi occupied their current location as early as the fifteenth century (Hilton 1962; Syme 1932).

My field research took place from July 1996 to April 1997 in and around the settlement of Zorse, which is located in the Bawku Central District of the Upper East Region (Mather 1999). I was joined by my wife, Rebecca Brundin-Mather, and Cletus Anabiga. Our research efforts included performing a shrine survey and compiling a list of shrines for the purpose of creating a typology. We interviewed the heads of 156 compounds. Apart from gathering essential information about the structure, function, and meaning of shrines, we gathered basic information on Kusasi society and on the spatial and social divisions and history of the settlement of Zorse.

Once we completed our shrine list, we drew a sample of twenty-seven compounds and recorded their layouts using compasses, measuring tapes, and stakes; we plotted in the shrines that were located within and

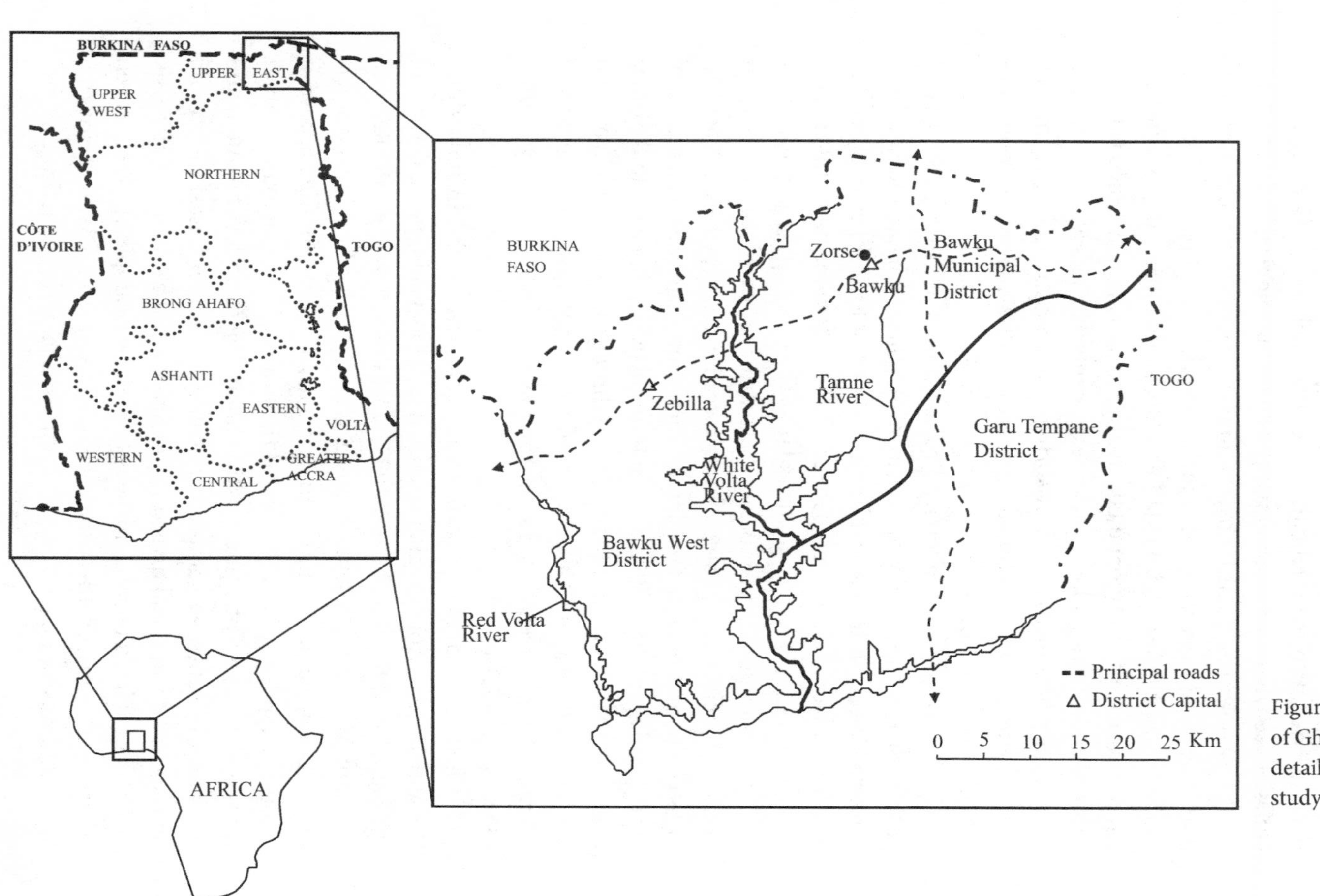

Figure 5.1. Map of Ghana with detail of the study area.

around each compound. We then conducted second interviews with the compound heads in order to determine how they—or the previous head of the compound—had chosen shrine locations.

The compound is the center of Kusasi existence, the seat of daily tasks and activities, of economic enterprise, child rearing, eating, and sleeping, and the site of significant life events including birth, marriage, and death. Individuals achieve and acquire their identities and destinies by virtue of their belonging to a compound; hence a compound is both a physical and a psychological shelter.

The compound is also central to the lives of the neighboring Tallensi, as detailed in the classic ethnographic work of Meyer Fortes (1949:46), who argues that a

> Taleŋ's home is his castle in the psychological rather than the material sense. It is the centre of his major interests, his dominant purposes, his deepest emotional attachments, and his whole scheme of values; it is his shelter, his storehouse, the stage of his life's drama. . . . His sex life, in maturity, is centred there. His children, the supreme object of his aspirations, are born and grow up in his home under his care and control. He worships his immediate forebears there. *His personal destiny, past, present, and future, revolves about his home, its stages perpetuated in the many shrines and other ritual objects that are housed in it* [emphasis added].

Like the Tallensi homestead, a Kusasi compound is a starting and an end point of life. Personal and collective identities, destinies, and histories stem from the compound, finding expression and embodiment in the shrines housed within it.

Shrines link architectural space to social organization; they form part of the built environment that both structures and is structured by human activity. As territorial markers, shrines divide physical space according to social divisions (different lineages, different domestic groups), thereby differentiating and separating groups. Conversely, as ceremonial locales, shrines bring different groups together into unified collectives. In this chapter I demonstrate how Kusasi utilize ancestors as referents for talking and thinking about social and spatial organization. Ancestors have different types of shrines, and ancestors and their associated shrines perform different roles when it comes to delimiting the social and spatial divisions within Kusasi society.

Defining Ancestors and Ancestor Shrines

The Kusasi recognize both maternal and paternal ancestors, and they honor them by enshrining them in objects that they refer to as "rooms within the house." An ancestor is a deceased person recognized by the living as having living descendants. As spiritual agents, ancestors play causal roles in the lives of their descendants—they can cause calamity or bring good fortune. The goal of enshrinement, of pouring libations and making animal sacrifices at shrines, is to establish and maintain positive social relations with ancestors in the hopes of motivating them to act on behalf of the living. The Kusasi refer to libations and sacrifices as "serving"; thus a man will "serve his ancestors" to ensure a good crop, virility, good health for his wives and children, positive business transactions, and the like.

Shrines are made from various materials, including animal horns and tails, iron rods, ceramic vessels, trees, stones, and calabashes (figure 5.2). Ancestor shrines take many physical forms, though they fall into two broad classes: paternal and maternal ancestor shrines. Paternal shrines include the *ya na'am*, a plural term that roughly translates as "grandfathers," which consist of stones roughly the size of billiard balls that people set into plastered mounds on the external walls of the compound next to the front entrance.[1] Although other shrines consist of or include stones, the stones that make up the paternal ancestor shrines are always located in the same place near the compound's front entrance. The Kusasi will enshrine up to three generations of their paternal ancestors. A compound head will serve his direct ancestors—his father and mother, *ba-bagr* and *ma-bagr* (a shrine for a single ancestor is *bagr*). The eldest grandson serves grandfathers and grandmothers (*ya-bagr* and *ya po'a-bagr*), and the eldest great-grandson serves his great-grandfathers and great-grandmothers (*yabya-bagr* and *yabya po'a-bagr*).

Maternal ancestor shrines go by the name *bugr*, or horn. Members of the patriline receive the *bugr* from the natal patrilines of their wives and mothers. The *bugr* is not a static entity. The shrines change over time, and each change involves the incorporation of other objects. The transfer of a *bugr* shrine from one patriline to the next is connected to bridewealth and other marital prestations (see Awedoba 1989a, 1989b, 1989c). Marriage exchange is a matter of one group giving its daughters—both their productive and reproductive capacity—in exchange for gifts (including cows, chickens, guinea fowl, tobacco, kola nuts, and fabric). The exchange

Figure 5.2. A set of objects that make up at least three different shrines. From left to right, the objects are a gourd rattle used by soothsayers to summon their divining spirits, carapaces from two turtles, a cow's tail, a soothsayer's stick (leaning on the wall), a canvas bag in which the contents on the ground are usually contained, a cow's horn, a knife for cutting the throat of sacrificial animals, a wild animal's horn, a cow's horn, a goat's horn, unknown metal object, horns from an oryx, a mound inside of which there is a stone, and the remains of two chameleons. On the wall above the mound is a stylized image of a chameleon. In total, the complex of shrines includes a *bakalogo* (soothsayer's shrine with all of its associated paraphernalia), a chameleon or *dendet* shrine, a *win* shrine, and a *ma-bugr*.

occurs over many years, due in part to economic factors. The party receiving the bride might not have the required number of cows at the time of marriage and may negotiate a schedule of payment. Completion of the exchange usually occurs after the wife has two or three children, ensuring that her husband's group has gotten what they paid for, and the wife-giving group is content that their daughter has a safe home and that she and her children are provided for.

Reproductive and productive capacity stem from personal destiny or *win*, the spiritual capacity that the individual inherits from forebears and ultimately Na Win, the chief of personal destiny. Marital prestations include the transfer of spiritual capacity; this process is part of the beliefs and behaviors that make up the cults of ancestors. The transfer begins when members of the husband's patriline take a sacrificial goat to the wife's natal patriline. The two groups sacrifice the animal at a shrine for a patrilineal ancestor of the woman's natal patriline and take its hide to fashion into a bag in which they put one of the animal's horns. Together, the objects enshrine a spirit whose central purpose is to guard and protect the wife's descendants. The spirit and the shrine, the immaterial and the material, are conflated by the Kusasi, who may refer to a shrine as "grandfather," for example. The *bugr* is thus both material object and social persona of the deceased.

When the woman for whom the spirit was transferred dies, the spirit returns to her natal patriline. To retrieve the spirit, the woman's descendants have to go to her natal patriline and reenact the rituals that their forebears conducted when the spirit was originally transferred to the shrine. The return and transfer of the *bugr* provide opportunities for members of the two patrilines who conducted the first marriage exchange to revisit, maintain, and solidify their relationship. In pragmatic terms, it also gives the two parties an opportunity to address the balance of their initial exchange (e.g., whether the payment of animals has occurred in full, whether the woman had a sufficient number of children). When the *bugr* returns to the patriline of the deceased woman's husband, her senior son will serve the shrine and will refer to it as his *ma-bugr*, or mother's horn.

If a man responsible for serving a *ma-bugr* dies, and he is the last member of his generation, the shrine passes to the senior member of the succeeding generation and the shrine goes by the name *ba-bugr*, or father's horn. As with the transition from *bugr* to *ma-bugr*, this pattern of inheritance occurs following the reenactment of the rites of transferring the shrines. When the shrine becomes a *ba-bugr*, the spiritual capacity continues to guard and protect the descendants of the wife who married into the patriline in the previous generation. In subsequent generations, that pattern of shrine transfer and inheritance stays the same; the resulting shrine goes by the term *tengbana bugr*, literally "skin of the earth horn." The English term used by Kusasi for the shrine is "horn of the landgod" (see Mather 2003 on this class of shrines).

The final matrilineal ancestor shrine is the *bakalogo*. This shrine is connected to the *bugr* in that one cannot have a *bakalogo* unless one also has a *bugr*. The phrase "the *bakalogo* moves with the *bugr*" encapsulates the relationship between the shrines and their associated spirits. Acquisition of the *bakalogo* can occur by way of inheritance—when a shrine holder dies, his shrines pass to his genealogical juniors—or by way of religious vision. The most common type of vision involves seeing a wild horned animal. The person who sees the animal should try and capture it, kill it, and then keep the horns. If the person who has the vision has a *bugr*, he—the vast majority of people with the *bugr* and *bakalogo* are men—will put the horns of the *bakalogo* with the *bugr*. If he does not have a *bugr*, he must get one. Indeed, the vision and successful hunt are proof that a *bugr* shrine is "calling" the man; that is, the spirit of the shrine wishes to guard and receive service from the individual. The soothsayers known as *bakalogo-sup* gain their powers from the spirits housed within the *bugr* and *bakalogo* shrines. Thus the courtyard shrine can also become a divining shrine (Mather 1999). The *bugr* and *bakalogo* shrines play important roles in the lives of cognatic descendants. They start as courtyard shrines, evolve into compound shrines, and over time can end up providing supernatural protection for very large patrilines. At this point in time the shrines are no longer located within a single compound but rather are built where the first man to serve the shrines had his compound. The location of the abandoned compound is marked by a large tree at the foot of which sits the *kugr*, the stone that enshrines the spirit. The *bugr* shrine is emblematic of the patriline even though it originates from outside that patriline.

The Physical Layout of Kusasi Compounds

A Kusasi compound, or *yir*, is a circular and/or rectilinear closed arrangement of buildings joined by walls of about 1.5 to 1.75 meters in height (figure 5.3). Figure 5.4 is the plan of a typical compound. It has one entrance, a gate that faces west onto the *saman* or front yard, an area outside the compound for public greeting and conversing. Granaries and graves are located in the front yard, along with different shrines. The *suk*, a light wooden frame structure with a thatch roof, provides a shaded sitting area where the *yirana*, or compound head, relaxes and converses with guests.

Within the compound, building entrances face the center. Walls subdivide the compound. The primary wall runs north–south, abutting various

Figure 5.3. Photo of a typical compound from the front yard.

structures or rooms, including that of the compound head. West of the wall is the *zampak*, or animal yard, that contains piles of animal dung and household refuse. Goats, sheep, and fowl find shelter within the buildings that face the yard. East of the wall is the living area proper.

The wall running south from the compound head's room is about a half meter in height and serves as the entrance to the living area. Internal walls running from the compound head's room to his second wife's room divide the interior into two courtyards. Each courtyard, or *zak*, consists of a wife's personal sleeping chambers, an indoor cooking area, an outdoor cooking area, and a bathing area. The senior wife's first son may be old enough to have his own room within her courtyard. The wall that separates the courtyards is the same height as the external walls. According to a compound head in Zorse, the height of internal walls reflects the relationship between wives. This man's wives do not get along well and thus the internal walls create entirely separate courtyards. In cases where wives do get along, internal walls are short enough that residents can easily step over them.

The location of a husband's room varies according to how many wives he has and whether members of an earlier generation reside within the

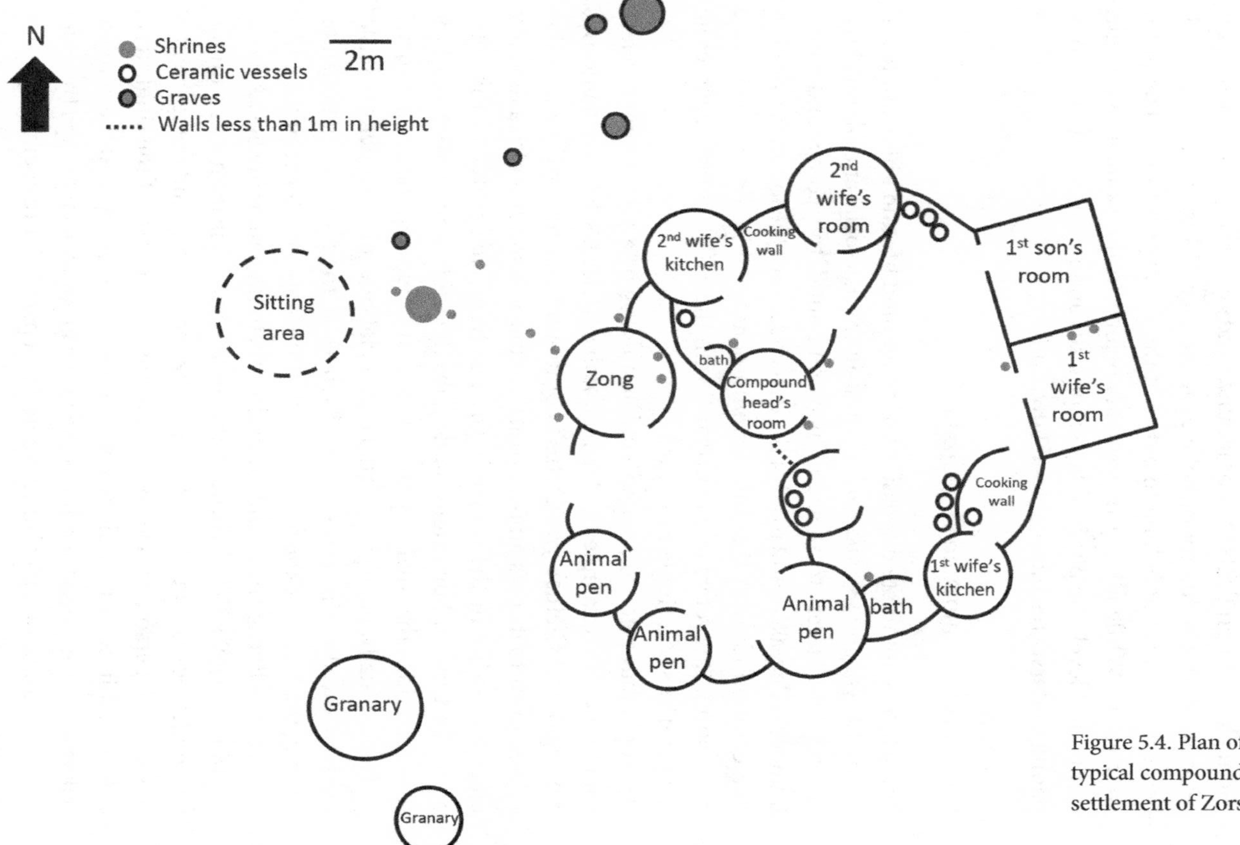

Figure 5.4. Plan of a typical compound in the settlement of Zorse.

compound. In figure 5.4 the compound head's room is located at the center of the compound, roughly between the courtyards of his wives. The room placement reflects the compound head's central position within the residential group; his room belongs to neither of his wives' courtyards because he does not belong to either of the social groups that live in the courtyards. While all of the residents belong to the same group at the compound level, the physical layout of walls and rooms within the compound underscores internal social divisions.

Principles of Compound Organization

Three terms dominate discussions of compound life and kin relations: (1) *dabog*, (2) *yir*, and (3) *zak*. Each of these terms has social and physical referents. *Dabog* refers to an abandoned compound, to a compound whose founder is deceased, and to all of the descendants of the founder. *Yir* refers to a compound; with the suffix *-diim* it denotes all of the members of a compound. *Zak* refers to a courtyard; with the suffix *-diim* it denotes all the members of a single courtyard.

People may refer to a compound as a *dabog* or a *yir*. My interpreter's compound, for example, is Anabiga *dabog* (Cletus's father's name was Anabiga) and Cletus's *yir*. Cletus's compound is a historical entity that existed prior to its present occupants, Anabiga *dabog*. It is also a dynamic place that exists in the present—*yir*. The term *dabog* situates the compound in time and by extension denotes the origins and structure of the social relations that make up the residential group and the social order.

Conceptually, *dabog* is a spatial and social category that defines settlement or dwelling in terms of the dwellers or their social relationships. Among the Dogon, Lane found a similar concept in the term *ginna*, which refers to the lineage head and, by extension, to the minor lineage. According to Lane (1994:205), "Through the use of this single term . . . an important homology is established between the social group and the residential space of the person who leads it." In Kusasi society, use of the single term *dabog* establishes a homology between the social group and the residential space of the ancestor who founded the group. Social groups trace descent to a common apical ancestor and to a particular residential space or common house.

Implicitly, the term *dabog* refers to human mortality. An occupied compound becomes a *dabog* once its founder is deceased. The death of a founder is conceptually equivalent to abandonment; both events lead to the establishment of a *dabog*. Whether a physical space or a social group, a *dabog* owes its existence to the death of some person or homestead. While it expresses an awareness of mortality and transience, the term *dabog* refers also to persistence and permanence. Physically and socially, the *dabog* exists prior to and subsequent to the lives of its individual members. Each person is born into a *dabog*. Membership in a *dabog* offers participation in something greater than one's own transient life. When a compound becomes a *dabog*, it becomes a monument to the past, to "an eternal and imperishable social order" (Parker Pearson and Richards 1994:3).

The Kusasi use *dabog* to refer to lineages, but they lack qualifiers for distinguishing between segments within a lineage. People rely on context to determine the social groups that speakers refer to in conversation. Understanding context is essentially a matter of knowing the history of the compounds that make up the settlement, and this involves knowing the names of the forebears or progenitors of the current population. Kusasi society is historically oriented; Kusasi look to the past to understand the present, which is, in part, why ancestors are so important.

The four-generation kin network in figure 5.5 depicts a descent group or patriline with the name Akiint *dabog*. For the sake of simplicity, the figure is limited to lines of descent of only two of Akiint's five sons and only includes adult males—those after whom the descent groups get their names. Each individual belongs to a nested series of descent groups. Cletus belongs to, or traces his descent through, Anabiga *dabog*, Anatuum *dabog*, and Akiint *dabog*. Akiint *dabog* is the social group that Cletus identifies when he refers to his lineage. Using Fortes's (1949:9) analytical approach as a guide, Akiint *dabog* is a nuclear lineage wherein "male members have a common interest in, and joint rights of inheritance to particular patrimonial farmlands; and the head of the lineage bears the formal jural responsibility for any of the members in such matters as the payment of bride wealth."

The Tallensi trace the apical male ancestor of the nuclear lineage back from four to six generations. In the case of Akiint *dabog*, the apical male ancestor is three generations removed from Cletus. When the junior member of Cletus's generation dies, the nuclear lineage will fission. The nuclear lineage is not necessarily limited to a single compound but may subsume several residential groups. In Fortes's terms (1949:9), the residential group is an effective minimal lineage, the narrowest lineage segment that people

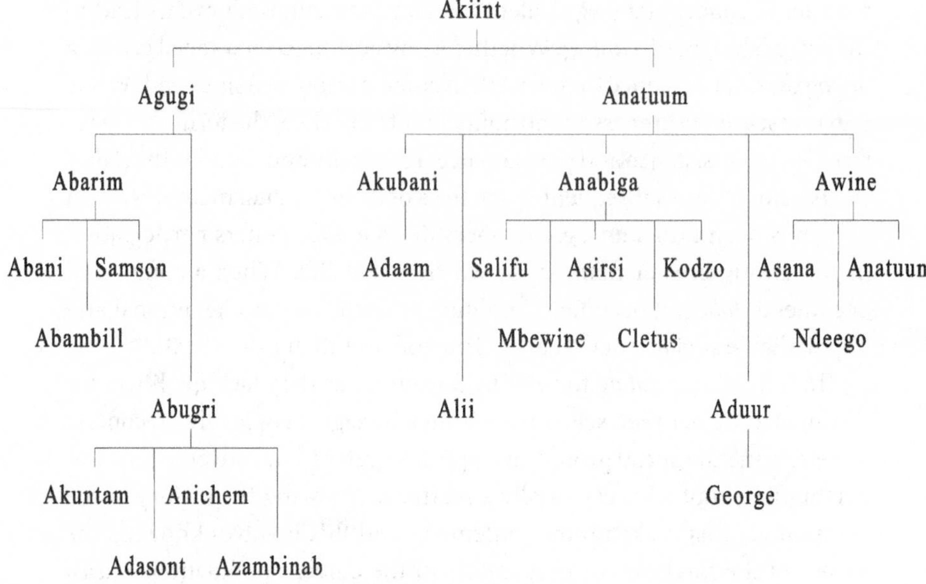

Figure 5.5. Diagram of a patrilineal descent group known as Akiint *dabog*.

recognize in corporate activities. The social structure is not static. As individuals age and die, the larger groups to which they belong fission. Thus the lineage Akiint *dabog* will split into different nuclear lineages when the senior member of the fourth generation of Akiint's descendants dies.

Figure 5.6 provides a diagram of Anatuum *dabog* with Cletus as ego. The diagram includes the women who have married into the descent group. Each tie of marriage within the kin network is a point of fission, division, or segmentation. It marks the introduction of blood from a foreign descent group, that of the wife's natal patriline. Descent is physically expressed in the layout of Cletus's compound (figure 5.7), which is divided into two courtyards, one for each of Cletus's father's wives who remained living there following his death. In one courtyard we find Cletus, his wife, mother, siblings of the same mother, and children, while in the second courtyard we find Cletus's father's second wife, her sons, and the sons' wives and children. If social proximity is the degree to which individuals share the same blood, then social proximity corresponds to spatial proximity. Residential members from the same family, offspring from the same mother and father, live in the same courtyard. Similarly, spatial segmentation is a reflection of social segmentation. Members from

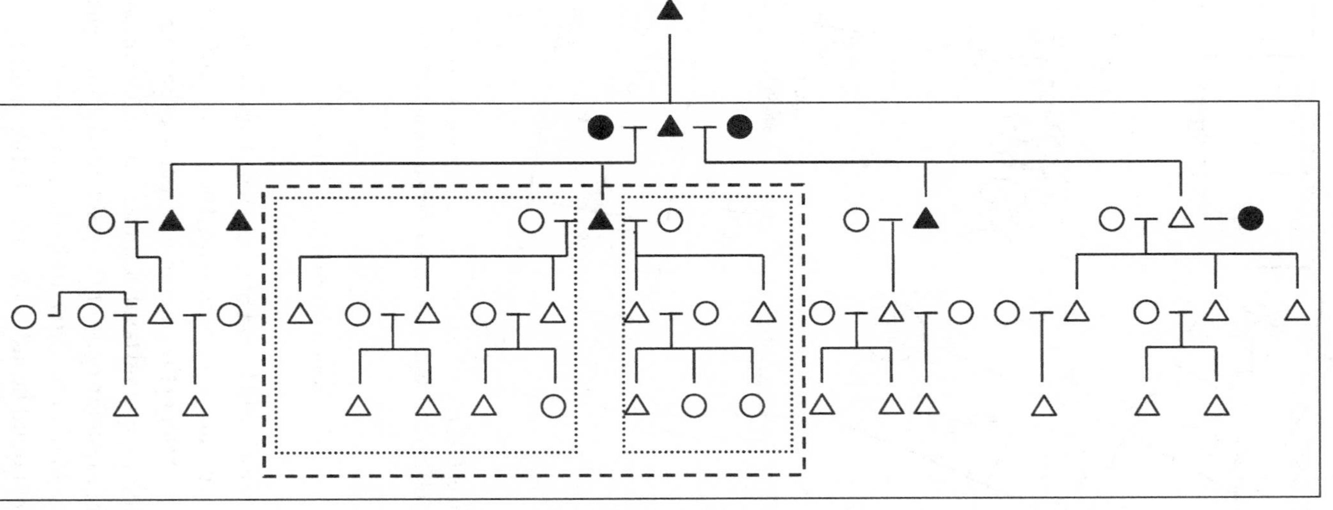

Residential sub-groups within Cletus *yir* or Anobiga *dabog*

Includes members of Anabiga *dabog*

Includes members of Anatuum *dabog*

Figure 5.6. Kin network for the lineage known as Anatuum *dabog*.

Figure 5.7. Plan of the compound of Cletus Anabiga showing two courtyards, one for each wife of Cletus's father, her children and their spouses, and her children's children.

different families, offspring from different maternal bloodlines, live in different courtyards.

Figure 5.8 illustrates the compound layout of a man who has two wives and hence two residential subgroups, each represented by a courtyard. An arrangement of shrines at the center of the compound separates the courtyards. As discussed above, the compound head occupies a central location that symbolizes his position as senior male of the residential group. His room is ideally connected to all of the courtyards in the compound.

A primary role of the compound head is to mediate between his residential group and the larger descent group(s) and between the residential group and the spiritual world by leading sacrifices and rituals at shrines.

When sacrifices are conducted, he mediates between the generations before and after him, though some members are no longer living.[2]

There are two contrary forces at work in the social and spatial structure of Kusasi compounds. The first force is centralization embodied in the mediating role played by the senior male in the descent group or residential group. The second force is segmentation, a logical consequence of marriage that ultimately gives rise to more courtyards within the residential group and more bloodlines within the descent groups. According to Fortes (1949:45), in Tallensi society social relations within the residential group move along two planes: (1) the plane of lineage relations where "the canon of agnatic descent dominates corporate action and directs individual conduct" and (2) "the plane of domestic relations, in which the bonds of marriage and parenthood, and the bilateral ties of kinship in

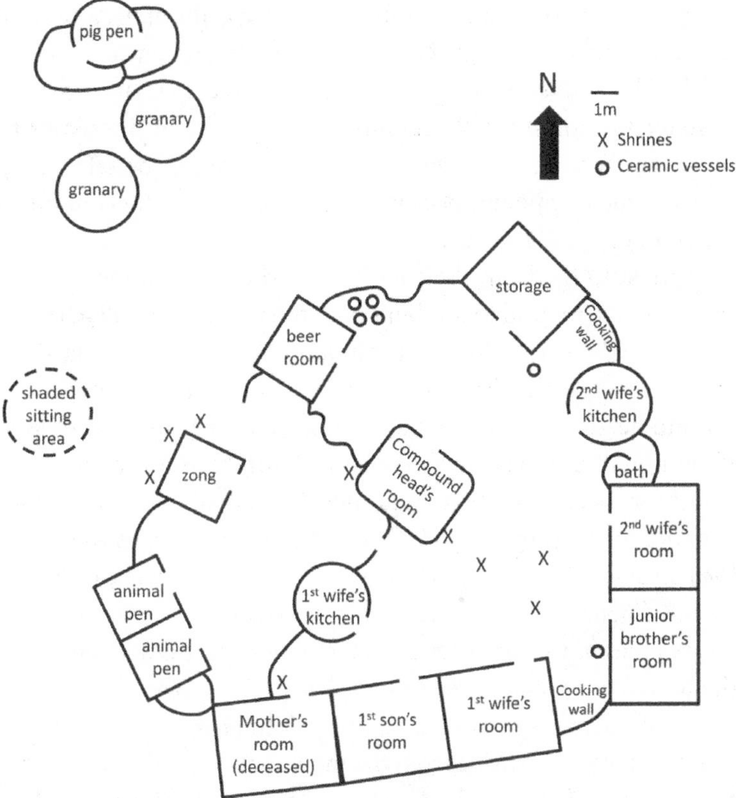

Figure 5.8. Plan of a compound in the settlement of Zorse.

the narrowest sense, control the behavior of people towards one another." These same complementary and contrary forces are at work in Kusasi society. Lineage relations define the residential group and promote solidarity and common interests while domestic relations define individual families and introduce stresses and divisions into the residential group. Lineage relations emphasize a shared bloodline while domestic relations are always segmentary.

Ancestor Shrine Distribution in Compound Space

The evolution of the *bugr* shrine mirrors the developmental cycle of the residential group and its lineage structure. A shrine (*bugr*) starts its existence in the personal room of the woman who has married into the compound; when she dies it moves to the personal room of her senior son (*ma-bugr*). An alternate location for the shrine is the *zong*, a room that serves as the spiritual center of the compound, but only when the senior son is also the *yirana*, or compound head. When the last member of the elder generation dies, the shrine moves to the *zong* of the senior male of the next generation (*ba-bugr*). As a *ba-bugr*, the shrine safeguards all residents of the compound because they are all descendants of the man who first inherited the shrine.

In contrast to the *bugr*, the *bagr* is located outside of the compound and paved into a mound that is built onto the foot of the wall of the *zong*. The *ba-bagr* (the shrine for the compound head's father) is farthest to the left followed by the shrine for his wife or wives, the *ma-bagr* (for the compound head's mother or junior mother). Shrines for the compound head's grandfather(s) (*ya-bagr*) come next with shrines for their wives (*ya po'a bagr*) occurring directly to their left. Finally, the shrine for the great-grandfather (*yabya bagr*) is followed by shrines for his wife or wives (*yabya po'a bagr*). A compound head serves the *bagr* when he is the senior son of his generation, serves the *ya-bagr* when he is the senior grandson, and serves the *yabya bagr* when he is the senior great-grandson.

The Kusasi only serve three generations of *bagr*. When the last great-grandson of the ancestor enshrined in a *yab ya bagr* passes away, his descendants remove the shrine from the mound and toss the stone into the bush. Members of the patriline no longer serve the spirit. According to some of my informants, these are the spirits that ultimately get passed in marriage exchange to other patrilines (these spirits will ultimately become *bugr* in other compounds). An alternate perspective is that these spirits look toward their cognatic descendants for individuals who can serve them as other types of spirits in other types of shrines, including *bakalogo*.

Shrines that serve as the abode for spirits that originate from outside the residential group are located inside the compound, while shrines that house spirits that originate from within the residential group are located outside the compound. As the paternal ancestors reach the stage where their descendants no longer serve them, the maternal ancestor shrines move from deeper to shallower spaces within the compound. The distribution patterns stem from the types of relationships that make up the residential group and larger social order. Like the physical layout of Kusasi compounds, lineage and domestic relations find expression in paternal and maternal ancestor shrines.

The paternal ancestor shrines embody centralization or the fact that all the residents of the compound belong to the same group. Located in the plastered mound on the exterior wall of the *zong*, the shrines enable the spirits to monitor both residents and visitors. The shrines have a collective existence as the *ya na'am*, and they are all in the same mound of plastered earth. As such, the shrines symbolize the collective nature of lineage relations.

Maternal ancestor shrines embody segmentation or the fact that residential groups are products of different lineages forging relationships through marriage exchange. As a *bugr*, a maternal ancestor shrine starts out in the personal room of the woman with whom it was transferred. It cannot be located in the same space as other maternal ancestor shrines, since those shrines house spirits from other lineages. Likewise, the *ma-bugr* resides in the personal room of the man who serves it. The preferred location of the *ba-bugr* is the *zong*, which is a private location, separate from both the paternal ancestor shrines and other maternal ancestor shrines. The maternal ancestor shrines have distinct spaces and thereby underscore the segmentary nature of domestic relations.

The placement of both paternal and maternal ancestor shrines around and in the *zong* highlights the interdependence of the different segments that make up the residential group. The *zong* embodies the ultimate reality of social life, that human beings are entangled in relationships and are members of groups that are simultaneously collaborative and competitive.

The Kusasi *zong* is comparable to the Anufo compound and the space known as *le*. According to Kirby (1986:69),

> It is from the centre of the compound looking through the *le* to the sunset that the cardinal points of direction are determined. Thus the house itself is a kind of shrine, though rarely sacral. It binds men to the ancestors, and the heart of the compound is a cosmic gateway to the ancestors.

The *zong* is a cosmological center that links the past to the present and the ancestors with the living. It is a liminal space that binds outside to inside, public to private, and paternal blood to maternal blood. The *zong* embodies the notion that the compound itself is a shrine. Its buildings house the future ancestors of the residential group, just as the many shrines in and around the compound house the current ancestors.

Conclusions

If ever there was a form of material culture that could be read like a text, it would be Kusasi ancestor shrines. The presence of paternal ancestor shrines is an index of the compound head's genealogical position and authority within the lineages to which he belongs. The presence of maternal ancestor shrines indicates the number of lineal segments within the residential group and is indicative of relationships with marriage exchange partners. For the compound head, competing obligations to the *bugr* and *bagr* shrines reflect on the one hand patrilineal solidarity and strength and on the other the principles of social fission and segmentation associated with the matriline.

The Kusasi evidence demonstrates descent may be materialized in distinct ways that are detectable archaeologically. Shrines of patrilineal ancestors occur in different locations within the compound space than those dedicated to matrilineal ancestors. Shrines also express principles of social organization. Paternal ancestor shrines signify centralization while maternal ancestor shrines are symbols of segmentation. Ultimately, the dichotomy between the shrines breaks down when the paternal ancestor is no longer served and the maternal ancestor is enshrined in the *tengbana bugr*. Despite the fact the Kusasi are patrilineal, it is the maternal ancestor shrine that serves as the durable symbol of the lineage.

Ancestor shrines are meaningful social, material, and spatial phenomena that, at least in the Kusasi case, produce durable patterns in material culture. Understanding the ways in which ancestors are represented, enshrined, and emplaced will allow archaeologists to both explain and interpret the material culture assemblages they encounter.

Notes

1. Some types of maternal ancestor shrines may include stones, but paternal ancestor shrines or *ya na'am/bagr* are always stones. While other types of shrines may also include stones, what makes the *ya na'am/bagr* unique is their location on the outside wall of the *zong*—they are always there.

2. People often say that they need to have children so that someone will be able to serve them when they are dead, that is, when they become ancestors. This rationale seems to exclude children from being ancestors. In a patrilineal polygynous society, children can be senior members of lineages because of their generational age, and in fact my interpreter had "grandfathers" who were much younger than he was. So, theoretically, if one of those people died, my interpreter could create a shrine and serve that person. However, the general rule may be situationally "violated." While it may be possible for children to become ancestors, I suspect that it would be a fairly rare occurrence.

References Cited

Awedoba, Albert

1989a Notes on Matrimonial Goods among the Atoende Kusasi, Part 1. *Research Review* 5(1):37–53.

1989b Matrimonial Goods among the Atoende Kusasi Contingent Prestations, Part 2. *Research Review* 5(2):1–17.

1989c Matrimonial Goods among the Atoende Kusasi: Matrimonial Prestations and Exploitation, Part 3. *Research Review* 6(1):49–56.

Fortes, Meyer

1949 *The Web of Kinship among the Tallensi*. International African Institute, Oxford University Press, London.

Hilton, T. E.

1962 Notes on the History of Kusasi. *Transactions of the Historical Society of Ghana* 6:79–96.

Kirby, Jon P.

1986 *God, Shrines, and Problem-Solving among the Anufo of Northern Ghana*. Dietrich Reimer Verlag, Berlin.

Lane, Paul J.

1994 The Temporal Structuring of Settlement Space among the Dogon of Mali: An Ethnoarchaeological Study. In *Architecture and Order: Approaches to Social*

Space, edited by M. Parker Pearson and C. Richards, pp. 196–216. Routledge, London.

Mather, Charles

1999 *An Ethnoarchaeology of Kusasi Shrines, Upper East Region, Ghana*. Unpublished PhD dissertation, Department of Archaeology, University of Calgary, Calgary, Alberta.

2000 Kusasi Ancestor Shrines as Historical and Social Maps. In *The Entangled Past: Integrating History and Archaeology, Proceedings of the 30th Annual Chacmool Archaeological Conference*, edited by M. Boyd, J. C. Erwin, and M. Hendrickson, pp. 136–143. Archaeological Association of the University of Calgary, Calgary, Alberta.

2003 Shrines and the Domestication of Landscape. *Journal of Anthropological Research* 59(1):23–45.

2005 Accusations of Genital Theft: A Case from Northern Ghana. *Culture, Medicine, and Psychiatry* 29(1):33–52.

2007 Personal, Social, and Cultural Dimensions of Health in Kusasi Ethnomedicine. In *Cultural Healing and Belief Systems*, edited by James Pappas, William Smythe, and Angelina Baydala, pp. 94–110. Detselig Enterprises, Calgary, Alberta.

Naden, Tony

1988 The Gur Languages. In *The Languages of Ghana*, edited by M. E. Kropp Dakubu, pp. 12–49. Occasional Publications no. 2, International African Institute, Kegan Paul, London.

Parker Pearson, Michael, and Colin Richards

1994 Ordering the World: Perceptions of Architecture, Space, and Time. In *Architecture and Order: Approaches to Social Space*, edited by M. Parker Pearson and C. Richards, pp. 1–37. Routledge, London.

Spratt, David H., and Nancy Spratt

1968 *Collected Field Reports on the Phonology of Kusaal*. Collected Language Notes no. 10. Institute of African Studies, University of Ghana, Legon.

1972 *Kusal Syntax*. Collected Language Notes no. 13. Institute of African Studies, University of Ghana, Legon.

Syme, J.G.G.

1932 *The Kusasis: A Short History*. Mimeo NRG 8/2/214. Accra, Ghana.

PART II

Discovering Ancestors

6

Landscapes of Ancestors

The Structuring of Space around Iron Age Funerary Monuments in Central Europe

MATTHEW L. MURRAY

The hero draws inspiration from the virtues of his ancestors.

Johann Wolfgang von Goethe

Humans are not proud of their ancestors,
and rarely invite them round for dinner.

Douglas Adams, author of the *Hitchhiker's Guide to the Galaxy*

An ancestor is a real or mythical member of a community who was celebrated and commemorated in death by the living. In society, ancestors are links in chains of related kin groups—threads that are woven to unite people in larger social classification tapestries (Fortes 1969; Goody 1969; Radcliffe-Brown 1941). Ancestors may form the basis of shared group identities (Helms 1998; Newell 1976). Prior to the development of the state, kinship and descent were authoritative and pervasive principles of social organization. Ancestors as identifiable elements in descent structures were fundamental sources of identity and power. In complex societies today, kinship and ancestry continue to be central social elements at local and regional scales of integration and differentiation, such as in the southern United States, where family heritage is a defining aspect of group identity and a source of social privilege and prestige (Billingsly 2004; Wilson 2006). These identities may be concretized on the landscape in places of group burial (Davies 1997:93–110), as illustrated for traditional societies such as the Merina of Madagascar (Bloch 1971) and the Berawan of

Figure 6.1. Location of the Heuneburg (Baden-Württemberg) and the Glauberg (Hessen) in Germany.

Borneo (Metcalf and Huntington 1991:144–151), as well as for other societies (Francis et al. 2005). Ancestral identities are literally encoded and incorporated into the earth during mortuary practice. Later actions at these places make reference to encoded identities.

In many societies the ancestors are—or were—*everywhere*. In prehistoric central Europe, the ancestors were embodied by the very earth, becoming landscapes themselves (see also Campbell, Hageman, this volume). In these embodied places, the living interacted with and experienced their kinship/descent structures, reinforced dominant social norms, and even engaged in a contentious discourse about them. At various times and places in the past, considerable energy and wealth were expended on creating complex theaters of action that linked the living to the dead—ancestral landscapes that resonated with agency for generations and were even potent places for social references in later societies.

In the early Iron Age, mortuary places, lineage tombs, burial sculpture, and associated features defined entire landscapes in terms of ancestral space. These landscapes were contexts for shared physical activities or "choreographies" of cultural experience. For the living, tombs and mortuary landscapes were significant investments of political and spiritual capital. They were also resources for social discourse, and they represented a continuum between present, past, and future—a form of "ancestor time" in which landscape and people were ritually and habitually fused. Fundamental in the creation of an ancestral landscape was the *corporealization* of the earth—the corporeality of place through mortuary practice. Mortuary monuments and cemeteries embodied the ancestors, who became a significant content of these places. Across these landscapes during the final millennium BC, a contest ensued between opposing societal and philosophical structures: the charismatic "hero" and the community.

In this chapter, I use a phenomenological landscape approach to explore early Iron Age mortuary spaces, which I argue are places of performance and discourse. I will illustrate my argument with two case studies in central Europe: the Heuneburg and the Glauberg (figure 6.1). I then suggest that art consumed in these places can be used to examine the rise and fall of communal versus individual roles in society and that this cycle is linked to the sociopolitical development of Iron Age communities.

Funerary Monuments of the Early Iron Age

Early Iron Age burial places from the seventh to the fourth centuries BC were contexts for diverse contemporary funerary performances, including cremation and inhumation, and placement of funerary remains in simple unmarked pits or in chambers beneath mounds or in enclosures (Murray 1992). One of the best illustrations of this diversity is the cemetery of Rottenburg, Germany (Reim 1988). Some enduring features of these places were mounds of earth—and sometimes stone—usually constructed over a primary grave. These mounds were often used as tombs for later secondary interments. Osteological and material culture analyses of collective mound tombs at Dattingen in southwestern Germany (Alt

Figure 6.2. The reconstructed paramount burial monument, the Hohmichele, near the Heuneburg. Photo by author.

et al. 1995) reveal that at least some of these monuments were family or lineage tombs. The largest collective tombs were up to 100 meters in diameter and contained as many as 126 graves, such as the Magdalenenberg in southwestern Germany (Spindler 1976). The Hohmichele, about 2,000 meters from the Heuneburg hillfort on the upper Danube River, is one of the largest mortuary monuments in continental Europe (figure 6.2). Anthropomorphic stone statuary uncovered at some burial mounds—such as the celebrated stela from Hirschlanden (Zürn 1970)—was most likely originally placed on the mound's crown. These monuments and statues were part of a concretized, incorporated memory of the dead. The monuments were further linked to the landscapes of the living in important ways (Arnold 2002; Murray 1996) that guided ritualized activities of descendant communities.

Ritual, Performance, and Choreography

Ritual is the undertaking of a complex sequence of symbolic acts (Turner 1969). Ritual is a structure that has logical social and cultural effects beyond religion, such as establishment of convention, making of a social contract, encoding of morality and order, construction of time and eternity, and representation of creation and ancestry (Rappaport 1999:27). Roy Rappaport (1999:32–49) defined the primary features of ritual as adherence to form, repetition, invariance, diachronic constancy, and the physical act of performance.

According to Victor Turner (1986:84), ritual is the presentation of a shared "lived experience," or *communitas*, which "embodies the response of the collective mind to the collective experience." This knowledge is acquired through participation in collective performances.

Unless there is a performance, there is no ritual (Rappaport 1999:37). Performance concretizes and habitualizes ritual, and the places and things of performance become the material correlates of ritual. Milton Singer (1972) used the term "cultural performance" to denote acts that encapsulated the essence of particular cultural systems. Each cultural performance has a structured time, a beginning and an end, an organized program of activities, a set of participants, and an audience. All of these structured elements are tied to a place and time of performance.

Since the early 1990s, my approach to past-ritualized performances in the landscape has been influenced by Paul Connerton's (1989) description of the intrinsically physical nature of the process through which societies remember and continuously rediscover themselves. Connerton argues that ritual performances communicate and sustain communal images and a shared knowledge of the past. This performative memory is transferred from the group to the individual and from generation to generation through repeated bodily actions undertaken within ritually prescribed spatial contexts. After all, rituals are repetitive, and repetition is a link to the past (Connerton 1989:45). Ritual is a formal performative "language" encoded in set postures, gestures, and other bodily actions that make it effective as a social mnemonic system (1989:58–59). Ritualized actions, or "incorporated practices," are habitual, recurrent performances that reinforce group identity and ideology and transmit collective memory. The spaces occupied during performance—and the flow of performances through space—are central to this process of social remembering (cf. Murray 1995:39, 1996).

An integral part of performance is choreography, which is a process of planning, directing, and coordinating the movements made by groups of performers. The essential physical nature of ritual and remembering elucidated by Connerton has particular utility for the archaeologist interested in landscapes. Built environments that leave lasting traces in the landscape present ritual performers with a matrix of boundaries, pathways, and places similar to the way that Christopher Tilley (1994) has explained a phenomenology of landscape. This matrix is analogous to the "theater" of collective cultural performance, a set designed to contain, determine, and direct the repeated staging of ritual performance. The choreography of social and cultural performances, therefore, is constituted in the corporeal and permanent structuring of space through conventions that either direct and focus performances or enclose them.

In *The Savage Mind* (1966), Claude Lévi-Strauss analyzed the practice of the dream-time among Australian Aborigines as an example of the structural opposition of mythic history (diachrony) and life history (synchrony). Alfred Gell (1992:26–29) discussed Aboriginal "ancestor time" as a parallel time when the past is both the present and the future. I suggest that there was a similar "ancestor time" in the early Iron Age of central Europe that linked a living people to a territory and its resources, its opportunities, and its layers of meanings and interpretations. The physical, corporeal world could be manipulated to incorporate "ancestor time," essentially re-creating the past so that it becomes the present and re-creating the present so that it melds with the past (Gell 1992:27).

Case Studies: The Heuneburg and the Glauberg

The physical corporeal world was intentionally manipulated during the early Iron Age in central Europe to incorporate ancestor time and space, and the lived experience of the ancestors was integral to the choreographies of daily life. The bodily incorporation of ancestors is illustrated by extensive built landscapes only recently uncovered at well-known early Iron Age elite centers such as the Heuneburg and Glauberg in southwestern Germany.

Landscape Choreography at the Heuneburg

One of the most dramatic changes in the past fifteen years of archaeological research in central Europe, where centuries of deep plowing have erased many surface features, is the discovery that some landscapes were structured on truly monumental proportions. Elite hillforts and paramount burial monuments appear to be at the core of these structures.

The Heuneburg bei Hundersingen, located on the upper Danube River south of Stuttgart in the state of Baden-Württemberg, is arguably one of the best excavated type-sites of the late Hallstatt period dating to the sixth and fifth centuries BC (Kimmig 1983; S. Kurz 2007). It was recently one of several early Iron Age centers included in a wide-ranging Deutsche Forschungsgemeinschaft (DFG) "focal point" project (www.fürstensitze.de) that examined the origin and development of early Iron Age power centers (Krausse 2004, 2008; Krausse and Bofinger 2004).

The Heuneburg is a small promontory at the western edge of the Danube River valley and about 65 meters above the valley floor. Here, after 600 BC, an early Iron Age polity erected a Mediterranean-style mud-brick fortification (Kimmig 1983:70–80). At least eleven known burial mound groups, including some of the largest monuments on the continent, lie within 3,000 meters of the hillfort; several of these monuments have yielded the remains of late Hallstatt elite burials (Kurz and Schiek 2002). Recent excavation of intact mounds in the Hohmichele mound group revealed that some mounds were used for several generations and became the focus of ancestor veneration (Arnold 2003, 2004; Arnold and Murray 2002; Arnold et al. 2000, 2001, 2003; Schneider 2003, 2007). Members of the Heuneburg mud-brick-wall dynasty may have been placed in some of these graves (Riek 1962); their monuments are enduring markers of ancestor space and elements of "ancestor time" (see figure 6.3).

In the past decade, research at the Heuneburg has focused particularly on landscape relationships beyond the well-known hillfort (Bofinger 2007; S. Kurz 2005, 2008). This work has yielded traces of monumental linear structures, including a network of intersecting ditch-and-wall systems (Bofinger and Goldner-Bofinger 2008; S. Kurz 1998; Reim 2001). The systems encompass numerous "outer" settlement areas that are roughly contemporary with the hillfort (Bofinger 2005, 2006; S. Kurz 2000, 2008; Kurz and Wahl 2006). The layout of the ditches and walls also suggests that they were designed to establish links between Heuneburg inhabitants and elite burial monuments (figure 6.4). As people passed through a substantial stone "chambered" gate that was recently uncovered at the foot of the Heuneburg (G. Kurz 2008), their attention and actions would have been focused on a group of large burial mounds at Gießübel-Talhau 400 meters west of the hillfort complex. Additional monumental linear features also appear to link the hillfort and outer settlements with other large mounds about 1,500 meters to the south at Lehenbühl and the Baumburg.

Figure 6.3. Excavation of Tumulus 18 near the Hohmichele in 2002. Photo by author.

Thus the Heuneburg and its outer settlements and mortuary monuments were once networked in an extensive complex of earthworks that directed movement and choreographed performances across the landscape and structured people's experiences of the past and present.

Landscape Choreography at the Glauberg

Since the early 1990s, large-scale fieldwork at the Glauberg, northeast of Frankfurt in the state of Hessen, incorporating aerial photography, topographic mapping, geophysical survey, field walking, and excavation, has revealed portions of a highly complex structured landscape similar to the Heuneburg (Baitinger 2008; Baitinger and Pinsker 2002; Hansen and Pare 2008; Posluschny 2007).

The Glauberg is a small basalt plateau that rises 60 to 100 meters above the surrounding terrain. The plateau was apparently fortified during the late Hallstatt and early La Tène periods in the sixth and fifth centuries BC. Although relatively little is known about settlement on the plateau (Baitinger 2008), the discovery in 2001 of three elite early La Tène burials at

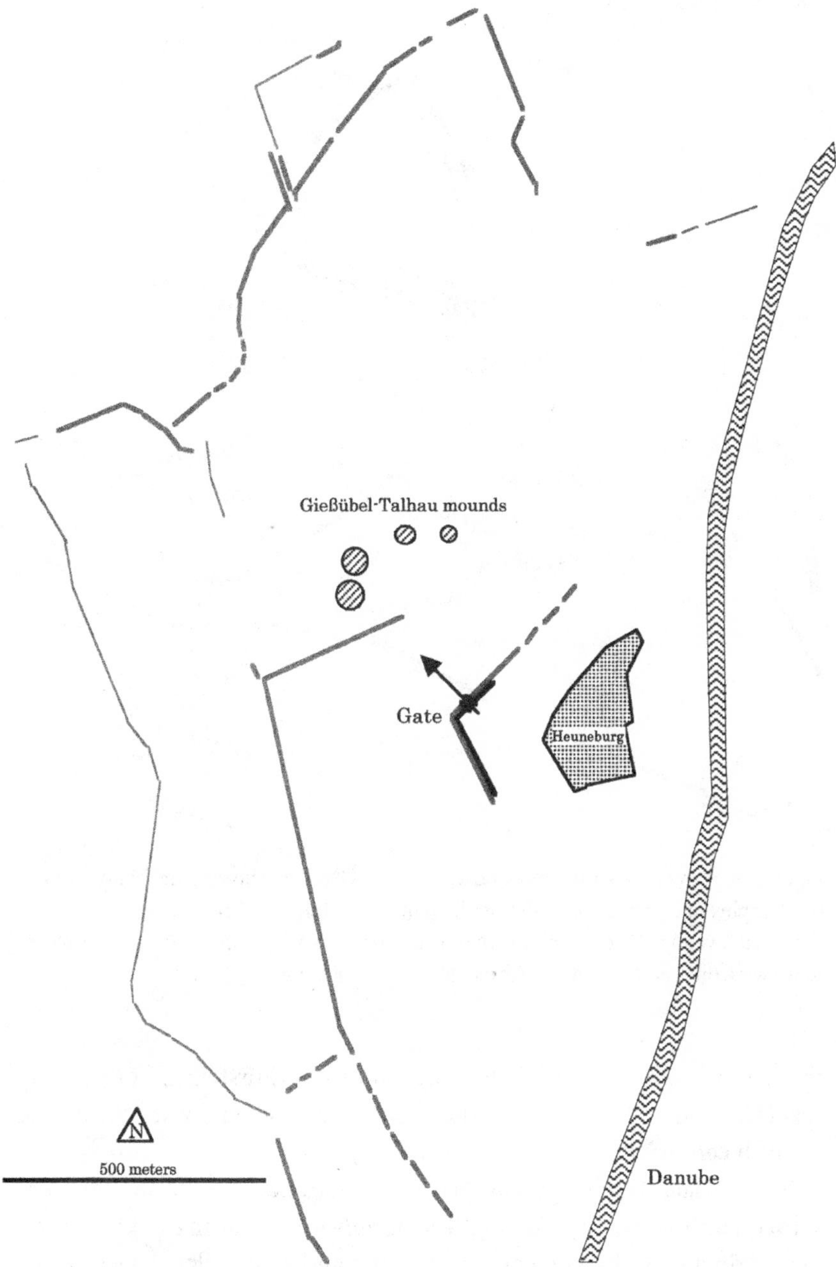

Figure 6.4. Plan of the structured landscape of the Heuneburg showing the hillfort and an extensive complex of earthworks, including the "chamber" gate and its orientation toward the burial mounds at Gießübel-Talhau. Ditches are shown in gray, and wall remnants are shown in black; dashed lines indicate suspected earthworks. Adapted from Siegfried Kurz 2008, fig. 1, and Gabriele Kurz 2008, fig. 10.

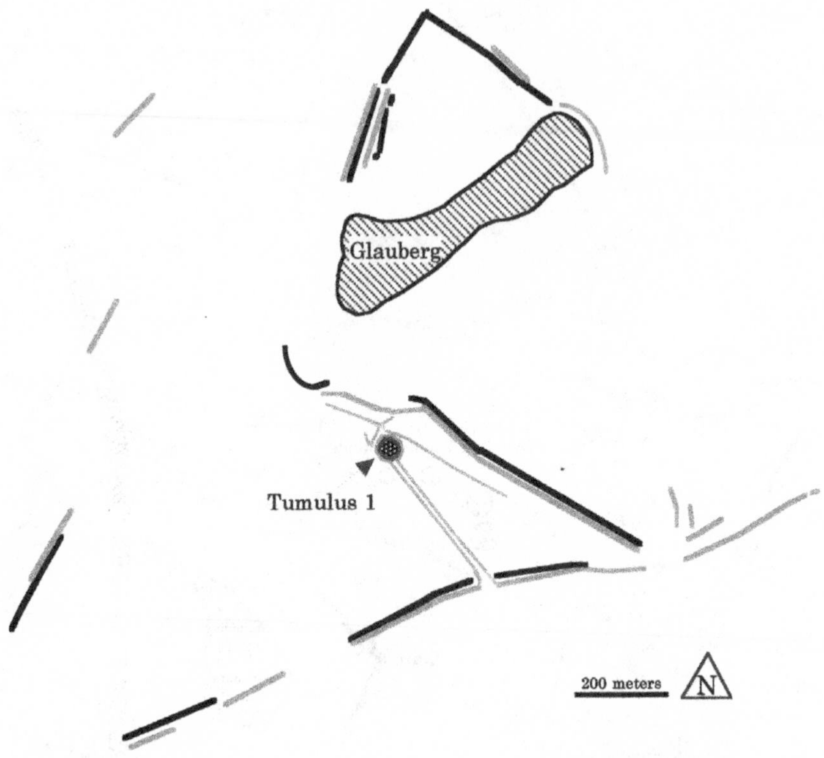

Figure 6.5. Plan of the structured landscape of the Glauberg showing the hillfort and the complex of earthworks, including the remains of Tumulus 1 at the northern end of a ditched "avenue." Ditches are shown in gray, and embankments are shown in black. Redrawn from Leif Hansen and Christopher Pare 2008, fig. 1.

the foot of the hill has led to its designation as a "Fürstensitz" or princely seat (Herrmann 2002:95). The graves were established toward the end of the fifth century BC.

The burials were originally placed beneath two tumuli, which were subsequently leveled by plowing. The tumuli are part of an extensive complex of ditches, walls, and enclosures south and west of the plateau (Hansen and Pare 2008; Herrmann 2002; Posluschny 2007). The now-famous stone statue, an apparent representation of the individual in Grave 1 under Tumulus 1 (based on the finds of a gold torque and shield in the grave that are signified on the *stela*), was found on the northwest side of the tumulus in the ditch along with fragments of two other sculptures.

Tumulus 1 appears to occupy a focal point of the Glauberg (figure 6.5). A primary unifying structural element of the complex is a massive ditch that surrounds the tumulus. On the south side of the mound, the ditch diverges to form a 10-meter-wide "avenue" that extends 350 meters south-southeast of the tumulus. At this point, the avenue opens abruptly onto the plain, and traces of the ditch and associated berm continue to the east and west roughly perpendicular to the avenue for a distance of about 750 meters in either direction. To the west, an interruption in the ditch marks the location of several urn burials and a tumulus grave. Evidence of settlement has been found primarily inside the complex on either side of the avenue and in the so-called annex below the northern slope of the Glauberg (Hansen and Pare 2008).

The earthworks would have created an effective barrier against direct movement to the north toward the Glauberg, channeling activity into the "avenue" and thus focusing attention and action on Tumulus 1 with its mortuary statues. In this way, the built elements of the landscape choreographed cultural performances by directing and coordinating action across well-defined pathways toward the monument. Ancestral space was linked with domestic space, and people were encouraged to *walk through*, experience, and "remember" their social conditions.

The structured landscapes of the Heuneburg and the Glauberg concentrated attention and action on monuments of the dead, creating "theaters" of collective cultural performance where links between the living and the ancestors were emphasized. The mortuary monuments were often parts of larger burial places, but it is evident that within these places, certain ancestors or ancestral groups were particularly emphasized through earthworks and statuary as well as through rich funerary accoutrements, such as wagons, feasting accessories, and personal adornment. Some of the most distinctive pieces of early Iron Age material culture were created for use in mortuary displays. In its mortuary landscape context, early La Tène art was an active element of social discourse and eventually social change.

Early La Tène Art in Its Landscape Context

The early La Tène of central Europe, as represented by the landscape of the Glauberg, is the dramatic finale of an era of societal fragmentation that began with the emerging late Hallstatt elites in the eighth century

BC. During this process, traditional Bronze Age symbols and practices that reflected and reinforced *community* were transformed by emerging elites and their competitive kin groups and allies (Murray 1992, 1995; see also Hageman, this volume). Individuals were celebrated and enshrined in monumental and heroic ways. Mortuary sculptures were erected that illustrated the accepted generalized features of a "heroic" ancestor, perhaps even displaying specific individual characteristics, such as in Grave 1 at the Glauberg. Entire landscapes were ditched, mounded, and banked to create links between hillforts, their territories, and ancestral burial grounds. Movement across these landscapes was choreographed to emphasize these links.

During the early La Tène, a radically new art style was fostered and consumed by elites (Megaw and Megaw 1989:51–107). The eccentric and one-of-a-kind nature of early La Tène cast bronze ornamentation celebrated the individual—the "hero" as a social ideal. Many of the most charismatic works are associated with indigenous adaptations of Mediterranean drinking and serving vessels placed in elite tombs, such as the remarkable spouted flagon from the Dürrnberg, Austria (Moosleitner 1985). Within the contexts of funeral performance, these unique pieces reinforced ideas of distinction and difference, and they were important functional and symbolic elements of Iron Age competitive feasting (Arnold 1999) as well as spiritual power (Green 1996:137–138).

But this new elite art also contained the ideological seeds of the eventual collapse of early Iron Age heroic society by the end of the fourth century BC (cf. Pauli 1978:455–460). These seeds of instability were sown in the theme of *interconnectedness*, in contrast to *opposition*, that was represented in early La Tène art on many existentialist levels—element and design, human and animal, time and being, individual and community. The art of *interconnectedness*—and its organic, vegetal essence—is particularly well represented in one of the last of the great elite tombs at Waldalgescheim, Germany (Joachim 1991; Megaw and Megaw 1989:113–114). As heroic early Iron Age society began to implode, partly as a result of the demands of competitive consumption and destruction of wealth (Cunliffe 1994), the ideology of the charismatic individual became increasingly entangled in twining tendrils and never-ending curves. Early Iron Age hillforts and burial places were abandoned. In many places across central Europe, later Iron Age communities eventually returned to symbols and practices in "ancestor time" that reflected and reinforced *community* identity rather than the *hero*.

Burial places of the later fourth to the third centuries BC in central Europe were primarily small groupings of flat inhumation and cremation graves with no evident monuments and comparatively little material differentiation, such as the "family" plots at Nebringen, Germany (Krämer 1964). By the time of the great *oppida* after the third century BC (Collis 1984), formal burial places largely disappeared across southern Germany, while select human remains were deposited in habitation contexts at places such as Manching in Bavaria, which may indicate that the bones of ancestors were maintained and manipulated in "domestic" spaces (Lange 1983; Murray 1992, 1995; Sievers 2003:100–103). Indeed, contrary to Douglas Adams's witty assertion that people are not proud of their ancestors, there are indications that people of the later Iron Age were actually including ancestors as "guests" at dinner.

Conclusion

As Christopher Tilley (1994) has argued, landscapes have agency in relation to people. We live in them, perceive them, experience them, influence them, and in turn are influenced by them (Tilley 2008:271). At sites such as the Heuneburg and the Glauberg, ancestors were part of day-to-day lived experiences because the ancestors were incorporated into and embodied landscapes. Landscapes were theaters of social performance, incorporated practices, and social memory. Artwork displayed and deposited during these activities encoded conflicting existential ideas of opposition and interconnectedness. The complex embodied and choreographed landscapes of the Heuneburg and the Glauberg reflect efforts of elites (individuals or groups of related individuals) to legitimize their power, inscribe land tenure, and establish and perpetuate social cosmologies on the very earth that people occupied. The subsequent destruction and burial of idiosyncratic mortuary statues at elite monuments, such as Tumulus 1 at the Glauberg, heralded the collapse of this heroic society.

In early Iron Age central Europe, the earth in the form of an embodied "landscape of ancestors" served as a source of knowledge and social agency through carefully choreographed experiences. The past was in the present and the present became part of the past. As advocates of populist neo-Celtic “wisdom” suggest, “The earth remembers everything” (Matthews and Matthews 1994:6).

Acknowledgments

Ancient ancestors were one of several cross-cultural topics explored during stimulating breakfast discussions that I had with Erica Hill at the European Archaeology Association meeting in Cork, Ireland, in 2005. I would like to thank Erica and Jon Hageman for their invitation to participate in the symposium, “Ancient Ancestors in Global Perspective,” at the Society for American Archaeology meeting in Austin, Texas, in 2007. The excavation of Tumulus 18 at the Hohmichele was part of the “Landscape of Ancestors” project initiated by Bettina Arnold (University of Wisconsin, Milwaukee). Fieldwork was supported by research grants from the National Geographic Society and the University of Wisconsin, Milwaukee.

References Cited

Alt, Kurt W., Martina Munz, and Werner Vach

1995 Hallstattzeitliche Grabhügel im Spiegel ihrer biologischen und sozialen Strukturen am Beispiel des Hügelgräberfeldes von Dattingen, Kr. Breisgau-Hochschwarzwald. *Germania* 73(2):281–316.

Arnold, Bettina

1999 “Drinking the Feast”: Alcohol and the Legitimation of Power in Celtic Europe. *Cambridge Archaeological Journal* 9(1):71–93.

2002 A Landscape of Ancestors: The Space and Place of Death in Iron Age West-Central Europe. In *The Space and Place of Death*, edited by Helaine Silverman and David B. Small, pp. 129–143. American Anthropological Association, Washington, D.C.

2003 Landscapes of Ancestors: Early Iron Age Hillforts and Their Mound Cemeteries. *Expedition: The Magazine of the University of Pennsylvania Museum of Archaeology and Anthropology* 45(1):8–13.

2004 Early Iron Age Mortuary Ritual in Southwest Germany: The Heuneburg and the Landscape of Ancestors Project. In *Spatial Analysis of Funerary Areas*, edited by Ladislav Šmejda and Jan Turek, pp. 148–158. University of West Bohemia, Plzeň, Czech Republic.

Arnold, Bettina, and Matthew L. Murray

2002 A Landscape of Ancestors in Southwest Germany. *Antiquity* 76:321–322.

Arnold, Bettina, Matthew L. Murray, and Seth A. Schneider

2000 Untersuchungen in einem hallstattzeitlichen Grabhügel der Hohmichelegruppe im "Speckhau," Markung Heiligkreuztal, Gemeinde Altheim, Landkreis Biberach. *Archäologische Ausgrabungen in Baden-Württemberg 1999*, pp. 64–67.

2001 Abschließende Untersuchungen in einem hallstattzeitlichen Grabhügel der Hohmichelegruppe im "Speckhau," Markung Heiligkreuztal, Gemeinde Altheim, Landkreis Biberach. *Archäologische Ausgrabungen in Baden-Württemberg 2000*, pp. 67–70.

2003 Untersuchungen in einem zweiten hallstattzeitlichen Grabhügel der Hohmichelegruppe im "Speckhau," Markung Heiligkreuztal, Gemeinde Altheim, Landkreis Biberach. *Archäologische Ausgrabungen in Baden-Württemberg 2002*, pp. 78–81.

Baitinger, Holger

2008 Der frühkeltische Fürstensitz auf dem Glauberg (Hessen). In *Frühe Zentralisierungs- und Urbanisierungsprozesse: Zur Genese und Entwicklung frühkeltischer Fürstensitze und ihres territorialen Umlandes*, edited by Dirk Krausse, pp. 39–56. Konrad Theiss, Stuttgart.

Baitinger, Holger, and Bernhard Pinsker

2002 *Glaube—Mythos—Wirklichkeit: Das Ratsel der Kelten vom Glauberg*. Konrad Theiss, Stuttgart.

Billingsly, Carolyn Earle

2004 *Communities of Kinship: Antebellum Families and the Settlement of the Cotton Frontier*. University of Georgia Press, Athens.

Bloch, Maurice

1971 *Placing the Dead*. Seminar Press, New York.

Bofinger, Jörg

2005 Archäologische Untersuchungen in der Vorburg der Heuneburg—Siedlung und Befestigungssysteme am frühkeltischen Fürstensitz an der oberen Donau, Gde. Herbertingen-Hundersingen, Kreis Sigmaringen. *Archäologische Ausgrabungen in Baden-Württemberg 2004*, pp. 82–86.

2006 Stein für Stein . . . Überraschende Befunde im Beriech der Befestigungssysteme der Heuneburg-Vorburg, Gde. Herberingen-Hundersingen, Kreis Sigmaringen. *Archäologische Ausgrabungen in Baden-Württemberg 2005*, pp. 73–79.

2007 *Flugzeug, Laser, Sonde, Spaten: Fernerkundung und archäologische Feldforschung am Beispiel der frühkeltischen Fürstensitze*. Landesamt für Denkmalpflege, Esslingen. http//www.denkmalpflege-bw.de/publikationen-und-service/publikationen/onlinepublikationen.html (accessed August 6, 2010).

Bofinger, Jörg, and Anita Goldner-Bofinger

2008 Terrassen und Gräben—Siedlungstrukturen und Befestigungssysteme der Heuneburg-Vorburg. In *Frühe Zentralisierungs- und Urbanisierungsprozesse: Zur Genese und Entwicklung frühkeltischer Fürstensitze und ihres territorialen Umlandes*, edited by Dirk Krausse, pp. 209–228. Konrad Theiss, Stuttgart.

Collis, John

1984 *Oppida: Earliest Towns North of the Alps*. Department of Prehistory and Archaeology, University of Sheffield, Sheffield.

Connerton, Paul
1989 *How Societies Remember*. Cambridge University Press, Cambridge.
Cunliffe, Barry
1994 Iron Age Societies in Western Europe and Beyond, 800–140 BC. In *The Oxford Illustrated Prehistory of Europe*, edited by Barry Cunliffe, pp. 336–372. Oxford University Press, Oxford.
Davies, Douglas James
1997 *Death, Ritual, and Belief: The Rhetoric of Funerary Rites*. Cassell, London.
Fortes, Meyer
1969 *Kinship and the Social Order: The Legacy of Lewis Henry Morgan*. Routledge and Kegan Paul, London.
Francis, Doris, Leonie Kellaher, and Georgina Neophytu
2005 *The Secret Cemetery*. Berg, London.
Gell, Alfred
1992 *The Anthropology of Time*. Berg, Oxford.
Goody, Jack
1969 *Comparative Studies in Kinship*. Routledge and Kegan Paul, London.
Green, Miranda A.
1996 *Celtic Art: Reading the Messages*. Calmann and King, London.
Hansen, Leif, and Christopher Pare
2008 Der Glauberg in seinem mikro- und makroregionalen Kontext. In *Frühe Zentralisierungs- und Urbanisierungsprozesse: Zur Genese und Entwicklung frühkeltischer Fürstensitze und ihres territorialen Umlandes*, edited by Dirk Krausse, pp. 57–96. Konrad Theiss, Stuttgart.
Helms, Mary W.
1998 *Access to Origins: Affines, Ancestors, and Aristocrats*. University of Texas Press, Austin.
Herrmann, Fritz-Rudolf
2002 Fürstensitz, Fürstengräber, und Heiligtum. In *Glaube—Mythos—Wirklichkeit: Das Ratsel der Kelten vom Glauberg*, edited by H. Baitinger and B. Pinsker, pp. 90–107. Konrad Theiss, Stuttgart.
Joachim, Hans-Eckart
1991 The Waldalgescheim Tomb. In *The Celts*, edited by Venceslas Kruta, Otto-Hermann Frey, Barry Raftery, and Miklós Szabó, p. 294. Rizzoli, New York.
Kimmig, Wolfgang
1983 *Die Heuneburg an der oberen Donau*. Konrad Theiss, Stuttgart.
Krämer, Werner
1964 *Das keltische Gräberfeld von Nebringen (Kreis Böblingen)*. Silberburg, Stuttgart.
Krausse, Dirk
2004 Frühkeltische Fürstensitze: Ein neues Schwerpunktprogramm der Deutschen Forschungsgemeinschaft am Landesdenkmalamt Baden-Württemberg. *Denkmalpflege in Baden-Württemberg* 33(4):237–245.
Krausse, Dirk (editor)
2008 *Frühe Zentralisierungs- und Urbanisierungsprozesse: Zur Genese und Entwick-*

lung frühkeltischer Fürstensitze und ihres territorialen Umlandes. Konrad Theiss, Stuttgart.

Krausse, Dirk, and Jörg Bofinger
2004 Neues DFG-Projekt: Genese und Entwicklung frühkeltischer Fürstensitze. *Archäologie in Deutschland* 4:4.

Kurz, Gabriele
2008 Ein Stadttor und Siedlung bei der Heuneburg (Gemeinde Herbertingen-Hundersingen, Kreis Sigmaringen). Zu den Grabungen in der Vorburg von 2000 bis 2006. In *Frühe Zentralisierungs- und Urbanisierungsprozesse: Zur Genese und Entwicklung frühkeltischer Fürstensitze und ihres territorialen Umlandes*, edited by Dirk Krausse, pp. 185–208. Konrad Theiss, Stuttgart.

Kurz, Siegfried
1998 Neue Ausgrabungen im Vorfeld der Heuneburg bei Hundersingen an der oberen Donau. *Germania* 76:527–547.
2000 *Die Heuneburg-Außensiedlung: Befunde und Funde*. Konrad Theiss, Stuttgart.
2005 Neue Forschungen im Umland der Heuneburg bei Herbertingen-Hundersingen, Kreis Sigmaringen. *Archäologische Ausgrabungen in Baden-Württemberg 2004*, pp. 87–91.
2007 *Untersuchungen zur Entstehung der Heuneburg in der späten Hallstattzeit*. Konrad Theiss, Stuttgart.
2008 Neue Forschungen im Umfeld der Heuneburg. Zwischenbericht zum Stand des Projektes "Zentralort und Umland: Untersuchungen zur Struktur der Heuneburg-Außensiedlung und zum Verhältnis der Heuneburg zu umgebenden Höhensiedlungen." In *Frühe Zentralisierungs- und Urbanisierungsprozesse: Zur Genese und Entwicklung frühkeltischer Fürstensitze und ihres territorialen Umlandes*, edited by Dirk Krausse, pp. 163–184. Konrad Theiss, Stuttgart.

Kurz, Siegfried, and Siegwalt Schiek
2002 *Bestattungsplätze im Umfeld der Heuneburg*. Konrad Theiss, Stuttgart.

Kurz, Siegfried, and Joachim Wahl
2006 Zur Fortsetzung der Grabungen in der Heuneburg-Außensiedlung zuf Markung Ertingen-Binzwangen, Kreis Biberach. *Archäologische Ausgrabungen in Baden-Württemberg 2005*, pp. 78–82.

Lange, Günter
1983 *Die menschlichen Skeletreste aus dem Oppidum von Manching*. Die Ausgrabungen in Manching, vol. 7. Franz Steiner, Wiesbaden.

Lévi-Strauss, Claude
1966 *The Savage Mind*. University of Chicago Press, Chicago.

Matthews, Caitlín, and John Matthews (editors)
1994 *The Encyclopaedia of Celtic Wisdom: The Celtic Shaman's Sourcebook*. Element, Shaftesbury, UK.

Megaw, Ruth, and Vincent Megaw
1989 *Celtic Art: From Its Beginnings to the Book of Kells*. Thames and Hudson, New York.

Metcalf, Peter, and Richard Huntington
1991 *Celebrations of Death: The Anthropology of Mortuary Ritual.* Cambridge University Press, Cambridge.
Moosleitner, Fritz
1985 *Die Schnabelkanne vom Dürrnberg: Ein Meisterwerk keltischer Handwerkskunst.* Museum Carolino Augusteum, Salzburg.
Murray, Matthew L.
1992 The Archaeology of Mystification: Ideology, Dominance, and the Urnfields of Southern Germany. In *Ancient Images, Ancient Thought: The Archaeology of Ideology*, edited by A. Sean Goldsmith, Sandra Garvie, David Selin, and Jeannette Smith, pp. 97–104. University of Calgary Archaeological Association, Calgary, Alberta.
1993 The Landscape Survey, 1990–1991. In *Settlement, Economy, and Cultural Change at the End of the European Iron Age: Excavations at Kelheim in Bavaria, 1987–1991,* edited by Peter S. Wells, pp. 96–134. International Monographs in Prehistory, Ann Arbor, Michigan.
1995 Archaeological Landscapes and Social Development: Late Bronze and Iron Age Settlement around Kelheim an der Donau, Germany. Unpublished PhD dissertation, Harvard University, Cambridge, Massachusetts.
1996 Socio-Political Complexity in Iron Age Temperate Europe: A Dialectical Landscape Approach. In *Debating Complexity*, edited by Daniel A. Meyer, Peter C. Dawson, and Donald T. Hanna, pp. 406–414. University of Calgary Archaeological Association, Calgary, Alberta.
Newell, William H. (editor)
1976 *Ancestors.* Aldine, Chicago.
Pauli, Ludwig
1978 *Der Dürrnberg bei Hallein III*, vol. 1. C. H. Beck'sche, Munich.
Posluschny, Axel
2007 From Landscape Archaeology to Social Archaeology: Finding Patterns to Explain the Development of Early Celtic "Princely Sites" in Middle Europe. In *Digital Discovery: Exploring New Frontiers in Human Heritage*, edited by Jeffrey T. Clark and Emily M. Hagemeister, pp. 131–141. Archaeolingua, Budapest.
Radcliffe-Brown, A. R.
1941 The Study of Kinship Systems. *Journal of the Royal Anthropological Institute* 71:49–89.
Rappaport, Roy A.
1999 *Ritual and Religion in the Making of Humanity.* Cambridge University Press, Cambridge.
Reim, Hartmann
1988 Das keltische Gräberfeld bei Rottenburg am Neckar, Grabungen 1984–1987. *Archäologische Informationen aus Baden-Württemberg 3.* Landesdenkmalamt Baden-Württemberg, Stuttgart.
2001 Grabungen im befestigten Vorwerk der frühkeltischen Heuneburg bei Her-

bertingen-Hundersingen, Kreis Sigmaringen. *Archäologische Ausgrabungen in Baden-Württemberg 2000*, pp. 63–67.

Riek, Gustav

1962 *Der Hohmichele: Ein Fürstengrabhügel der späten Hallstattzeit bei der Heuneburg.* Walter de Gruyter, Berlin.

Schneider, Seth A.

2003 Ancestor Veneration and Ceramic Curation: An Analysis from Speckhau Tumulus 17, Southwest Germany. Unpublished MA thesis, University of Wisconsin, Milwaukee.

2007 Ashes to Ashes: The Instrumental Use of Fire in West-Central European Early Iron Age Mortuary Ritual. In *Fire as an Instrument: The Archaeology of Pyrotechnologies*, edited by Dragos Gheorghiu, pp. 85–95. BAR International Series 1619, Archaeopress, Oxford.

Sievers, Susanne

2003 *Manching—Die Keltenstadt.* Konrad Theiss, Stuttgart.

Singer, Milton

1972 *When a Great Tradition Modernizes.* Praeger, New York.

Spindler, Konrad

1976 *Der Magdalenenberg bei Villingen: Ein Fürstengrabhügel des 6. vorchristlichen Jahrhunderts.* Konrad Theiss, Stuttgart.

Tilley, Christopher

1994 *A Phenomenology of Landscape: Places, Paths, and Monuments.* Berg, Oxford.

2008 Phenomenological Approaches to Landscape Archaeology. In *Handbook of Landscape Archaeology*, edited by Bruno David and Julian Thomas, pp. 271–276. Left Coast Press, Walnut Creek, California.

Turner, Victor

1969 *The Ritual Process: Structure and Anti-Structure.* Aldine, Chicago.

1986 *The Anthropology of Performance.* PAJ, New York.

Wilson, Charles Reagan (editor)

2006 *Myth, Manners, and Memory. The New Encyclopedia of Southern Culture.* Vol. 4. University of North Carolina Press, Chapel Hill.

Zürn, Harwig

1970 *Hallstattforschungen in Nordwürttemberg.* Müller & Graf, Stuttgart.

7

Royal Ancestor Construction and Veneration in the House of Habsburg

ESTELLA WEISS-KREJCI

There are many types of ancestors extant in the ethnographic and historic record (e.g., Ahern 1973; Antonaccio 1995; Bryant 2003; Fortes 1965; Freedman 1966; Gluckmann 1937; Hardacre 1987; Kopytoff 1971; Long 1987) and distinctions should be made among them. In this chapter, I focus on ancestors and ancestor construction in the royal House of Habsburg. Royal ancestors differ considerably from ancestors of commoners and even those of lesser nobles because while some are biologically related through the patri- or matriline, others are entirely fictive. Further, Habsburg ancestors left historically visible traces in genealogies and art.

I have selected the House of Habsburg for two reasons. First, the mortuary behavior of this house has been the focus of my past research (Weiss-Krejci 2001, 2004, 2005, 2008, 2010, 2015); second, a large body of published data concerning Habsburg ancestors exists, some of which has been translated (e.g., Wrandruszka 1964) or discussed in the English-language literature (e.g., Bietenholz 1994; Emerson 2004; Silver 2008). This will enable archaeologists who are unfamiliar with the German language to further engage with the problem of royal ancestor construction in a European context.

I focus on two people: Rudolph I (AD 1218–1291), the first Habsburg to become German king of the Holy Roman Empire, and his patrilineal descendant Emperor Maximilian I (AD 1459–1519), who set the stage for the Habsburg world empire. The construction of ancestry through Rudolph I's marriage politics, Maximilian I's emphatic relationship with forebears, and the manipulation of deceased "ancestors" and appropriation of their burial sites are the topics of this chapter.

Predecessors of the Habsburgs in Austria: The Babenberg Dynasty

In 976 Babenberg Leopold I (Luitpold) was given a small margravate in the present-day province of Lower Austria. The region in which the margravate was located was a sparsely settled area with a population of predominantly Bavarian and Slavic origin. The territory had been gained back from the Avars under Charlemagne (d. 814) at the beginning of the ninth century, but it soon suffered from renewed attacks by the Magyars. After the split of the Frankish Empire and formation of a new empire under German kings, the Magyar invasion came to an end, although the region continued to be contested (Friesinger 1976; Gutkas 1976:5–8; Lechner 1976; Mitscha-Märheim 1976; Vajda 1986; Zöllner 1976).

Twelve Babenberg rulers from nine generations controlled these territories for almost 270 years. Seven Babenbergs ruled as margraves of Ostarrichi and five as dukes of Austria. Eight times the reign passed from father to son, three times, in generations two, six, and eight after Leopold I, from older to younger brother (Lechner 1976; Pohl 1995). The Babenberg dynasty pushed the eastern frontier down the Danube River valley and colonized the lands on either side of the river. They moved their residence from Pöchlarn to Melk and then from Melk to Gars (figure 7.1).

The sixth margrave, Leopold III (d. 1136, generation 5), moved even farther east and founded a residence at Klosterneuburg (Gutkas 1976; Röhrig 1976:235–237). Leopold was married to Agnes (d. 1143), a princess from the Salian dynasty. At the time of their wedding in 1106, Agnes and her widowed stepmother, Praxedis (d. 1109), were the highest ranking women in the Holy Roman Empire. Agnes was the daughter of Emperor Henry IV, sister of Emperor Henry V, and widow of the Swabian duke Frederick I (Staufen dynasty) (figure 7.2). One of her sons from her first marriage was elected German king in 1138 (Conrad III). Through her marriage with Leopold III, Agnes became the female link between the Salian, Staufen, and Babenberg dynasties. If the sources can be trusted (Weller 2004:197–200), Agnes was a woman of almost unparalleled fecundity. She gave birth to more than twenty children, of which seventeen came from her second marriage. Two of her sons with Leopold III (Leopold IV and Henry II)

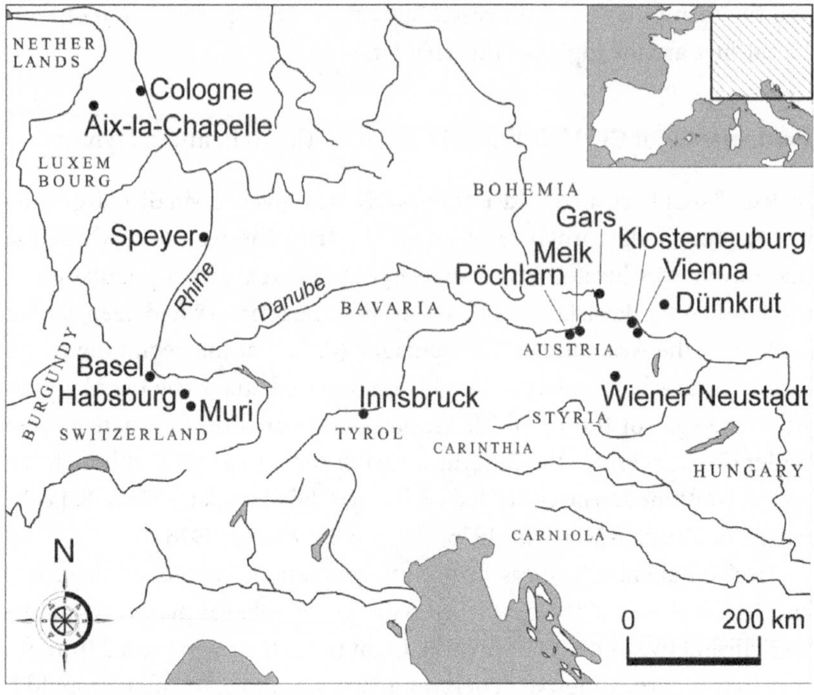

Figure 7.1. Sites and regions mentioned in the text.

became margraves and dukes. Agnes died at the age of seventy (Gerbert et al. 1772:4/1:34; Gutkas 1976:17–25; Röhrig 1976:239; Wacha 1976:612).

In 1156, under the eighth Babenberg ruler, Henry II (d. 1177), Ostarrichi became the duchy of Austria and Vienna the duke's residence (Lechner 1976:11–12, 355). With the death of the twelfth and last Babenberg duke, Frederick II (generation 9), in 1246, the male Babenberg line died out. Two women became involved in the struggle for the Babenberg inheritance. One was Frederick II's older sister, Margaret, widow of King Henry VII of Sicily from the Staufen dynasty and mother of his heir. The other was Gertrud, daughter of Frederick II's older brother, Count Henry the Cruel. The right of succession and inheritance of land through the female line was granted in the *privilegium minus*, the deed from 1156 issued by the emperor to elevate the margravate to a duchy (Ferenczy 1977:32–34; Gutkas 1976:26; Lechner 1976:155–156). Since the aristocracy would not accept a woman ruling in her own right, a wedding race began.

Gertrud married three times within six years. Her first husband, whom she married shortly after Frederick II's death, was Vladislaus of Moravia,

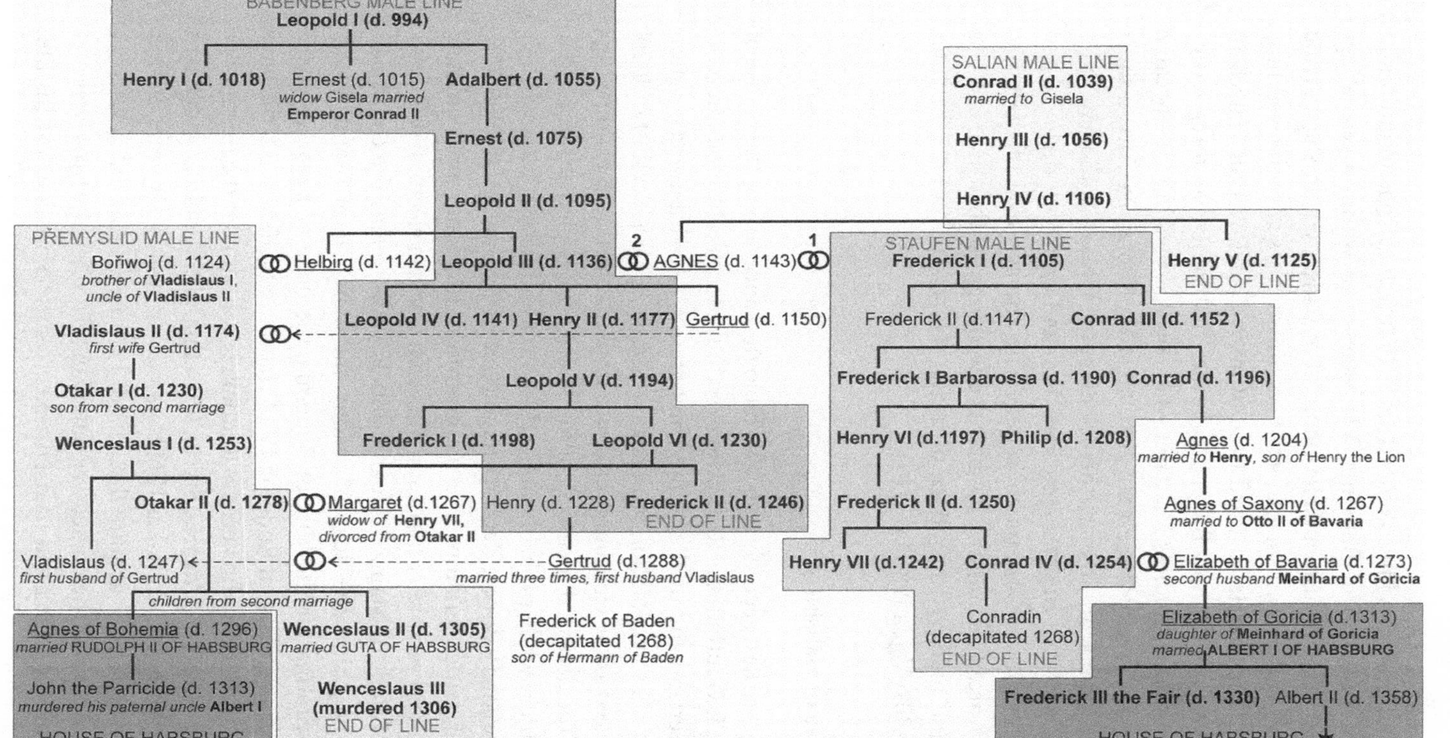

Figure 7.2. Dynastic succession lines in the Salian, Staufen, Babenberg, Přemyslid, and Habsburg dynasties. Highest-ranking individuals in each generation are bolded. The importance of women as dynastic links between different patrilines is apparent; when dynasties died out in the male line, intermarriage with a female heir often provided inheritance of new rights and territories. When widowed, these women usually remarried (e.g., Agnes, Gertrud, Margaret).

son of the Bohemian king Wenceslaus I (Přemyslid dynasty) and older brother of Otakar II of Bohemia. Vladislaus died within a year at age twenty. Her second husband, Hermann VI of Baden, whom she married in 1248 and with whom she had a son, died two years after the wedding. When Gertrud married a third time, Roman Danylovich of Halych in 1252, she was not the only Babenberg bride. That same year, forty-seven-year-old and now childless Margaret—her son had died in 1251—became the wife of the twenty-three-year-old Otakar II of Bohemia. After a short struggle, the pope and the aristocracy accepted Otakar as the new ruler of the duchy. When Gertrud conceded, Roman Danylovich divorced her.

Margaret did not fare much better. With the approval of the pope, Otakar divorced her nine years after the wedding. At that time she was fifty-six and unlikely to produce offspring (Gutkas 1976:41–43; Lechner 1976:299–307; Vajda 1986:147–149).

The House of Habsburg

One of the earliest securely traceable biological ancestors of the House of Habsburg is Guntram the Rich, who lived in the tenth century in present-day Switzerland and died at some point after 973 (Habsburg generation 1). One of his sons, Radbot, built the Habsburg (= hawk's castle) in 1020, which served as the Habsburg residence until the thirteenth century (figure 7.3). The deceased members of the house were buried at Muri Monastery, which, while probably not a Habsburg foundation, became their house monastery during Radbot's reign (Gut 1999:95; Jackman 1990:47).

In 1273, ten generations after Guntram the Rich and approximately three hundred years after his death, the seven German electoral princes—the archbishops of Mainz, Cologne, and Trier, as well as the count palatine of the Rhine, the duke of Saxony, the margrave of Brandenburg, and, substituting for the king of Bohemia, the duke of Bavaria—chose fifty-five-year-old Count Rudolph IV of Habsburg (generation 11) as their new king. Rudolph (who became Rudolph I) was granted the former Babenberg territories of Austria, Styria, Carinthia, and Carniola, which had been under the rule of Otakar II of Bohemia for twenty-six years. It took Rudolph five years to acquire these lands because Otakar did not accept Rudolph's election. The matter was settled in 1278 when the two rivals met in battle on the Marchfeld near Dürnkrut, Austria. Otakar lost his life,

Figure 7.3. Habsburg Castle, Switzerland, seen from the southwest. The castle was founded by Count Radbot around 1020, but the buildings from the eleventh century are now in ruins. The large tower to the left dates to around 1200 and the living quarters in the center to 1250, the time when Rudolph was count.

and Rudolph finally became the uncontested ruler of the Austrian lands (Agnew 2004:21–22; Barber 2004:393; Vajda 1986:154–161).

The period between Rudolph I's death in 1291 and his third great-grandson's accession to king of the Holy Roman Empire in 1438 (Albert II, generation 16) saw a prolonged struggle between the houses of Habsburg, Luxembourg, and Wittelsbach over the German throne. Of eleven German kings who reigned in the fourteenth and early fifteenth centuries, only two came from the House of Habsburg: Albert I, d. 1308 (generation 12) and Frederick the Fair, d. 1330 (generation 13). The rest of the house ruled as dukes of Austria, Styria, and the Tyrol. Although Albert II was king only for one year—he had gained the German throne through intermarriage with the House of Luxembourg, which had died out in 1437—the Habsburgs established themselves as emperors. Albert II's second cousin, Duke Frederick V, was elected Frederick III in 1440 and crowned emperor in 1452. In 1477, Frederick III's son Maximilian (generation 17, emperor in 1508) married Mary of Burgundy and as a result inherited the Netherlands, Luxembourg, and Burgundy. Maximilian also reunited Austria, Styria, and the Tyrol, after the Austrian and Tyrolean Habsburg lines had died out. After his father's death in 1493, Maximilian I's children intermarried with the Spanish house of Trastámara (Philip I and Joana in 1496), and in 1516 the House of Habsburg inherited Spain. Maximilian's grandchildren intermarried with the Polish house of Jagiello (double wedding of 1515) and with the Portuguese house of Avis (Eleanor and Manuel I in 1519; Charles V and Isabella in 1526). These illustrious matches linked the Habsburg family with the most powerful dynasties in Europe.

Strategies of Ancestor Appropriation

Fabricating Genealogies

Once being elevated to the ranks of a royal dynasty, the House of Habsburg was in dire need of proper ancestors. "Sacredness of the blood" (= *Geblütsheiligkeit*) is of primary concern to European noble houses (Hauck 1950:187). After Rudolph I's accession to "king of the Romans" in 1273 and his acquisition of the Austrian lands in 1278, the royal family found that the Muri Monastery no longer met their needs as a burial place; they also gave up their residence at the Habsburg (Gut 1999:96–97). As happened with many other medieval houses, the only reminder of their origin is their house name, which the family retained (Schmid 1957).

In order to enhance their position, the Habsburgs used the strategy of "genealogical appropriation" (= *Ansippung*) (Hauck 1950; Schmid 1957:57; Weiss-Krejci 2015:310). Heroes, saints, and kings were incorporated into the line of descent. While these "ancestors" were not biological, their association with the house lent it historicity and status. When anti-Habsburg propaganda emphasized Rudolph I's low status and lack of royal ancestors (see also Hageman, this volume) by referring to him as "pauper comes" (poor count) and "comes minus ydoneus" (improper count), the House of Habsburg sought to counter this slander (Lenz 2002:69; Lhotsky 1944). On one hand, Rudolph's accession to the throne was supported by prophecies predicting his election (Lenz 2002:71). On the other, contemporary chronicler Ulrich Krieg traced back Rudolph I's ancestry to the ancient

Roman Anician house without backing it up with a detailed genealogy (Schmit 1858:1).

Two centuries later, during Emperor Maximilian I's reign, when the House of Habsburg was on its way to create a "world" empire, a more systematic approach to Habsburg ancestry developed. Like his father, Frederick III, and other medieval sovereigns before him, Maximilian used heraldic territorial signs to demonstrate his sovereign rights and to stake new territorial claims (Schauerte 2011). However, with the aid of the best printers and artists of the empire (e.g., Albrecht Dürer) Maximilian exploited the power of texts and illustrations, pressing his claims to imperial rank and noble blood (Michel and Sternath 2012; Silver 2008). The emperor also employed several genealogists, including Ladislaus Sunthaym, Jacob Mennel, Abbot Trithemius, John Stabius, Konrad Peutinger, and John Cuspinianus, who devoted their time to the great genealogical enterprise of establishing the prestige and antiquity of the house. Some of their genealogies developed into extremely bold constructions that instigated debate about coherence and accuracy between the historiographers (Bietenholz 1994:200; Emerson 2004:80; Kellner and Webers 2007:124; Pollheimer 2006; Schauerte 2011; Silver 2008).

In the early stages, Maximilian favored a theory of descent from different branches of Roman nobility, such as the Colonna and Pierleoni families (Bietenholz 1994:200; Kellner and Webers 2007:137). Later the Roman connection was downplayed in favor of Merovingian descent from Troy. The development of a Trojan founding myth for the Habsburg dynasty is of particular interest because descent from Troy also demonstrated the antiquity of other ruling European houses, including the Valois of France, who contested Habsburg government in the Burgundian Netherlands. Descent from Troy had already been claimed by the Merovingians. In the version of the seventh-century chronicler Fredegar, King Priam—not Paris—abducted Helen, which led to the fall of Troy. The Trojan refugees who settled in northern Europe called themselves Franks, after their king Francio, who built a new Troy near the Rhine River. King Priam of Troy was supposedly descended from Shem, Noah's son (Bietenholz 1994:190). Priam's relationship would allow the Merovingians and everybody else descending from them to claim descent from the kings of Israel.

In Mennel's *Fürstliche Chronik*, which was presented to Maximilian in 1518, the Habsburgs are direct descendants of the Merovingians through the fictive count Ottbert, son of Theodpert. In an earlier version, Ottbert

Figure 7.4. The cenotaph of Emperor Maximilian I at the Hofkirche, Innsbruck, is surrounded by twenty-eight larger-than-life bronze figures representing real and mythical kin.

Figure 7.5. Bronze figures at the Hofkirche, Innsbruck. *Left to right*: Albert II (d. 1358), grandson of Rudolph I; Rudolph I of Habsburg (d. 1291) in his coronation harness; Philip the Fair, Maximilian's son (d. 1506); and Clovis, king of the Franks (d. 511). These four figures were cast between 1516 and 1550.

had been the son of Odoberth, a direct descendent of Chlotar I (AD 555–561), also known as Clotaire, king of the Franks. After being criticized by John Stabius, Mennel replaced Ottbert with Theodbert, the king of Burgundy, who may be the Merovingian king Theudebert II (595–612), the ruler of Austrasia (Kellner and Webers 2007:139–143; Schauerte 2011:348–349). The ultimate goal of Maximilian's genealogies, which were modified and adapted many times and eventually demonstrated Habsburg descent from Noah, was to show that the House of Habsburg embodied, in the person of Maximilian, the blood and power of ancient Israel, Rome, and Troy.

The ultimate realization of Maximilian's interest in genealogy is his tomb in Innsbruck (figures 7.4, 7.5). It was completed many years after his death and not according to the original plan. There were to be a hundred statues of saints and thirty-four busts of Roman emperors. Of the forty statues that were to surround his body and represent Maximilian's real and ideal ancestors (e.g., King Arthur, Theodoric, Theobert, Julius Caesar, Charlemagne), only twenty-eight survive. Several were eliminated from the plan by later emperors (Bietenholz 1994:201; Lauro 2007:151–166; Oberhammer 1935; Pollheimer 2006). The tomb remains empty; Maximilian himself was buried very humbly at Wiener Neustadt (Lauro 2007:95; Weiss-Krejci 2008:186).

Marriage as a Genealogical Corrective Measure

In dynastic Europe, marriage was a way not only to improve the future bloodline but also to forge relations with specific people and houses of the past. Through intermarriage of his children (Rudolph II, Guta, and Albert I) with important contemporary royal houses (Přemyslid, Goricia), Rudolph I of Habsburg indirectly and retroactively—through his grandchildren—was able to create a link between himself and the Salian, Staufen, and Babenberg dynasties, which at that time had all died out. The marriage project started no later than one day after Rudolph's coronation at Aix-la-Chapelle in 1273 when two of his daughters (Matilda and Agnes) were married to two of the electoral princes (count palatine of the Rhine Ludwig II of Bavaria and duke of Saxony Albert II). In 1274, one year after his coronation, Rudolph's nineteen-year-old son Albert married Elizabeth of Goricia, the daughter of Meinhard of Goricia and Elizabeth of Bavaria, who was a member of the Wittelsbach dynasty by birth.

Elizabeth of Goricia's mother was not only a former empress and widow of the Staufen king, Conrad IV, but was also descended from the Salian princess Agnes in the female line.

Around 1278, after the death of Rudolph's enemy Otakar II, his eight-year-old son, also named Rudolph, was betrothed to nine-year-old Agnes of Bohemia, the daughter of Otakar II, and seven-year-old Guta (Judith) to Otakar's son Wenceslaus, who at that time was also seven years old. These marriages not only connected the Habsburgs with the Přemyslids, but additionally served as indirect links with the Babenberg and Salian dynasties through several Babenberg men and women who had previously intermarried with the Přemyslid dynasty. Babenberg heir Margaret, although divorced from Otakar II, could be considered one link. Other connections existed through Helbirg (d. 1142), a sister of margrave Leopold III, who married the Bohemian duke Bořiwoj (d. 1124), and Gertrud (d. 1150), daughter of Leopold III and Agnes, who was the first wife of King Vladislaus II (d. 1174).

By the time of Rudolph I's death in 1291, the dynastic marriages had already come to fruition. Five of his grandchildren were born and four of them were boys. Nine-year-old Rudolph (future Rudolph I, king of Bohemia), two-year-old Frederick (future Frederick III, German Roman king), and one-year-old Leopold (Leopold I, Duke of Austria and Styria) were Rudolph's grandsons through Albert I. One-year-old John "the Parricide" (Duke of Austria and Styria) was the son of Rudolph II. He would murder his uncle, Albert I, many years later (see Weiss-Krejci 2008:181–182).

Entering the Graves of the Ancestors

Rudolph had never founded a new burial place for the Habsburgs. His wife, Queen Anna, and two of his sons had already been buried at Basel Cathedral, which Anna had probably chosen to ameliorate damage that her husband had done to the episcopate before becoming king (Gut 1999:100). Rudolph himself aspired to a more majestic burial place. Speyer Cathedral was a Salian foundation and had served as burial place for the Holy Roman emperors of that dynasty between 1039 and 1125. It housed the bodies of Conrad II (d. 1039) and his wife, Gisela (d. 1043), Henry III (d. 1056), Henry IV (d. 1106) and empress Bertha (d. 1087), and Henry V (d. 1125). Between 1184 and 1213, the Staufen dynasty, biologically connected to the Salians through Leopold III's spouse, Agnes, reused the place. Beatrice, wife of Frederick I Barbarossa, and her little daughter Agnes (both d. 1184) as well as King Philip of Swabia (d. 1208) were buried there.

One day before his death on July 14, 1291, seventy-three-year-old Rudolph was on his way to Speyer by horse. At Germersheim he supposedly spoke the following famous words, which were written down by chronicler Mathias of Neuenburg: "On to Speyer, where more of my forebears are, who have also been kings" (my translation after Meyer 2000:19).

By riding to Speyer, terminally ill Rudolph had increased his chances of being buried at the cathedral with the former emperors. The association with the kings through joint burial at the same place helped to legitimize his and his house's claim to kingship. Since Frederick I Barbarossa's assigned burial location had been vacant for a century, Rudolph took it for himself (Gut 1999:103; Klimm 1953:55; Meier 2004). Barbarossa had wished to be buried at the cathedral but had drowned in Seleucia during the Third Crusade in 1190. In order to make his bones fit for transport back to Germany, his corpse was boiled and the bones were defleshed (*mos teutonicus*). His intestines were probably buried at Tarsus and his flesh at St. Peter in Antioch. However, his bones—probably lost—were not returned to Germany. Their final fate has been a matter of debate for centuries (see Prutz 1879; Schäfer 1920).

Ancestral burial places were also of great interest to Emperor Maximilian. In 1514 he ordered the search for the corpse of Habsburg king Frederick the Fair, who had died in 1330 and been buried at the monastery of Mauerbach near Vienna. Frederick was not a direct ancestor but Maximilian's great-great-grandfather's brother. Two coffins were encountered; one belonged to Frederick and the other to Frederick's daughter Elizabeth (d. 1336). Accompanied by liturgical chanters, the bones were rinsed with wine and placed on specially prepared biers. Maximilian ordered the manufacture of a new mortuary monument for the king and his daughter. However, as with a project for Speyer Cathedral (Schmid 1984), the plan never materialized and the bones remained in storage in the vestry. When the Turks plundered the abbey in 1529, the remains were thrown out but later collected by inhabitants of the area. After several further exhumations, they were finally deposited at St. Stephen's in Vienna in the eighteenth century (Lauro 2007:49–50; Meyer 2000:70–72; Weiss-Krejci 2011a:figure 4.3).

While canonization of royal relatives was a salient feature of many

European royal houses (e.g., France and Portugal) until the late fifteenth century, the House of Habsburg did not have a saint in its tree of ancestors. First attempts to canonize Babenberg Leopold III had already been under way in the fourteenth century, but only in 1485, during the reign of Maximilian's father, Frederick III, was his canonization finally achieved. On the one hand, Leopold incorporated the virtue of pietas because he had rejected the imperial crown in 1125 (Kovács 1992; Samerski 2006:254; Vajda 1986:72). On the other hand, his canonization was a posthumous reward for political success, abundant offspring, and the foundation of monasteries. The ritual of translation, in which the burial vault beneath the Klosterneuburg chapter house was emptied and the bones moved into a silver shrine, took place in 1506 and was attended by Maximilian I.

The Remains of the Dead, Ancestor Construction, and the Legitimization of Governance

In the royal house of Habsburg, at least three kinds of ancestors existed: (a) matri- and patrilineal consanguineal forebears; (b) appropriated members of illustrious royal families; and (c) mythical persons from the distant past. While drawing connections with mythic ancestors merely required skilled genealogists, genealogical appropriation of historically prominent people needed a good matchmaker. As I have shown, in this process, the remains of the dead also played an important role. When Rudolph I claimed members of the Salian and Staufen dynasties as his ancestors and usurped their burial places, he legitimized his royal status and that of his house. St. Leopold (Leopold III), on the other hand, connected the Habsburgs not only with the idea of Holy Roman kingship (through the Salians) but also with the rulership of Austria (through the Babenbergs). For this reason, Leopold's saintly relics continued to be of relevance in rituals related to Habsburg enthronement and coronation.

In 1604 an embroiderer was paid for making a textile crown for St. Leopold's skull. In 1616 Archduke Maximilian III of the Tyrol commissioned a bust reliquary for the head (figure 7.6) and a much heavier metal and textile crown, the so-called Archducal Hat. St. Leopold's head was crowned with this crown in 1616 (Röhrig 1976:238). Through the onetime coronation and physical contact with the saint's head, the Archducal Hat itself became a relic (a third-class or contact relic). It was utilized by ten emperors from the Habsburg dynasty between 1620 and 1835 during the

Figure 7.6. Bust and skull of St. Leopold (Leopold III) at Klosterneuburg (d. 1136, canonized 1485). The bust was manufactured at the beginning of the seventeenth century; the skull wrapping dates to 1677; the crown on the skull is a copy of the Archducal Hat (Herrgott and Heer 1760, plate 2).

oath of allegiance ceremony, which was usually held at St. Stephen's Cathedral in Vienna after the emperor's accession (Cernik 1958:39–41; Wacha 1963). The hat was either carried in front or placed beside the emperor during the ceremony, as if it were a person in its own right.

The involvement of Leopold's relics in enthronement rituals calls to mind the skulls of the Three Magi at Cologne Cathedral. In 1164 these relics had been carried off by Emperor Frederick I Barbarossa after the storming of Milan and were brought to Cologne by Archbishop Rainald of Dassel. By 1200, Otto IV of Brunswick—son of Duke Henry the Lion and maternal nephew of King Richard the Lionhearted—had adorned the skulls of the magi with valuable crowns. By paying homage to the magi, King Otto, whose reign was constantly endangered, tried to secure the support of these divine authorities in his claim for rulership. It became a tradition for the Holy Roman emperors of the later Middle Ages to visit the shrine of the Three Magi after their coronation at Aix-la-Chapelle (Legner 2003:108–110).

Grave usurpation is a common phenomenon throughout the world. It can encompass visits and the deposition of objects during elaborate ceremonies, the placement of new bodies, exhumation and reuse of human remains, and the destruction of mortuary monuments and incorporation of tomb fragments into new buildings. Ancient Maya kings frequently reentered tombs of earlier kings and performed "tomb renewal" ceremonies, which could involve torches, incense, and bones (see Hageman, this volume). These rites may represent the desire to revivify a burial place (Stuart 1998:418). While in some instances these rituals took place 260 days or a few years after burial, in other instances centuries passed between the death and the rites of commemoration (Fitzsimmons 1998, 2006; Martin and Grube 2008; Weiss-Krejci 2011b:23–24). Some of these rites were probably directed at true consanguineal ancestors, but the veneration of appropriated ancestors and mythical persons may also have occurred. Like European noble houses, the ancient Maya aristocracy emphasized blood lines and invested a lot of energy into situating royal persons within long genealogies (Houston and McAnany 2003:37; Martin and Grube 2008). While ancestor worship was an important activity among all sectors of ancient Maya society, ancestor veneration by the ruling classes was qualitatively different from that practiced by commoners (McAnany 1995:7–8; see also Hageman, this volume).

The reuse of ancient burial places and mortuary monuments after long time gaps is also known from prehistoric Europe (Bradley 1993:117–121; Díaz-Guardamino et al. 2015). Megalithic monuments of the Neolithic have frequently been used for the deposition of the dead at a later date, primarily during the Bronze and Iron Ages. A crucial issue in the interpretation of tomb reuse is *who* is initiating the activity. Whitley (2002:123) suggests that at least in British and Irish prehistory, the reuse and reinterpretation of ancient monuments may not be the result of ancestor commemoration; rather, Iron Age people may have venerated what they believed to be the sites and remains of the "old gods" or of earlier mythic inhabitants of the area, such as a fairy race of Irish legend. The considerable quantities of bronze, silver, and gold that were deposited around the entrance to the tomb of Newgrange in the fourth and fifth centuries AD, according to Whitley, could be evidence for the presence of elites, who may have publicly sought to link themselves to past events or individuals.

An excellent historical example has been captured in a painting—today in the National Museum of Stockholm—by the Swedish artist Johan

Figure 7.7. Painting by Johan Way 1836, *Carl XIV Johans besök vid Uppsala högar 1834* (Carl XIV Johan's visit to the Uppsala mounds in 1834). Reprinted with permission of the National Museum of Stockholm, NM 4813.

Way (figure 7.7). It depicts Swedish king Carl XIV Johan visiting the Iron Age burial mounds of Old Uppsala in the company of scholars and student unions of Uppsala University. The highly politicized royal visit took place in 1834, at a time when the members of universities became the leading interpreters of the past (Rowley-Conwy, 2006:106–112). That the burial mounds were considered graves of the entire nation's ancestors is suggested by the letter that the two young students (right foreground) are writing: "On the graves of our forefathers before the King of kings we swear Your Maj[esty] an unwavering allegiance" (deciphered and translated from Swedish with the aid of Alison Klevnäs). The evocation of ancestors who represented the Old Norse past played a crucial role in the building of the nation in nineteenth-century Sweden (Weiss-Krejci

2015:314–318). According to Katherine Verdery (1999:160), nationalism is just another form of ancestor cult.

Conclusions

The "royal ancestor" is a highly variable construct. Royal Habsburg ancestors were named and anonymous, real and mythical, male and female, human and divine; they encompassed recently deceased and dead from the distant past. The borderline between ancestors and Whitley's (2002) semidivine races and "old gods" often is quite murky. Of what value are these constructed ancestors for us in our attempts to reconstruct the past? I believe that these constructions can provide lots of valuable information if we focus on the actors involved in veneration and not so much on the objects of veneration. Habsburg genealogies from the time of Emperor Maximilian, while not helpful to the reconstruction of Merovingian or Trojan histories, provide a great deal of information about Maximilian I and the political situation in Europe at the time when the genealogies were constructed. Similarly, studying patterns of reuse of Neolithic mortuary monuments in the Bronze and Iron Ages will tell us little about the Neolithic and the original occupants of the tombs, but reveal much about those later populations and how they perceived their relationships to the dead, the landscape, and each other (see Campbell, this volume, for examples of this phenomenon in China). In my opinion, the best way to work toward a definition of kinds of ancestors in archaeology is to ask what purpose ancestors fulfilled and how they were used by the living in a specific historical context.

References Cited

Agnew, Hugh L.
2004 *The Czechs and the Lands of the Bohemian Crown*. Hoover Institution Press, Stanford, California.

Ahern, Emily M.
1973 *The Cult of the Dead in a Chinese Village*. Stanford University Press, Stanford, California.

Antonaccio, Carla M.
1995 *An Archaeology of Ancestors: Tomb Cult and Hero Cult in Early Greece*. Rowman and Littlefield, London.

Barber, Malcolm

2004 *The Two Cities: Medieval Europe, 1050–1320*. 2nd ed. Routledge, New York.

Bietenholz, Peter G.

1994 *Historia and Fabula: Myths and Legends in Historical Thought from Antiquity to the Modern Age*. E. J. Brill, Leiden, Netherlands.

Bradley, Richard

1993 *Altering the Earth: The Origins of Monuments*. Society of Antiquaries of Scotland, Edinburgh.

Bryant, Clifton D.

2003 Hosts and Ghosts: The Dead as Visitors in Cross-Cultural Perspective. In *The Presence of Death: Handbook of Death and Dying*, vol. 1, edited by Clifton D. Bryant, pp. 77–86. Sage, Thousand Oaks, California.

Cernik, Berthold

1958 *Das Augustiner Chorherrenstift Klosterneuburg: Statistische und geschichtliche Daten*. Floridus Druck, Vienna.

Díaz-Guardamino, Marta, Leonardo García Sanjuán, and David Wheatley (editors)

2015 *The Lives of Prehistoric Monuments in Iron Age, Roman, and Medieval Europe*. Oxford University Press, Oxford.

Emerson, Catherine

2004 *Olivier de la Marche and the Rhetoric of 15th-Century Historiography*. Boydell Press, Woodbridge, UK.

Ferenczy, Heinrich

1977 Heinrich II. Jasomirgott—Herzog von Österreich. In *Gedächtnisschrift anlässlich des 800. Todestages Herzog Heinrichs II. Jasomirgott*, the Monastery of the Scots, Vienna, pp. 27–42. Schottenstift, Vienna.

Fitzsimmons, James L.

1998 Classic Maya Mortuary Anniversaries at Piedras Negras, Guatemala. *Ancient Mesoamerica* 9:271–278.

2006 Classic Maya Tomb Re-Entry. In *Jaws of the Underworld: Life, Death, and Rebirth among the Ancient Maya*, Proceedings of the 7th European Maya Conference, British Museum, London, edited by Pierre R. Colas, Geneviève LeFort, and Bodil Liljefors Persson, pp. 33–40. Verlag Anton Saurwein, Markt Schwaben, Germany.

Fortes, Meyer

1965 Some Reflections on Ancestor Worship in Africa. In *African Systems of Thought*, edited by Meyer Fortes and Germaine Dieterlen, pp. 122–142. Oxford University Press, London.

Freedman, Maurice

1966 *Chinese Lineage and Society: Fukien and Kwangtung*. Athlone Press, New York.

Friesinger, Herwig

1976 Vorbabenbergerzeitliche und babenbergerzeitliche Archäologie in Niederösterreich. In *1000 Jahre Babenberger in Österreich*, edited by Amt der Niederösterreichischen Landesregierung, pp. 50–59. Katalog des Niederösterreichischen Landesmuseums, Neue Folge 66. Ferdinand Berger & Söhne, Horn, Austria.

Gerbert, Martin, Marquard Herrgott, and Rustenus Heer

1772 *Taphographia Principum Austriae: Monumenta Augustae Domus Austriacae*, Vol. 4. Abbey St. Blasien, St. Blasien, Germany.

Gluckmann, Max

1937 Mortuary Customs and the Belief in Survival after Death among the South-Eastern Bantu. *Bantu Studies* 11:117–136.

Gut, Johannes

1999 Memorialorte der Habsburger im Südwesten des Alten Reiches: Politische Hintergründe und Aspekte. In *Vorderösterreich: Nur die Schwanzfeder des Kaiseradlers? Die Habsburger im deutschen Südwesten*. Württembergisches Landesmuseum Stuttgart, pp. 94–113. Süddeutsche Verlagsgesellschaft, Ulm, Germany.

Gutkas, Karl

1976 *Die Babenberger in Österreich*. Wissenschaftliche Schriftenreihe Niederösterreich. Niederösterreichisches Pressehaus, St. Pölten, Austria.

Hardacre, Helen

1987 Ancestor Worship. In *Encyclopedia of Religion*, vol. 1, edited by Mircea Eliade, pp. 263–268. Macmillan, New York.

Hauck, Karl

1950 Geblütsheiligkeit. In *Liber Floridus: Mittellateinische Studien. Paul Lehmann dargebracht zum 65. Geburtstag*, edited by Bernhard Bischoff and Suso Brechter, pp. 187–240. Eos Verlag, St. Ottilien, Germany.

Herrgott, Marquard, and Rustenus Heer

1760 *Pinacotheca Principum Austriae: Monumenta Augustae Domus Austriacae*, vol. 3, part 1. Satron, Freiburg, Germany.

Houston, Stephen D., and Patricia A. McAnany

2003 Bodies and Blood: Critiquing Social Construction in Maya Archaeology. *Journal of Anthropological Archaeology* 22:26–41.

Jackman, Donald C.

1990 *The Konradiner: A Study in Genealogical Methodology*. Klostermann, Frankfurt/Main.

Kellner, Beate, and Linda Webers

2007 Genealogische Entwürfe am Hof Kaiser Maximilians I (am Beispiel von Jakob Mennels *Fürstlicher Chronik*). *Genealogische Diskurse, Zeitschrift für Literaturwissenschaft und Linguistik* 37(147):122–149.

Klimm, Franz

1953 *Der Kaiserdom zu Speyer*. Verlag Jaeger, Speyer, Germany.

Kopytoff, Igor

1971 Ancestors as Elders in Africa. *Africa* 41:129–142.

Kovács, Elisabeth

1992 Die Heiligen und heiligen Könige der frühen Habsburger (1273–1519). In *Laienfrömmigkeit im späten Mittelalter*, edited by Klaus Schreiner, pp. 93–126. Schriften des historischen Kollegs, Kolloquien 20. Oldenbourg, Munich.

Lauro, Brigitta
2007 *Die Grabstätten der Habsburger: Kunstdenkmäler einer europäischen Dynastie.* Christian Brandstätter Verlag, Vienna.

Lechner, Karl
1976 *Die Babenberger: Markgrafen und Herzöge von Österreich, 976–1246.* Böhlau, Vienna.

Legner, Anton
2003 *Kölner Heilige und Heiligtümer: Ein Jahrtausend europäischer Reliquienkultur.* Greven Verlag, Köln, Germany.

Lenz, Martin
2002 *Konsens und Dissens: Deutsche Königswahl (1273–1349) und zeitgenössische Geschichtsschreibung.* Formen der Erinnerung, vol. 5. Vandenhoeck & Ruprecht, Göttingen, Germany.

Lhotsky, Alphons
1944 Apis Colonna: Fabeln und Theorien über die Abkunft der Habsburger. *Mitteilungen des Instituts für österreichische Geschichtsforschung* 55:171–246.

Long, Charles
1987 Mythic Ancestors. In *Encyclopedia of Religion*, vol. 1, edited by Mircea Eliade, pp. 268–270. Macmillan, New York.

Martin, Simon, and Nikolai Grube
2008 *Chronicle of the Maya Kings and Queens: Deciphering the Dynasties of the Ancient Maya,* rev. ed. Thames and Hudson, London.

McAnany, Patricia
1995 *Living with the Ancestors: Kinship and Kingship in Ancient Maya Society.* University of Texas Press, Austin.

Meier, Thomas
2004 Ambivalenz im Raum: Zur Disposition mittelalterlicher Herrschergräber. In *The European Frontier: Clashes and Compromises in the Middle Ages*, edited by Jörn Staecker, pp. 127–144. Lund Studies in Medieval Archaeology 33. Almquist & Wiksell, Lund, Germany.

Meyer, Rudolf J.
2000 *Königs- und Kaiserbegräbnisse im Spätmittelalter.* Beihefte zu J. F. Böhmer, Regesta Imperii, vol. 19. Böhlau, Köln, Germany.

Michel, Eva, and Marie Luise Sternath (editors)
2012 *Emperor Maximilian I and the Age of Dürer.* Prestel Verlag, Munich.

Mitscha-Märheim, Herbert
1976 Babenberger und Ebersberger und ihre Erben im und um das Poigreich. In *Babenberger Forschungen*, pp. 216–234. Jahrbuch für Landeskunde von Niederösterreich, Neue Folge 42. Verein für Landeskunde von Niederösterreich und Wien, Vienna.

Oberhammer, Vinzenz
1935 *Die Bronzestandbilder des Maximiliangrabes in der Hofkirche zu Innsbruck.* Tyrolia Verlag, Innsbruck.

Pohl, Walter
1995 *Die Welt der Babenberger: Schleier, Kreuz, und Schwert*, edited by Brigitte Vacha. Verlag Styria, Graz, Austria.

Pollheimer, Marianne
2006 Wie der jung weiß kunig die alten gedachtnus insonders lieb het. Maximilian I, Jakob Mennel und die frühmittelalterliche Geschichte der Habsburger in der "Fürstlichen Chronik." In *Texts and Identities in the Early Middle Ages*, edited by Richard Corradini, Rob Meens, Christina Pössel, and Philip Shaw, pp. 165–176. Forschungen zur Geschichte des Mittelalters 12. Austrian Academy of Sciences, Vienna.

Prutz, Hans
1879 *Kaiser Friedrich I. Grabstätte: Eine kritische Studie*. Ernst Gruihn, Danzig.

Röhrig, Floridus
1976 Stift Klosterneuburg. In *1000 Jahre Babenberger in Österreich*, edited by Amt der Niederösterreichischen Landesregierung, pp. 267–268. Katalog des Niederösterreichischen Landesmuseums, Neue Folge 66. Ferdinand Berger & Söhne, Horn, Austria.

Rowley-Conwy, Peter
2006 The Concept of Prehistory and the Invention of the Terms "Prehistoric" and "Prehistorian": The Scandinavian Origin, 1833–1850. *European Journal of Archaeology* 9:103–130.

Samerski, Stefan
2006 Hausheilige statt Staatspatrone: Der mißlungene Absolutismus in Österreichs Heiligenhimmel. In *Die Habsburgermonarchie, 1620–1740: Leistungen und Grenzen des Absolutismusparadigmas*, edited by Petr Mat'a and Thomas Winkelbauer, pp. 251–278. Franz Steiner, Stuttgart.

Schäfer, Dietrich
1920 Mittelalterlicher Brauch bei der Überführung von Leichen. *Sitzungsberichte der preussischen Akademie der Wissenschaften* 26:478–498.

Schauerte, Thomas
2011 Heraldische Fiktion als genealogisches Argument. Anmerkung zur Wiener Neustädter Wappenwand Friedrichs III und zu ihrer Nachwirkung bei Maximilian. In *Erzählen und Episteme: Literatur im 16. Jahrhundert*, edited by Beate Kellner, Jan-Dirk Müller, and Peter Strohschneider, pp. 345–364. Walter de Gruyter, Berlin.

Schmid, Karl
1957 Zur Problematik von Familie, Sippe und Geschlecht, Haus und Dynastie beim mittelalterlichen Adel. *Zeitschrift für Geschichte des Oberrheins* 105:1–62.
1984 "Andacht und Stift." Zur Grabmalplanung Kaiser Maximilians I (Mit einem Anhang von Dieter Mertens). In *Memoria: Der geschichtliche Zeugniswert des liturgischen Gedenkens im Mittelalter*, edited by Karl Schmid and Joachim Wollasch, pp. 750–786. Münstersche Mittelalter-Schriften, vol. 48. Wilhelm Fink Verlag, Munich.

Schmit, Carl Ritter von Tavera
1858 *Geschichte des Hauses Habsburg bis zum Tode Maximilian I. Bibliographie zur Geschichte des österreichischen Kaiserhauses*. Part 1, 1. L. W. Seidel, Vienna.
Silver, Larry
2008 *Marketing Maximilian: The Visual Ideology of a Holy Roman Emperor*. Princeton University Press, Princeton, New Jersey.
Stuart, David
1998 "The Fire Enters His House": Architecture and Ritual in Classic Maya Texts. In *Function and Meaning in Classic Maya Architecture*, edited by Stephen D. Houston, pp. 373–425. Dumbarton Oaks, Washington, D.C.
Vajda, Stephan
1986 *Die Babenberger: Aufstieg einer Dynastie*. Orac, Vienna.
Verdery, Katherine
1999 *The Political Lives of Dead Bodies: Reburial and Postsocialist Change*. Columbia University Press, New York.
Wacha, Georg
1963 Reliquien und Reliquiare des hl. Leopold. *Jahrbuch des Stiftes Klosterneuburg*, Neue Folge 3:9–25.
1976 Das Nachleben Leopold III. In *1000 Jahre Babenberger in Österreich*, edited by Amt der Niederösterreichischen Landesregierung, pp. 612–625. Katalog des Niederösterreichischen Landesmuseums, Neue Folge 66. Ferdinand Berger & Söhne, Horn, Austria.
Weller, Tobias
2004 *Die Heiratspolitik des deutschen Hochadels im 12. Jahrhundert*. Böhlau, Köln, Germany.
Weiss-Krejci, Estella
2001 Restless Corpses: "Secondary Burial" in the Babenberg and Habsburg Dynasties. *Antiquity* 75:769–780.
2004 Mortuary Representations of the Noble House: A Cross-Cultural Comparison between Collective Tombs of the Ancient Maya and Dynastic Europe. *Journal of Social Archaeology* 4:368–404.
2005 Excarnation, Evisceration, and Exhumation in Medieval and Post-Medieval Europe. In *Interacting with the Dead: Perspectives on Mortuary Archaeology for the New Millennium*, edited by Gordon Rakita, Jane Buikstra, Lane Beck, and Sloan Williams, pp. 155–172. University Press of Florida, Gainesville.
2008 Unusual Life, Unusual Death, and the Fate of the Corpse: A Case Study from Dynastic Europe. In *Deviant Burial in the Archaeological Record*, edited by Eileen Murphy, pp. 169–190. Oxbow Books, Oxford.
2010 Heart Burial in Medieval and Early Post-Medieval Central Europe. In *Body Parts and Bodies Whole*, edited by Katharina Rebay-Salisbury, Marie Louise Stig Sørensen, and Jessica Hughes, pp. 119–134. Oxbow Books, Oxford.
2011a The Formation of Mortuary Deposits: Implications for Understanding Mortuary Behavior of Past Populations. In *Social Bioarchaeology*, edited by Sabrina C. Agarwal and Bonnie Glencross, pp. 68–106. Wiley-Blackwell, Chichester, UK.

2011b The Role of Dead Bodies in Ancient Maya Politics: Cross-Cultural Reflections on the Meaning of Tikal Altar 5. In *Living with the Dead: Mortuary Ritual in Mesoamerica*, edited by James Fitzsimmons and Izumi Shimada, pp. 17–52. University of Arizona Press, Tucson.

2015 The Plot against the Past: Reuse and Modification of Ancient Mortuary Monuments as Persuasive Efforts of Appropriation. In *The Lives of Prehistoric Monuments in Iron Age, Roman, and Medieval Europe*, edited by Marta Díaz-Guardamino, Leonardo García Sanjuán, and David Wheatley, pp. 307–324. Oxford University Press, Oxford.

Whitley, James

2002 Too Many Ancestors. *Antiquity* 76:119–126.

Wrandruszka, Adam

1964 *The House of Hapsburg: Six Hundred Years of a European Dynasty*. Translated by Cathleen and Hans Epstein. Doubleday, Garden City, New Jersey.

Zöllner, Erich

1976 Die Dynastie der Babenberger. In *1000 Jahre Babenberger in Österreich*, edited by Amt der Niederösterreichischen Landesregierung, pp. 9–25. Katalog des Niederösterreichischen Landesmuseums, Neue Folge 66. Ferdinand Berger & Söhne, Horn, Austria.

8

Images of Ancestors

Identifying the Revered Dead in Moche Iconography

ERICA HILL

The study of ancestors has occupied anthropologists since the late nineteenth century and Edward Tylor's 1870 work on comparative religion. Since then, the ethnographic study of ancestors and the roles they play among the living have followed complex trajectories in Africa and East Asia. The work of twentieth-century British social anthropologists such as Meyer Fortes (1965, 1976), Jack Goody (1962), and Maurice Bloch (1971) provided the foundation upon which current understandings of African ancestors are built. In China, Maurice Freedman (1958, 1966) set the tone for English-language studies of Asian ancestors with his paradigmatic publications on kinship and lineage organization. Although ancestors made occasional appearances in archaeology in the twentieth century, notably in Kenyon's work at Jericho (1954, 1957; Kenyon and Tushingham 1953), they were not truly established in the discipline until the publication of two landmark books: McAnany on the Maya (1995) and Helms (1998) using a comparative framework.

Late twentieth-century and twenty-first-century archaeologists working in the Americas and Europe have turned to now classic ethnographies of African and Asian ancestors and to McAnany and Helms for interpretive insights on ancient ancestors. In the Americas, increasing attention to ancestors is a product in part of the more general interest in the archaeology of ritual and religion (Fogelin 2007, 2008). Ritual and ancestors are complementary research pursuits. Indeed, a concern with ritual behaviors, especially as manifested in funerary materials, "special" deposits, and topography and architectural remains, distinguishes the archaeological study of ancestors. Examples from the Andes include the identification of offerings to ancestors in niched halls at Wari sites (Glowacki and Malpass 2003) or Hastorf's evidence from the site of Chiripa, Bolivia, for the reopening of burial pits to feed and tend to the dead (Hastorf 2003).

While archaeologists working in Mesoamerica (Hageman, this volume) and the Andes have found ancestors to be a fruitful interpretive turn, a parallel trend in European prehistory has raised concerns that archaeologists are assuming that ancestors existed in past societies, rather than demonstrating their existence using material evidence (Whitley 2002). Fortunately, Andeanists have a wealth of ethnographic, ethnohistoric, archaeological, and iconographic evidence with which to evaluate the question of ancestor veneration in the region's past.

Andean Ancestors

The Central Andes have long been recognized as a place where ancestors existed prior to European contact. Ethnohistoric documents describing the treatment of Inca mummies are among the richest descriptions of ancient ancestor worship in the world (e.g., Arriaga 1968 [1621]; Cobo 1990 [1653]). Sophisticated historical (e.g., Doyle 1988; MacCormack 1991; Sallnow 1987) and archaeological studies (e.g., Buikstra 1995; DeLeonardis and Lau 2004; Isbell 1997; Lau 2002, 2008, 2011; Salomon 1995) have generated a scholarly atmosphere in which ancestors are very much a part of reconstructions of the Andean past.

Andean archaeologists have used several forms of material culture to identify ancestors, including architecture and landscapes, human remains, and sculpture. However, as George Lau (2008:1029) notes, this is largely proxy evidence: "Paradoxically, very few studies of ancestor veneration have examined the ancestor itself." Lau (2008, 2011) has been one of the most productive and thoughtful scholars of Andean ancestors, arguing that anthropomorphic Recuay monoliths were stone embodiments of ancestors who oversaw daily life, participated in rituals, consumed food and drink, and mediated between the living and other types of beings. Monoliths of Recuay ancestors, like Chinese ancestor tablets and or Kusasi shrines (Mather, this volume), functioned as "pervasive references to descent and entitlement" (DeLeonardis and Lau 2004:90). They were material instantiations of a complex set of social relations linking the living to both the ancestor and to the lineage and its history more generally.

While later Andean prehistory seems saturated with ancestors, their origins in Andean cosmologies remain murky, contrary to the implication that mere preservation of the body represents ancestor veneration (e.g., Guillén 2005:149; Kaulicke 2000:290–294). Reserving the term "ancestor" for the revered dead who remain active in the lives of their descendants, rather than extending it to include the dead more generally, is critical to identifying venerative practices in the archaeological record and reconstructing the roles of ancestors in past societies. While Lau has demonstrated that ancestor veneration was a key component of Recuay ritual practice, similar comprehensive evaluations of the evidence do not yet exist for the contemporary Moche and Nasca. However, both iconographic and bioarchaeological studies have either argued for or hypothesized the existence of Moche and Nasca ancestors. Nasca trophy heads have been the subject of considerable attention, with bioarchaeological attempts to evaluate their use as objects of ancestor veneration inconclusive (Forgey and Williams 2005). On the basis of iconography, Carmichael (1994, 1995) has suggested that trophy head manipulation was part of a mortuary program involving ancestor worship. Proulx (2001, 2006:203), however, remains unconvinced by available evidence that ancestor worship was part of Nasca religious practice. On the basis of burial ritual and archaeological features at Cahuachi, Silverman (Silverman and Proulx 2002:218–220) suggests that the Nasca evidence for ancestor veneration is accumulating, though she remains cautious in her interpretations.

Archaeologists studying the Moche have made tangential references to the existence of ancestors in the Moche past—implying that the Moche practiced human sacrifice in order to appease the ancestors and ensure agricultural fertility (Bourget 1997:98, 2001; Bourget and Newman 1998) or that ceramics were ritual paraphernalia used to maintain relationships between the living and the dead (Russell and Jackson 2001:171–172). Based on his work on elite architecture, Uceda (2001:62) has stated the case as follows:

> We now feel that the rebuildings [of platforms and enclosures] were linked to veneration of ancestors, and that the architectural renovations served to reinforce ancestral and priestly power at Huaca de la Luna [in the Moche valley]. . . . It is our view that in Moche society power came from the ancestors, and that the latter materialized themselves through their representatives, the priests. When a priest

> died, his replacement would have undertaken the construction of a new structure, where the deceased priest was then buried. The deceased priest would become a powerful ancestor, the monument would be energized by his presence and the new priest would gain respect as the new living representative of the ancestor.

Uceda (1997a, 2001) thus links ancestor veneration to the ritual burial of architectural features, a practice documented at other Moche sites, such as Huaca Colorada (Swenson 2012), and elsewhere in the Andes. Uceda's interpretation relies primarily on architectural and burial evidence and, presumably, the fact that ancestor veneration was a documented contact-era practice among the Inca and therefore part of a long Andean tradition.

More recently, Bourget has cited Fortes's definition of an ancestor as "a named, dead forebear" receiving "ritual service and tendance"(Fortes 1965:124, 1987:68), thus making a clear distinction between the revered dead and the dead more generally. Acknowledging that ancestor veneration appears to have been widespread in the Andes, Bourget (2006:62)—echoing Proulx (2006:203)—concluded that "such a specific belief cannot be confidently demonstrated for the Moche at the moment." Despite the wealth of suggestive architectural, iconographic, and mortuary data, then, the evidence for a belief in ancestors among the Moche remains ambiguous.

In the remainder of this chapter, I explore the iconographic evidence for Moche ancestors, directing attention to a recurrent set of images in Moche iconography—bundled figures seated under gabled-roof structures. I evaluate the idea that these seated figures represent the revered dead—individuals singled out for special treatment as ancestors—and briefly discuss painted and modeled ceramic structures found on stirrup-spout vessels. The structures in these scenes have architectural parallels in the daises, or raised platforms, excavated in elite precincts at several Moche sites. The correspondence between iconography and architecture suggests that ancestor veneration may have been ritually performed within platform mound enclosures at many Moche sites at least as early as the Middle Moche period.

While my discussion focuses on Moche iconography and architecture, my perspective has been influenced by the significance of ancestor veneration among the Inca. Drawing comparisons between the Inca and earlier Andean societies is both tempting and problematic—the danger of *lo andino*, the tendency to conflate disparate belief systems into an overarching Andean worldview. As Lau (2013) has pointed out, "alterity" was an organizing concept in the ancient Andes, both between the living and the dead and between social groups. My emphasis on Andean parallels is intended only to highlight a widespread concern with materializing ancestors, not to promote a synchronic view of the Andean past. As the introduction and chapters in this volume demonstrate, ancestor veneration takes myriad ritual and material forms and requires study from perspectives both particularist and synthetic.

Moche Ancestors

Overlapping temporally with Recuay (AD 1–700) during the Early Intermediate period, the Moche inhabited the river valleys of the Peruvian coastal desert between AD 1 and 850 (figure 8.1). Their society was socially complex and hierarchical with a religious system that involved elaborate treatment of the dead, manipulation of body parts and skeletal remains, and representational art illustrating humans and deities, the living and the dead, and the ritual performances through which they interacted.

Moche art is found on monumental murals and friezes associated with corporate architecture, as at the site of Huaca de la Luna; however, the primary iconographic source material is painted and modeled ceramics, many of which, unfortunately, are devoid of archaeological context, though in all likelihood, the majority originated in interments or elite tombs. Both men and women are depicted in Moche iconography, with hair and clothing generally signaling female sex and/or feminine gender and tasks. The images described here contain no explicit representations of female genitalia, so my assumption that women are depicted is based on the association of hairstyle, clothing, and context (i.e., gender markers and roles) with female sex. These gendered markers have been discussed in some detail by scholars (Arsenault 1991; Benson 1988; Hocquenghem and Lyon 1980; Lyon 1978; Scher 2010; Vogel 2003). Absent current evidence to the contrary, I assume that gendered hair and clothing denoted "women" to Moche viewers.

The women in question are involved in a scene, repeated on multiple vessels, involving a bound prisoner, vultures, and a dais or structure with a gabled roof. Stylized Moche clubs adorn the roof. As is typical in Moche art, key motifs in the scene are depicted more frequently than the entire

Figure 8.1. Map of Moche region, north coast of Peru.

scene itself. Figure 8.2, a "roll-out" of the painted vessel (Donnan and McClelland 1999:figure 1.15) shows two women on the far left. A vulture perches in the center of the image, separated from the women by a gabled-roof structure that houses vessels. Presumably these contain offerings of food or drink similar to the ones commonly found in Moche tombs.

Figure 8.2. Roll-out of scene depicting two women, a vulture, a gabled-roof structure containing vessels, and what appear to be three supplicants (Donnan and McClelland 1999:fig. 1.15). Roll-out by Donna McClelland. Christopher B. Donnan and Donna McClelland, Moche Archive, 1963–2011, Image Collections and Fieldwork Archives, Dumbarton Oaks, Trustees for Harvard University, Washington, D.C., ref. no. PH.PC.001_192-TAG-78-NC.

The women consistently appear with bound prisoners, intended victims of sacrifice (de Bock 2005:92; Scher 2010:187–188), as in the modeled example in figure 8.3, in which the women crouch on either side of the prisoner, identified by the rope around his neck. In some scenes, the two women are involved in the dismemberment of the prisoner (figure 8.4). The gabled-roofed structure appears on the right, housing a seated figure.

Figure 8.3. Modeled ceramic vessel of bound prisoner. Museo Larco Herrera, Lima; cat. no. 02048.

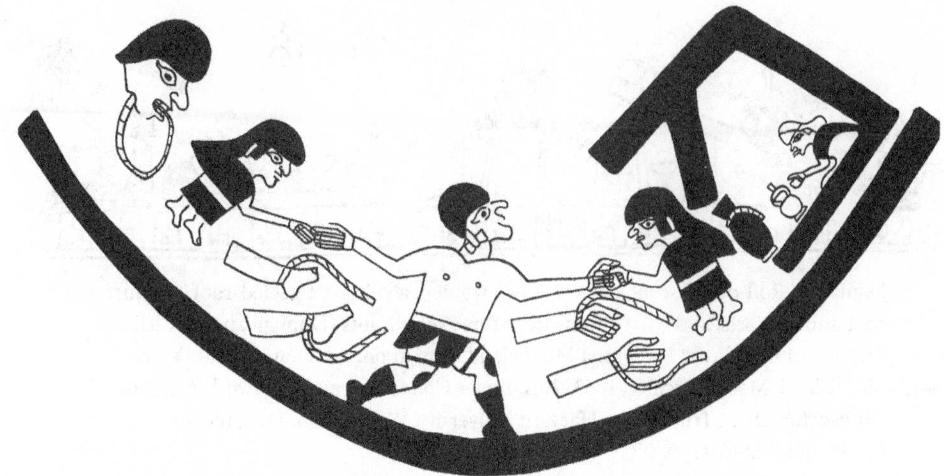

Figure 8.4. Roll-out of prisoner dismemberment. Note the small figure, apparently observing, from beneath the gabled roof. Adapted from Gerdt Kutscher 1983, figs. 120 and 121.

Immediately in front of the seated figure are two ceramic vessels. Several versions of this image exist (e.g., Bourget 2006:figures 2.126, 2.129, 2.130, 2.131), and in each case, the two women are associated with gabled-roof structures, vultures, and vessels.

I suggest below that the seated or kneeling figure under the gabled-roof structure is an ancestor—possibly an actual mummified individual or perhaps the instantiation of an ancestor analogous to the forms suggested by Lau (2002) for the Recuay.

In a complex and frequently published scene including women and vultures, naked male prisoners, presumably captured in combat, run or process to the left, toward an elite figure seated atop a stepped platform or pyramid. On the upper right is a sacrifice in progress—two figures expose the throat of a prisoner. In the center of the lower register is a female figure with a full burden bag. She appears to be leaving behind a prisoner who exchanges a dish with an anthropomorphized vulture. In the upper register in the center of the image is an unadorned gabled-roof structure with a woman offering a goblet to a seated figure. Behind her, to the left, is a naked prisoner. Several anthropomorphized birds—vultures or condors—hover nearby.

Figure 8.5 is a detail of the image of the woman and the prisoner. The woman offers a vessel or goblet to a seated or kneeling figure who, I

Figure 8.5. A woman making an offering to a bundled figure; this detail is part of a larger, more complex scene of prisoner procession and sacrifice. Adapted from Gerdt Kutscher 1983, fig. 123.

suggest, represents an ancestor. Researchers such as Bourget, who have explicitly linked women with death and the afterlife, have posited that Moche ritual involved the collection and perhaps the consumption of human blood (Bourget 2006:154–155, 177; see also Kaulicke 2000:269). Other painted and modeled vessels clearly show women involved in sacrificial bloodletting. Human blood residue has been identified in Moche goblets recovered in tomb contexts (Bourget and Newman 1998). The blood may have been offered to or poured out for ancestors, just as Inca ancestors received libations of *chicha*, or maize beer.

The contents of the vessel are actually of less concern to my argument than the ritual being performed. Some form of offering or exchange appears to be in progress, and whether it involves blood, *chicha*, or some other food or beverage is secondary to the ritual act itself and to my argument that the figure receiving the offering is an ancestor. Certainly, if the vessel contains blood, this is highly relevant to our understanding of the nature of the Moche body, the role of prisoners in Moche belief, and Moche cosmology more generally. Bourget (2006:138) has suggested that blood is associated with reciprocity, a perspective that my analysis of this scene supports. However, in contrast to Bourget, who suggests that menstrual blood is linked in an inverted and symbiotic way to fertility, sex, and the sacrificial blood of prisoners, I view the blood (or *chicha*) as a materialization of reciprocal relations between ancestors and members of Moche society more generally. The persistent association of *chicha* with ancestors, offerings, and veneration (Doyle 1988) makes it an ideal means of linking the living and the dead, as the fermentation process parallels the decomposition of the body and subsequent transformation into an ancestor (Lau 2015:228).

Bourget (see also de Bock 2005:92) is almost certainly correct, however, that the role of women—as opposed to men, who tend to dominate

Moche iconography—is ritually significant. Excavation of a Moche tomb at the site of San José de Moro has demonstrated through contextual evidence that women performed rituals both in large public settings *and* in small-scale domestic ritual contexts (Donnan and Castillo 1994). The iconographic evidence supports the interpretation that such roles were widespread and not limited to elite women, such as the prominent "priestess" figure in a ritual scene called the "Sacrifice Ceremony" (Castillo 2006; Castillo and Rengifo Chunga 2008; Donnan and Castillo 1994).

The role of women in domestic, or household-based, ritual, specifically the care of ancestors, has been demonstrated cross-culturally in both ethnographic and archaeological contexts. Freedman (1970:173–175), for example, has noted that twentieth-century Chinese women had primary responsibility for the "routine tendance" of ancestors, including the provision of offerings and the care of tablets placed on household altars. Women also interpreted behavior by ancestors, especially behavior that indicated displeasure. A similar pattern has been documented in nineteenth- and twentieth-century Japan, where women played critical roles in the daily ritual routine of attending the ancestors. While the male head of the household had formal charge of the ancestors' care, women handled day-to-day responsibilities. Women were also the most likely to become victims of spirit possession or to suffer retribution if the ancestors were unhappy with their treatment (Yonemura 1976:184–185). McAnany (1995:33) describes a similar set of responsibilities for post-Classic Maya women, who offered food and drink to the ancestors within the context of domestic shrines, usually in association with the physical remains of the deceased.

Ethnohistoric sources from Peru following Spanish contact describe a range of activities associated with the ancestral dead, including offerings of food and *chicha*. Women were the primary brewers and distributors of *chicha* (Bray 2003; Gero 1992; Hastorf 1991; Silverblatt 1987) and played major roles in the care of shrines (Bauer and Stanish 2001:236–237). Divination was a role undertaken by high-ranking Inca women, one of whom was reported to care for the mummy of her kinsman and interpret his responses to questions (MacCormack 1991:70–71).

In a seventeenth-century illustration (figure 8.6), Felipe Guaman Poma de Ayala depicts the mortuary practices of people from the Chinchay *suyo* (or *suyu*), the northwest quarter of the Inca empire—the region that included the Moche River valleys (Adorno 1980, 2000; Salomon 1995).

Figure 8.6. "Entiero de Chinchaisuios," interment in the style of the Chinchay suyo (region or "quarter") of the Inca empire, Guaman Poma de Ayala ([1615] 2001), folio 289 [291]; drawing 113. Kongelige Biblioteck (Royal Library), Copenhagen MS GKS 2232 4⁰.

Marked similarities exist between this image and the Moche gabled-roof scene, providing a glimpse of what a similar Moche-era ritual may have looked like. Notable here is the presence of a woman—in this case, a widow—the flexed figure of the deceased (*aya*), and the procession toward or past a tomb or *pucullo*, in which skeletonized remains are visible. Moore (2004:107) identifies the stone or mud-brick structure as a *machay* and associates it with highland funerary practices rather than coastal. However, he also observes that the *machay* "was fronted by a small open area, a *cayan*, in which ancestral ceremonies could take place." The Moche, several centuries earlier than Guaman Poma's illustration, may have practiced a form of ancestor veneration that shared key components with fifteenth- and sixteenth-century Andean rituals, among them, the delineation of sacred space, focus on either the body or simulacrum of a deceased ancestor, and sacrificial rites.

These three components of Inca ritual—sacred space, the materialization of the ancestor in some form, and sacrificial offerings involving libations, gifts of food, or the sacrifice of humans or animals—have cross-cultural analogs in societies in which ancestor veneration has been well documented ethnographically or historically. In suggesting that Moche ritual may have involved similar practices, then, I am drawing an analogy not only to the Inca but also to patterns in venerative rites more generally.

The architecture of sacred space is a particularly fruitful avenue of inquiry. The shrine or burial place-as-house metaphor is particularly salient in the Andes, where the concept of a home or dwelling place for ancestors was marked both architecturally through burial structures and linguistically (Ramírez 1996:144–145). During the Inca period, the deceased might inhabit a *chullpa* (Isbell 1997; Nielsen 2008), burial house or tower; a *pucullo*, burial house; or *aya huasi*, house of the dead (Isbell 1997; Salomon 1995:322).

The gabled-roof structure depicted in Moche iconography is clearly not a stone structure like a *chullpa*. But, like a *chullpa*, the structure was a locus of ritual activity, perhaps including the feeding and care of ancestors. In the Central Andes during the pre-Hispanic period, venerative rites focused on mummy bundles (*mallquis*) and may have taken place at the mortuary structures where deceased were interred. Mantha (2009:161) interprets such loci as centers of memory, social identity, and group solidarity. Moche rites may have fulfilled similar functions and taken place in metaphorical houses—gabled-roof structures—where the ancestors resided. Donnan (1978:79–82) identified such structures as ritual loci in Moche iconography, distinguishing between open and closed types and roof styles.

Wiersema's (2010) study of ceramic vessels and architectural models called *maquetas* established a clear correspondence between Moche sculptural forms and monumental architecture at Moche sites. Wiersema (2010:181) concluded that gabled-roof structures were of ideological and religious significance and associated them with ritual sacrifice. Similarly, Benson (2012:44) interprets painted house images and ceramic architectural models as "cosmic" houses associated with sacred power and sacrifice, and McClelland (2010) has demonstrated that the shape and structure of Moche *maquetas* reproduce elite ceremonial precincts, not residential architecture.

One function of the gabled-roof structure may have been as a shrine, or *huaca adoratorio*—a place where the revered dead interacted with the living through the medium of sacrificial ritual. Thus, in addition to the burial rites that involved interment of the deceased in a grave or tomb, Moche conducted another set of rites focused on select deceased who were not interred but were maintained in their own structures and tended by women. Proximity and interaction with these "living" dead likely occurred within the ceremonial precincts depicted in Moche iconography (Donnan and McClelland 1999:59; Wiersema 2010, 2011) and constructed at major Moche sites, such as Huaca de la Luna (Tufinio Culquichicón 2008), Huaca Cao Viejo (Franco Jordán et al. 2005), and Huaca Colorada (Swenson 2012).

These precincts are located within larger enclosures atop mud-brick platforms and associated with plazas, generally dated to Moche IV or V, the Middle and Late Moche periods. Access to the precincts tends to be limited or controlled by the surrounding walls, ramps, and corridors that generally lead through a series of switchbacks (Gálvez Mora and Briceño Rosario 2001; Uceda 2001); restricted access is also marked on ceramic architectural models (Wiersema 2010:375). At one end of the enclosure is a raised dais. Based on the presence of columns or post holes, the dais was likely gable-roofed (Swenson 2012:11). At several sites, such as Galindo in the Moche valley (Lockard 2008:289) and Huaca Cao in Chicama (Gálvez Mora and Briceño Rosario 2001), the dais is associated with polychrome murals or friezes. One or more walls associated with the dais tend to be white or have a white background (see reconstruction in Franco Jordán et al. 2005:17). The well-preserved dais at Huaca Colorada in the Jequetepeque River valley was the focal point of "elaborate rites centered on presentation, procession, feasting, and sacrifice" (Swenson 2012:11). Human and animal remains, apparently sacrifices, have been recovered in floor deposits in front of the daises. At Huaca Colorada, these included two humans, a dog, and a cache of copper (Swenson 2012). Human deposits at the Huaca de la Luna occur in the forms of prisoner sacrifice (Verano 2001), interment of children (Bourget 2001), and in elite tombs (Uceda 2001). These practices apparently continued among the Sicán and Chimú inhabitants at Túcume, where both humans and camelids were routinely sacrificed in the plaza in front of a small temple housing a monolith (Toyne 2015).

If feasting and sacrificial rituals were performed in front of the daises, the ancestral dead may have attended and participated through their presence beneath gable-roof structures. Their presence as mummy bundles would be consistent with what we know of Sicán, Chimú, and Inca practices, but both ethnological data for ancestor worship (Hageman and Hill, this volume) and archaeological evidence indicate that human remains need not be present for venerative ritual to occur. Work at Recuay (Lau 2002) and Sicán sites (Matsumoto 2014; Shimada et al. 2015; Toyne 2015) supports the idea that ancestor-related rituals, such as feasting, may have occurred far from funerary loci[1] and focused on simulacra or surrogates, rather than on actual bodies.

Anthropomorphic figures—some of whom may be ancestors—are shown in sculptured form on many Moche vessels (e.g., Wiersema 2010:figures 5.2, 5.17, 5.22). *Maquetas* associated with the Chimú period, which postdates the Moche, clearly represent similar figures in association with roofed structures, offerings, and attendants (Uceda 1997b). According to Wiersema (2010: 370–371, 376), human figures begin to appear within ceramic Moche architectural models in the Middle Moche period (i.e., Moche III). By Moche IV, an indisputable link had been established between architectural structures, offerings, and sacrifice. In Moche IV, the figure within the structure occasionally appears wearing a collar and ear spools and is sometimes fanged (Wiersema 2010:386), a trait associated with a deity-like personage called Aia Paec, or Wrinkle Face. This apparent transformation of an ancestor figure into a deity may reflect larger social processes occurring in Moche society. As elites centralized power and developed an ideological system based on prisoner sacrifice, rites that may once have been small-scale domestic acts directed toward ancestors may have become public spectacles meant to appease deities. Like elites among the Inca and the Shang of China (Campbell, this volume), Moche leaders may have appropriated the conceptual logic and ritual practice of ancestor veneration and reimagined it on a much larger scale. Rites that had once been lineage- or household-based and directed toward specific deceased may have become public or semipublic displays of power—the power to sacrifice human life and to communicate directly with those who ordered the Moche cosmos.

The Moche iconographic and architectural evidence is highly suggestive of ancestor veneration. However, to my knowledge, the actual remains of ancestors, as mummy bundles, for example, have not been identified at Moche sites. If ancestor veneration was practiced and focused on human remains—rather than simulacra in some other form—then such remains have not been preserved, have not yet been recovered, or have been recovered but not identified as such. Interaction with the dead was a routine practice among the Moche, as it was among the Inca, Recuay (Lau 2013), Sicán (Matsumoto 2014; Shimada et al. 2004; Shimada et al. 2015), and other Andean societies (Shimada and Fitzsimmons 2015; Takigami et al. 2014). Such interaction took multiple forms, reflecting the diverse ethnicities and socioeconomic statuses of people in the Andean past. While mummy bundles were the focus of venerative ritual among the Inca, the Moche may have revered their dead in some other form.

As Lau (2013:140) has observed, "Native Andeans were apparently quite comfortable with dead bodies." Abundant Moche evidence exists both for the curation of entire bodies (Nelson 1998) and for the manipulation of human body parts (Cordy-Collins 1997; Hecker and Hecker 1992; Hill 2003, 2005, 2006; Millaire 2004; Verano et al. 1999). Disarticulated human remains are frequently recovered in Moche contexts, including the graves of other individuals. Whether some of these bodies or body parts were considered Moche ancestors is unclear. Such remains could be parts of the ancestral dead, *sacra* that, for whatever reason, were removed from ritual circulation and interred. As Nelson (1998) has demonstrated, the Moche curated bodies in order to inter them at a later date; this may have been the case with ancestors, who were venerated until they, or their body parts, were placed in the graves of their kin, whether biological or fictive. DNA analysis could potentially demonstrate whether disarticulated body parts recovered from funerary contexts belong to kin of the primary decedent.

Conclusions

Iconography alone cannot conclusively demonstrate that the Moche practiced ancestor veneration during the Middle and Late Moche periods. When combined with architectural and burial evidence, however, the case becomes somewhat stronger. Clearly gabled-roof structures are associated with sacrificial ritual. Such ritual may have been directed toward ancestors. Alternatively, or additionally, deities may have been the intended recipients of sacrificial offerings as Moche elites consolidated political power.

The iconographic association between women, vultures, sacrifice, and gabled-roof structures appears secure, though the identification of the kneeling or bundled figure seated beneath the structure remains inconclusive. Perhaps for the Moche, representing an "ancestor" iconographically was unnecessary—the combination of women, vultures, and a gabled-roof structure may have signaled "ancestor" to viewers. Perhaps the structure is a shrine, and instead of painting or modeling an ancestor figure, the Moche focused on showing women engaged in their customary duties to ancestors. Such a representation would have reinforced and normalized the "proper" activities of a Moche woman to viewers who were already familiar with iconographic conventions regarding ancestors.

If ancestor veneration did take place, its elite practice within ritual precincts atop pyramid mounds likely had a smaller-scale parallel in household contexts. Just as Chinese lineage rites occurred both at home and in the corporate shrine, Moche veneration may have taken place on a daily basis in the homes of non-elites, who poured *chicha* and used modeled clay figurines—recovered in abundance at Moche sites—to represent ancestors or sacrificial human and animal offerings. At the same time, elites within their enclosures may have enacted rites involving the sacrifice of actual human prisoners. Such rites may have occurred in front of daises upon which the ancestors sat. Female attendants may have cared for the revered dead, provided *chicha,* and, if the Inca analogy is appropriate, interpreted their wishes.

In conclusion, the question of whether Moche ancestors existed is still unresolved, but this question may be answered in the future through further iconographic study, excavation, and contextual analysis. While the iconography is insufficient by itself, together with cross-cultural data, iconography can show us what to look for in the archaeological record and help us recognize it when we find it.

Acknowledgments

I thank Go Matsumoto and Juliet Wiersema for kindly providing offprints of their work. Shalimar White provided essential assistance with an image from Dumbarton Oaks.

Note

1. Even if the bodies of the ancestors themselves were not present, Moche ritual participants may have focused their attention on the ancestor in an alternative material form, a transportable and manipulable proxy in which the ancestor's essence inhered. Such proxies, or simulacra, could include masks, stone effigies, ceramic figurines, and figurative vessels (Lau 2008, 2015:229–230; MacCormack 1991:191–193; Salomon and Urioste 1991:§319). The Chinese tablet analogy is relevant here, as are the anthropomorphic bamboo rods used to represent the ancestral dead in Ghana (Goody 1962:224–230). Thus, even if the Moche were painting images of ancestors on their pottery, those ancestors may not have taken a recognizably human form in the archaeological record.

References Cited

Adorno, Rolena

1980 *The Nueva Corónica y Buen Gobierno*: A New Look at the Royal Library's Peruvian Treasure. *Fund og Forskning* (Copenhagen) 24:7–28.

2000 *Guaman Poma: Writing and Resistance in Colonial Peru*. 2nd ed. University of Texas Press, Austin.

Arriaga, Pablo José de

1968 [1621] *The Extirpation of Idolatry in Peru*. Translated by L. Clark Keating. University of Kentucky Press, Lexington.

Arsenault, Daniel

1991 The Representation of Women in Moche Iconography. In *The Archaeology of Gender: Proceedings of the 22nd Annual Chacmool Conference*, edited by D. Walde and N. D. Willows, pp. 313–326. Archaeological Association of the University of Calgary, Calgary, Alberta.

Bauer, Brian S., and Charles Stanish

2001 *Ritual and Pilgrimage in the Ancient Andes: The Islands of the Sun and the Moon*. University of Texas Press, Austin.

Benson, Elizabeth P.

1988 Women in Mochica Art. In *The Role of Gender in Precolumbian Art and Architecture*, edited by V. E. Miller, pp. 63–71. University Press of America, Boston.

2012 *The Worlds of the Moche on the North Coast of Peru*. University of Texas Press, Austin.

Bloch, Maurice

1971 *Placing the Dead: Tombs, Ancestral Villages, and Kinship Organization in Madagascar*. Seminar Press, London.

Bourget, Steve

1997 Le colère des ancêtres. In *À l'ombre du Cerro Blanco*, edited by C. Chapdelaine, pp. 83–99. Université de Montréal, Les Cahiers d'anthropologie, no. 1, Montréal.

2001 Children and Ancestors: Ritual Practices at the Moche Site of Huaca de la Luna, North Coast of Peru. In *Ritual Sacrifice in Ancient Peru*, edited by E. P. Benson and A. G. Cook, pp. 93–118. University of Texas Press, Austin.

2006 *Sex, Death, and Sacrifice in Moche Religion and Visual Culture*. University of Texas Press, Austin.

Bourget, Steve, and Margaret E. Newman

1998 A Toast to the Ancestors: Ritual Warfare and Sacrificial Blood in Moche Culture. *Baessler-Archiv* 46(1):85–106.

Bray, Tamara L.

2003 Inka Pottery as Culinary Equipment: Food, Feasting, and Gender in Imperial State Design. *Latin American Antiquity* 14(1):3–28.

Buikstra, Jane E.

1995 Tombs for the Living or for the Dead: The Osmore Ancestors. In *Tombs for the Living: Andean Mortuary Practices*, edited by T. D. Dillehay, pp. 229–280. Dumbarton Oaks, Washington, D.C.

Carmichael, Patrick H.

1994 The Life from Death Continuum in Nasca Imagery. *Andean Past* 4:81–90.

1995 Nasca Burial Patterns: Social Structure and Mortuary Ideology. In *Tombs for the Living: Andean Mortuary Practices*, edited by T. D. Dillehay, pp. 161–187. Dumbarton Oaks, Washington, D.C.

Castillo, Luis Jaime

2006 Five Sacred Priestesses from San José de Moro: Elite Women Funerary Rituals on Peru's Northern Coast. *Arkeos: Revista Electrónica de Arqueología PUCP* 1(3).

Castillo, Luis Jaime, and Carlos E. Rengifo Chunga

2008 Identidades Funerarias Femeninas y Poder Ideológico en las Sociedades Mochicas. In *Los Señores de los Reinos de la Luna*, edited by K. Makowski. Banco de Crédito del Perú, Lima. Available online at http://sanjosedemoro.pucp.edu.pe/descargas/articulos/Identidadesfemeninas.pdf.

Cobo, Bernabe

1990 [1653] *Inca Religion and Customs*. Translated by R. Hamilton. University of Texas Press, Austin.

Cordy-Collins, Alana

1997 The Offering Room Group. In *The Pacatnamu Papers*, vol. 2, *The Moche Occupa-*

tion, edited by C. B. Donnan and G. A. Cock, pp. 283–292. Fowler Museum of Cultural History and the University of California, Los Angeles.

de Bock, Edward K.

2005 *Human Sacrifices for Cosmic Order and Regeneration: Structure and Meaning in Moche Iconography*. BAR International Series 1429, Oxford.

DeLeonardis, Lisa, and George F. Lau

2004 Life, Death, and Ancestors. In *Andean Archaeology*, edited by H. Silverman, pp. 77–115. Blackwell, Oxford.

Donnan, Christopher B.

1978 *Moche Art of Peru*. Museum of Cultural History, University of California, Los Angeles.

Donnan, Christopher B., and Luis Jaime Castillo

1994 Excavaciones de Tumbas de Sacerdotisas Moche en San José de Moro, Jequetepeque. In *Moche: Propuestas y Perspectivas*, edited by S. Uceda and E. Mujica, pp. 415–424. Travaux de l'Institut Français d'Etudes Andines, Lima.

Donnan, Christopher B., and Donna McClelland

1999 *Moche Fineline Painting: Its Evolution and Its Artists*. Fowler Museum of Cultural History, University of California, Los Angeles.

Doyle, Mary E.

1988 The Ancestor Cult and Burial Ritual in Seventeenth- and Eighteenth-Century Central Peru. Unpublished PhD dissertation, Department of History, University of California, Los Angeles.

Fogelin, Lars

2007 The Archaeology of Religious Ritual. *Annual Review of Anthropology* 36:55–71.

Fogelin, Lars (editor)

2008 *Religion in the Material World*. Center for Archaeological Investigations, Southern Illinois University, Carbondale.

Forgey, Kathleen, and Sloan R. Williams

2005 Were Nasca Trophy Heads War Trophies or Revered Ancestors? Insights from the Kroeber Collection. In *Interacting with the Dead: Perspectives on Mortuary Archaeology for the New Millennium*, edited by G.F.M. Rakita, J. E. Buikstra, L. A. Beck, and S. R. Williams, pp. 251–276. University Press of Florida, Gainesville.

Fortes, Meyer

1965 Some Reflections on Ancestor Worship in Africa. In *African Systems of Thought*, edited by M. Fortes and G. Dieterlen, pp. 122–142. Oxford University Press for the International African Institute, London.

1976 An Introductory Commentary. In *Ancestors*, edited by W. H. Newell, pp. 1–16. Mouton, The Hague.

1987 *Religion, Morality, and the Person: Essays on Tallensi Religion*. Cambridge University Press, Cambridge.

Franco Jordán, Régulo, César Gálvez Mora, and Segundo Vásquez Sánchez

2005 *El Brujo: Pasado Milenario*. Fundación Augusto N. Wiese, Instituto Nacional de Cultura, and the Universidad Nacional de Trujillo, Trujillo.

Freedman, Maurice

1958 *Lineage Organization in Southeastern China*. Athlone, London.

1966 *Chinese Lineage and Society: Fukien and Kwantung*. London School of Economics Monographs on Social Anthropology 33. Athlone, New York.

1970 Ritual Aspects of Chinese Kinship and Marriage. In *Family and Kinship in Chinese Society*, edited by M. Freedman, pp. 163–187. Stanford University Press, Stanford, California.

Gálvez Mora, César, and Jesús Briceño Rosario

2001 The Moche in the Chicama Valley. In *Moche Art and Archaeology in Ancient Peru*, edited by J. Pillsbury, pp. 141–157. Yale University Press, New Haven, Connecticut, and National Gallery of Art, Washington, D.C.

Gero, Joan M.

1992 Feasts and Females: Gender Ideology and Political Meals in the Andes. *Norwegian Archaeological Review* 25:1–16.

Glowacki, Mary, and Michael Malpass

2003 Water, Huacas, and Ancestor Worship: Traces of a Sacred Wari Landscape. *Latin American Antiquity* 14(4):431–448.

Goody, Jack

1962 *Death, Property, and the Ancestors: A Study of the Mortuary Customs of the LoDagaa of West Africa*. Stanford University Press, Stanford, California.

Guaman Poma de Ayala, Felipe

2001 [1615] *El Primer Nueva Corónica y Buen Gobierno*. GKS 2232 40 vols. Det Kongelige Bibliotek / Royal Library, Copenhagen.

Guillén, Sonia E.

2005 Mummies, Cults, and Ancestors: The Chinchorro Mummies of the South Central Andes. In *Interacting with the Dead: Perspectives on Mortuary Archaeology for the New Millennium*, edited by G.F.M. Rakita, J. E. Buikstra, L. A. Beck, and S. R. Williams, pp. 142–149. University Press of Florida, Gainesville.

Hastorf, Christine A.

1991 Gender, Space, and Food in Prehistory. In *Engendering Archaeology: Women and Prehistory*, edited by J. M. Gero and M. Conkey, pp. 132–159. Basil Blackwell, Oxford.

2003 Community with the Ancestors: Ceremonies and Social Memory in the Middle Formative at Chiripa, Bolivia. *Journal of Anthropological Archaeology* 22:305–332.

Hecker, Giesela, and Wolfgang Hecker

1992 Ofrendas de Huesos Humanos y Uso Repetido de Vasijas en el Culto Funerario de la Costa Norperuana. *Gaceta Arqueológica Andina* 6(21):33–53.

Helms, Mary W.

1998 *Access to Origins: Affines, Ancestors, and Aristocrats*. University of Texas Press, Austin.

Hill, Erica

2003 Sacrificing: Moche Bodies. *Journal of Material Culture* 8(3):285–299.

2005 The Body Intact, the Body in Pieces: Foucault and the Moche Prisoner. In *Art for Archaeology's Sake: Material Culture and Style across the Disciplines*, edited by A. Waters-Rist, C. Cluney, C. McNamee, and L. Steinbrenner, pp. 124–131. University of Calgary Archaeological Association, Calgary, Alberta.

2006 Moche Skulls in Cross-Cultural Perspective. In *Skull Collection, Modification, and Decoration*, edited by M. Bonogofsky, pp. 91–100. BAR International Series 1539, Archaeopress, Oxford.

Hocquenghem, Anne Marie, and Patricia J. Lyon

1980 A Class of Anthropomorphic Supernatural Females in Moche Iconography. *Ñawpa Pacha* 18:27–50.

Isbell, William H.

1997 *Mummies and Mortuary Monuments: A Postprocessual Prehistory of Central Andean Social Organization*. University of Texas Press, Austin.

Kaulicke, Peter

2000 *Memoria y Muerte en el Perú Antiguo*. Pontificia Universidad Católica del Perú, Lima.

Kenyon, Kathleen M.

1954 Excavations at Jericho. *Journal of the Royal Anthropological Institute* 84(1–2):103–110.

1957 *Digging Up Jericho: The Results of the Jericho Excavations, 1952–1956*. Praeger, New York.

Kenyon, Kathleen M., and A. Douglas Tushingham

1953 Jericho Gives Up Its Secrets. *National Geographic* 104(6):853–870.

Kutscher, Gerdt

1983 *Nordperuanische Gefässmalereien des Moche-Stils*. Verlag C. H. Beck, Munich.

Lau, George F.

2002 Feasting and Ancestor Veneration at Chinchawas, North Highlands of Ancash, Peru. *Latin American Antiquity* 13(3):279–304.

2008 Ancestor Images in the Andes. In *Handbook of South American Archaeology*, edited by H. Silverman and W. H. Isbell, pp. 1027–1045. Springer, New York.

2011 *Andean Expressions: Art and Archaeology of the Recuay Culture*. University of Iowa Press, Iowa City.

2013 *Ancient Alterity in the Andes: A Recognition of Others*. Routledge, London.

2015 The Dead and the Longue Durée in Peru's North Highlands. In *Living with the Dead in the Andes*, edited by Izumi Shimada and James L. Fitzsimmons, pp. 200–244. University of Arizona Press, Tucson.

Lockard, Gregory D.

2008 A New View of Galindo: Results of the Galindo Archaeological Project. In *Arqueología Mochica: Nuevos Enfoques*, edited by L. J. Castillo, H. Bernier, G. D. Lockard, and J. Rucabado Yong, pp. 275–294. Fondo Editorial de la Pontificia Universidad Católica del Perú, Lima.

Lyon, Patricia J.

1978 Female Supernaturals in Ancient Peru. *Ñawpa Pacha* 16:95–140.

MacCormack, Sabine

1991 *Religion in the Andes: Vision and Imagination in Early Colonial Peru*. Princeton University Press, Princeton, New Jersey.

Mantha, Alexis

2009 Territoriality, Social Boundaries, and Ancestor Veneration in the Central Andes of Peru. *Journal of Anthropological Archaeology* 28(2):158–176.

Matsumoto, Go

2014 El culto de veneración al ancestro Sicán: una aproximación y evidencias. In *Cultura Sicán: Esplendor preincaico de la costa norte*, edited by Izumi Shimada, pp. 191–211. Fondo Editorial del Congreso del Perú, Lima.

McAnany, Patricia A.

1995 *Living with the Ancestors: Kinship and Kingship in Ancient Maya Society*. University of Texas Press, Austin.

McClelland, Donald

2010 Architectural Models in Late Moche Tombs. *Ñawpa Pacha* 30(2):209–230.

Millaire, Jean-François

2004 The Manipulation of Human Remains in Moche Society: Delayed Burials, Grave Reopening, and Secondary Offerings of Human Bones on the Peruvian North Coast. *Latin American Antiquity* 15(4):371–388.

Moore, Jerry D.

2004 The Social Basis of Sacred Spaces in the Prehispanic Andes: Ritual Landscapes of the Dead in Chimú and Inka Societies. *Journal of Archaeological Method and Theory* 11(1):83–124.

Nelson, Andrew J.

1998 Wandering Bones: Archaeology, Forensic Science, and Moche Burial Practices. *International Journal of Osteoarchaeology* 8:192–212.

Nielsen, Axel E.

2008 The Materiality of Ancestors: *Chullpas* and Social Memory in the Late Prehispanic History of the South Andes. In *Memory Work: Archaeologies of Material Practices*, edited by B. J. Mills and W. H. Walker, pp. 207–231. School for Advanced Research Press, Santa Fe.

Proulx, Donald A.

2001 Ritual Uses of Trophy Heads in Ancient Nasca Society. In *Ritual Sacrifice in Ancient Peru*, edited by E. P. Benson and A. G. Cook, pp. 119–136. University of Texas Press, Austin.

2006 *A Sourcebook of Nasca Ceramic Iconography: Reading a Culture through Its Art*. University of Iowa Press, Iowa City.

Ramírez, Susan E.

1996 *The World Upside Down: Cross-Cultural Contact and Conflict in Sixteenth-Century Peru*. Stanford University Press, Stanford, California.

Russell, Glenn S., and Margaret A. Jackson

2001 Political Economy and Patronage at Cerro Mayal, Peru. In *Moche Art and Archaeology in Ancient Peru*, edited by J. Pillsbury, pp. 159–175. Yale University Press, New Haven and National Gallery of Art, Washington, D.C.

Sallnow, Michael J.
1987 *Pilgrims of the Andes: Regional Cults in Cusco*. Smithsonian Institution Press, Washington, D.C.

Salomon, Frank
1995 "The Beautiful Grandparents": Andean Ancestor Shrines and Mortuary Ritual as Seen through Colonial Records. In *Tombs for the Living: Andean Mortuary Practices*, edited by T. D. Dillehay, pp. 315–353. Dumbarton Oaks, Washington, D.C.

Salomon, Frank, and George L. Urioste (editors)
1991 *The Huarochirí Manuscript: A Testament of Ancient and Colonial Andean Religion*. University of Texas Press, Austin.

Scher, Sarahh E. M.
2010 Clothing Power: Hierarchies of Gender Difference and Ambiguity in Moche Ceramic Representations of Human Dress, CE 1–850. Unpublished PhD dissertation, Department of Art History, Emory University, Atlanta.

Shimada, Izumi, and James L. Fitzsimmons (editors)
2015 *Living with the Dead in the Andes*. University of Arizona Press, Tucson.

Shimada, Izumi, Ken-ichi Shinoda, Julie Farnum, Robert Corruccini, and Hirokatsu Watanabe
2004 An Integrated Analysis of Pre-Hispanic Mortuary Practices: A Middle Sicán Case Study. *Current Anthropology* 45(3):369–402.

Shimada, Izumi, Haagen D. Klaus, Rafael Segura, and Go Matsumoto
2015 Living with the Dead: Conception and Treatment of the Dead on the Peruvian Coast. In *Living with the Dead in the Andes*, edited by Izumi Shimada and James L. Fitzsimmons, pp. 101–172. University of Arizona Press, Tucson.

Silverblatt, Irene
1987 *Moon, Sun, and Witches*. Princeton University Press, Princeton, New Jersey.

Silverman, Helaine, and Donald A. Proulx
2002 *The Nasca*. Blackwell, Malden, Massachusetts.

Swenson, Edward
2012 Moche Ceremonial Architecture as Thirdspace: The Politics of Place-Making in the Ancient Andes. *Journal of Social Archaeology* 12(1):3–28.

Takigami, Mai K., Izumi Shimada, Rafael Segura, Sarah Muno, Hiroyuki Matsuzaki, Fuyuki Tokanai, Kazuhiro Kato, Hitoshi Mukai, Omori Takayuki, and Minoru Yoneda
2014 Assessing the Chronology and Rewrapping of Funerary Bundles at the Prehispanic Religious Center of Pachacamac, Peru. *Latin American Antiquity* 25(3):322–343.

Toyne, J. Marla
2015 Ritual Violence and Human Offerings at the Temple of the Sacred Stone, Túcume. In *Living with the Dead in the Andes*, edited by Izumi Shimada and James L. Fitzsimmons, pp. 173–199. University of Arizona Press, Tucson.

Tufinio Culquichicón, Moisés
2008 Huaca de la Luna: Arquitectura y Sacrificios Humanos. In *Arqueología Mochica:*

Nuevos Enfoques, edited by L. J. Castillo Butters, H. Bernier, G. D. Lockard, and J. Rucabado Yong, pp. 451–470. Fondo Editorial de la Pontificia Universidad Católica del Perú, Lima.

Tylor, Edward B.

1870 The Philosophy of Religion among the Lower Races of Mankind. *Journal of the Ethnological Society of London* 2(4):369–381.

Uceda, Santiago

1997a El Poder y la Muerte en la Sociedad Moche. In *Investigaciones en la Huaca de la Luna 1995*, edited by S. Uceda, E. Mujica, and R. Morales, pp. 177–188. Facultad de Ciencias Sociales, Universidad Nacional de La Libertad, Trujillo.

1997b Esculturas en Miniatura y una Maqueta en Madera. In *Investigaciones en la Huaca de la Luna 1995*, edited by S. Uceda, E. Mujica, and R. Morales, pp. 151–176. Facultad de Ciencias Sociales, Universidad Nacional de La Libertad, Trujillo.

2001 Investigations at Huaca de la Luna, Moche Valley: An Example of Moche Religious Architecture. In *Moche Art and Archaeology in Ancient Peru*, edited by J. Pillsbury, pp. 47–67. Yale University Press, New Haven, Connecticut, and National Gallery of Art, Washington, D.C.

Verano, John W.

2001 War and Death in the Moche World: Osteological Evidence and Visual Discourse. In *Moche Art and Archaeology in Ancient Peru*, edited by J. Pillsbury, pp. 111–125. Yale University Press, New Haven, Connecticut, and National Gallery of Art, Washington, D.C.

Verano, John W., Santiago Uceda, Claude Chapdelaine, Ricardo Tello, Maria Isabel Paredes, and Victor Pimentel

1999 Modified Human Skulls from the Urban Sector of the Pyramids of Moche, Northern Peru. *Latin American Antiquity* 10(1):59–70.

Vogel, Melissa A.

2003 Sacred Women in Ancient Peru. In *Ancient Queens: Archaeological Explorations*, edited by S. M. Nelson, pp. 117–135. Altamira Press, Walnut Creek, California.

Whitley, James

2002 Too Many Ancestors. *Antiquity* 76(291):119–126.

Wiersema, Juliet

2010 The Architectural Vessels of the Moche of Peru (CE 200–850): Architecture for the Afterlife. Unpublished PhD dissertation, Department of Art History and Archaeology, University of Maryland, College Park.

2011 La relación simbólica entre las representaciones arquitectónicas en las vasijas Mochica y su función ritual. In *Modelando el Mundo: Imágenes de la Arquitectura Precolumbina*, edited by Cecilia Pardo, pp. 165–191. Museo de Arte de Lima, Lima.

Yonemura, Shoji

1976 *Dōzoku* and Ancestor Worship in Japan. In *Ancestors*, edited by W. H. Newell, pp. 177–203. Mouton, The Hague.

9

Where the Ancestors Live

Shrines and Their Meaning among the Classic Maya

JON B. HAGEMAN

Archaeologists agree that ancestors figured prominently in the lives of the Classic Maya (AD 250–900), particularly in the Late Classic (600–900), the period for which we have a wealth of epigraphic, iconographic, and archaeological evidence. Most data are from monumental site centers where royalty were lavishly interred in large pyramids. Much less is known, however, of the roles ancestors buried in small, often rural, shrines played in the lives of commoners—the remaining 90–98 percent of the Classic era population. Still less is known regarding the origins and development of ancestral practices in the Lowland Maya area (figure 9.1). In this chapter I review archaeological evidence for ancient Maya ancestors rather than the deceased in general. I approach this from a chronological perspective, beginning with the earliest evidence of ancestors during the Preclassic (1000 BC–AD 250). In so doing I emphasize changes in burial practices, including body position, architecture, and symbolic elements of grave goods. I also evaluate practices of kings and commoners in the Classic era, with a focus on the ongoing use of various Preclassic symbols and practices in the continued creation of ancestors. My emphasis is on the material manifestation of these ancestors, the practices associated with them, and the resulting implications for our understanding of ancient Lowland Maya society.

What Is an Ancestor?

Anthropological studies of ancestors conclude that these beings are a subset of the dead. Ancestors are *created* through mortuary ritual. An

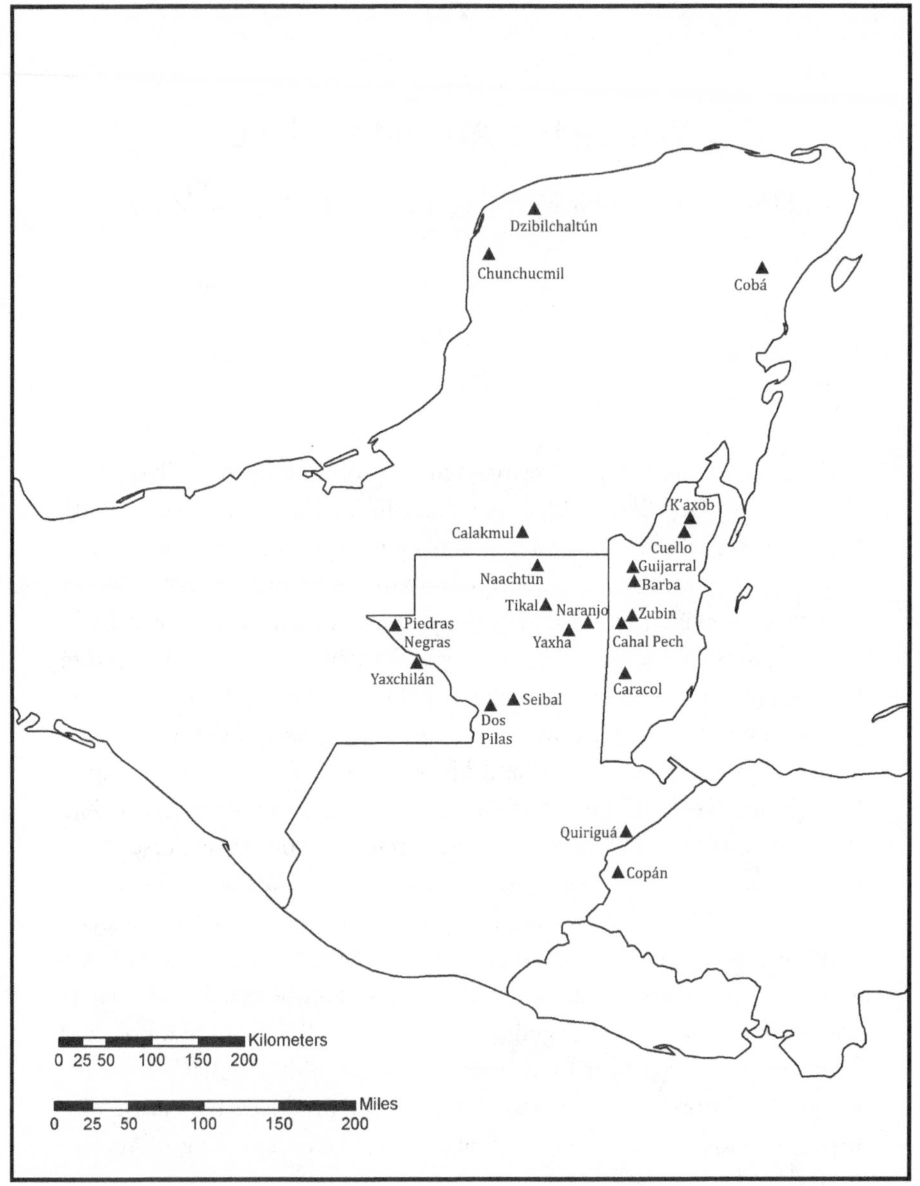

Figure 9.1. Map of Maya area showing sites mentioned in the text. After Brown and Witschey (2014).

ancestor may be the founder of a corporate group (Watson 1982:594), the first person who settled an area and cleared the land to create a cultural space (McCall 1995:258–259), or an important individual in the social group (Fortes 1953). Ancestors are revered and celebrated by their descendants through periodic group ritual.

Cross-culturally, death does not end a person's participation in the life and activities of the family, but instead inaugurates a different mode of participation (Freedman 1958:85; Fortes 1976:5). The dead continue to look after the living, and the living look after the dead. Death alone does not confer ancestorhood, however (Hageman and Hill, this volume). Elaborate funerary ceremonies are conducted as rites of passage that transform the deceased from a member of the world of the living into a being who is reincorporated into society in an ancestral and spiritual capacity. The reincorporation of the dead is often manifest as memorial tablets, effigies, shrines, or altars, which are placed in or near the ancestral hall or lineage home. These objects and structures are the material embodiment of the group within which the deceased are reinstated and, through their visible existence, act as a constant presence in the lives of the living (Fortes 1976:7). Since ancestors are usually considered to be part of the living group, they require sustenance. Food dependence and provision are the vital bonds that unite child to parent, and to share a meal is an expression of amity and trust (1976:10). Ancestors were owed a debt for the gift of life and sustenance (Freedman 1958:88). Feasting maintains relationships between the living members of the lineage and deceased ancestors. In return for ritual upkeep, ancestors may protect the living members of their lineage from natural and supernatural phenomena. Even ancestors are not omnipotent, however, and the living may still suffer misfortunes caused by witches, demons, sorcerers, or evil predestiny. Ancestors can also punish their descendants in cases of neglect (e.g., not "feeding" them) or for moral transgressions (Ahern 1973; Freedman 1958:89; Fortes 1976:13).

In summary, ancestors are *not* the entirety of the deceased population. Instead, ancestors are created through rituals conducted by their descendants (biological or not), who memorialize them in highly visible locations, often through interment or enshrinement. Ancestors are celebrated, often through feasting, and participate in the lives of their descendants through supernatural means. Ancestors also link people to place, as living descendants can indicate the shrine or monument that represents the presence or burial of several generations of ancestors.

Below I describe how some of the earliest Lowland Maya ancestors were created during the Preclassic. The best examples of ancestor creation come from sites that began as relatively egalitarian agricultural villages and were later transformed into larger, more hierarchically organized settlements. Most of these data have been recovered from northern Belize and in the Belize River valley.

Making Maya Ancestors in the Preclassic

During the Middle Preclassic (1000–400 BC), most Lowland Maya settlements consisted of relatively egalitarian farmsteads. Cuello and K'axob provide the best evidence of early ancestor creation through a mortuary record spanning over 1,000 years, from the Middle Preclassic through the Late Preclassic (400 BC–AD 250), and into the Early Classic (AD 250–600). Specifically, changes in burial location, grave goods, skeletal position, and to a certain extent the number of individuals interred suggest that ancestors were conceived at this time.

Early in the Middle Preclassic at Cuello, the deceased were buried under house floors. Men and women were buried together, in supine positions, with little differentiation in grave goods. These burials have been described as family mausolea (Hammond 1999; Robin and Hammond 1991; Storey 2004). Near the end of the Middle Preclassic, however, individual burials began to appear. One of the earliest of these, Burial 22, is that of a middle-aged to elderly adult male, who was interred with a ceramic bowl and eight shell beads (Robin 1989:199–200). In a break with previous mortuary patterns, this individual was not buried under the house floor but in the center of the plaza (Hammond 1991:103–104). Fire pits, which had been used for cooking by individual households prior to the interment of Burial 22, also disappear. This suggests a realignment of activities and the conversion of the plaza into a primarily public place.

In the Late Preclassic, at about 400–300 BC, several males were buried at Cuello in rubble fill that was then covered by a plaza floor much larger than its predecessor. This mass interment includes the primary burial of two adult males in seated positions (Burials 50 and 51) with bundles of human bones in their laps. The two males are associated with seven ceramic vessels and four deer bone tubes—probably fan handles—carved with the *pop*, or woven mat motif, quadripartite swirling smoke designs, and a reptilian or serpent design (figure 9.2). Twenty-nine additional

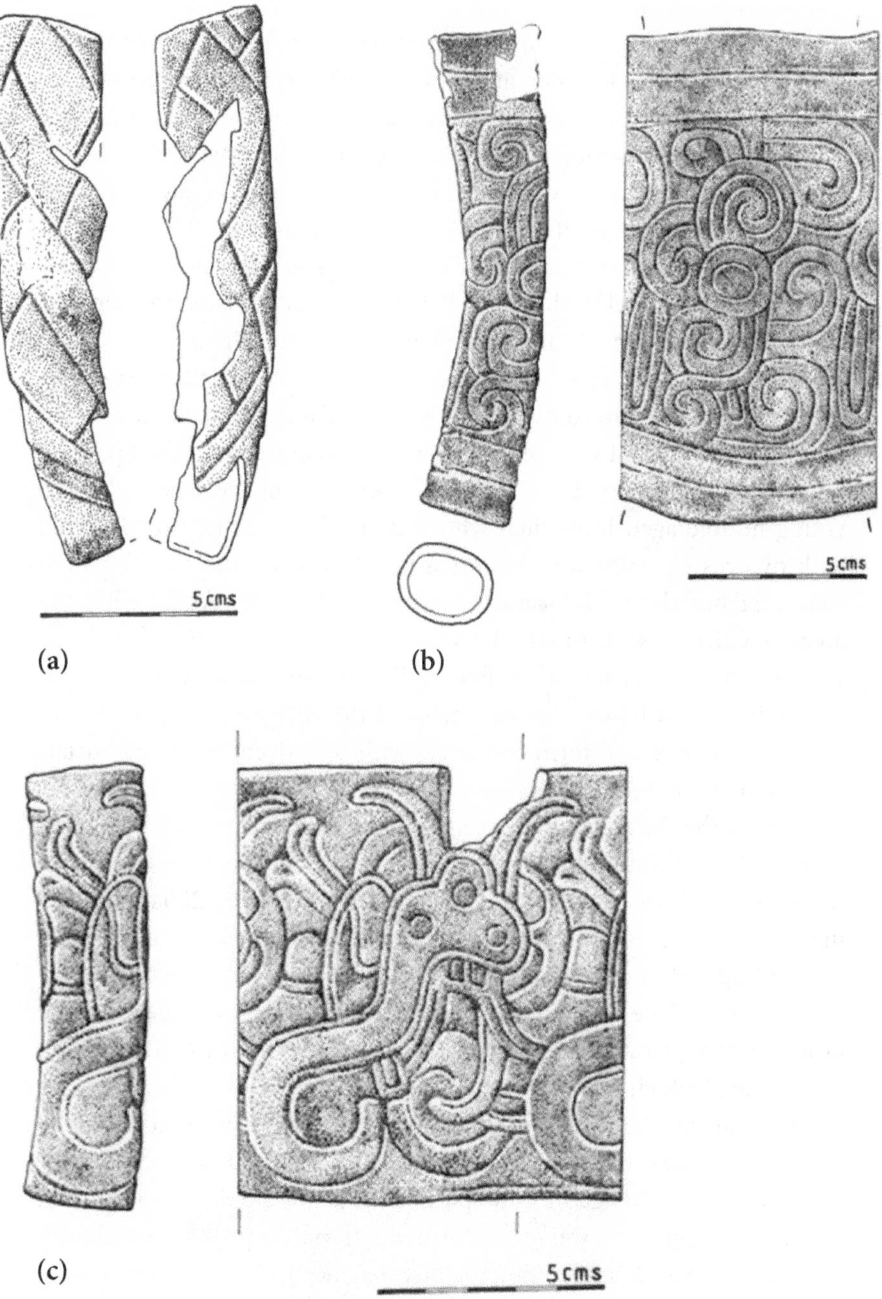

Figure 9.2. Preclassic deer bone fan handles from Cuello Burial 50: (a) *pop* motif; (b) quadripartite swirling smoke design; (c) reptilian or serpent design. Drawings by Sheena Hovarth, © Cuello Project, after Norman Hammond 1991, fig. 8.36.

disarticulated males and one possible female were also found in the pit (Robin 1989:240–246). Later, at about AD 100, a similar deposit was interred—also in construction fill—above the earlier mass burial. This later burial featured two seated adult males as primary interments (Burials 70 and 79) with human bone bundles in their laps, and an additional ten secondary burials of adult males (Robin and Hammond 1991). Burial 70 included four jade beads and four ceramic vessels, one of which was a broken tetrapod bowl (Robin 1989:272–274). Burial 79 featured chert and obsidian blade fragments and red ocher (Robin 1989:278–279).

At the contemporary village of K'axob, adult males buried in seated positions were also interred during the Late Preclassic; however, the seated burials are associated with ceramic bowls featuring a cross motif painted on the bottom (Storey 2004). Burial 1-1, whose primary deceased was a young-middle-aged individual who was "probably male," was interred with two vessels painted with a cross motif; this was the sixth of seven sequential burials in this location (Storey 2004:127–128). As at Cuello, the areas in which these distinctive burials occurred appear to have been converted into public spaces after their earlier use for domestic food preparation. Indeed, at K'axob, the expansion of the village and differentiation in residential size and form coincided with the advent of seated burials (McAnany et al. 1999:142–143).

Later in the Preclassic, the location and nature of these special interments changed—buildings, rather than plazas, become repositories for the deceased. This occurred not only at K'axob (Storey 2004) but also in the Belize valley (Aimers et al. 2000). At the Tolok Group near Cahal Pech, a Middle Preclassic round platform (Str. 14) contained two Late Preclassic burials. One was too fragmentary for sex to be estimated, but the other was that of a supine young adult female with two vessels (Song et al. 1994), one of which was a tetrapod bowl.

These unusual burials differ dramatically from previous practice while displaying remarkable within-group consistency. They mark space in plazas and signal a change in how space is used; areas that had been used for domestic activities were transformed into public places immediately accessible to surrounding inhabitants. Second, these interments were marked with artifacts featuring highly charged imagery, such as a serpent or reptilian motif. Saurian symbolism is a metaphor for cosmic realms and ritual actions. The Celestial Monster carries the sky on its serpent-like back, and the Vision Serpent represents the path that supernaturals, including ancestors, take to their earthly manifestation (Freidel et al. 1993:196; Schele and Freidel 1990:67–73; Schele and Miller 1986:45–47). Smoke symbolizes transformation and communication between human and supernatural realms (Freidel et al. 1993:214–218; Miller and Taube 1993:128–129).

Other powerful motifs include the *pop* symbol, crossed bands, and quadripartite imagery. The *pop* (mat) motif "symbolizes the pathways and portals between cosmic realms" (Looper 2006:93) and later underpins Classic era kingship. Crosses (or crossed bands) have an Olmec origin, where they are associated with rulership, the bundling of sacred items (Reilly 2006:7–18), and securing and protecting the essence or "soul force" believed to animate every human (Freidel and Guenter 2006:60). Crossed bands also symbolize the crossing point of the ecliptic and the Milky Way (Reilly 1995:36) or mark portals to the underworld (Guernsey Kappelman 2001:102). Another interpretation suggests this motif, along with the tetrapod bowls, represents a quincunx (four directions and a center) and signifies an *axis mundi* (McAnany et al. 1999). Headrick (2004:371) argues that "the crosses in the K'axob bowls refer to the idea of the center of the earth, the heart of the sky, the arch of the sun and the Milky Way, and even the blue-green bowl of water, which was a metaphor for the empty ocean at the beginning of time." In either interpretation, the crosses on the K'axob bowls are strongly linked to imagery and symbolism at the core of the Mesoamerican belief system (2004:377) and to the boundary between human and supernatural worlds.

Third, burial configuration changed after the appearance of quadripartite symbolism. The earliest cross symbolism at K'axob appeared in extended burials, but shifted to seated burials with symbols that were later linked to royal power, including the *pop* motif on shell and bone artifacts (e.g., Hammond 1999; Storey 2004). The seated position signified authority (McAnany et al. 1999:142); further, the crossed legs of the deceased replicated crossed bands, conveying the concepts of centrality, quadripartition, bundling, access to the underworld, and the *axis mundi*. Mere orientation of the body within the burial became part of a profound, cosmologically charged act.

Fourth, burials associated with cross/quadripartite symbolism were initially those of both adult males and females, but became dominated by adult males over a short period of time, such that seated burial became associated exclusively with adult males. Whether seated burial under plazas (e.g., Hammond 1999; Robin and Hammond 1991; Storey 2004) or extended burial in ceremonial structures (e.g., Aimers et al. 2000), the earliest Maya ancestors are for the most part adult males.

These changes demonstrate variation in the symbols used, but express a common and recognizable theme that is the basis for the creation and maintenance of ancestors and institutionalized inequality. Early indicators of ancestors persist and can be identified archaeologically in later periods. Ancestors are links to the past, and as such can confer legitimacy upon individuals within social groups. Interpretations of "the way of the ancestors" are subject to negotiation, and McAnany (1995) has argued that ancestors were one of the key factors in the creation of Maya divine kingship. Still, many nonroyal Maya appear to have revered their own ancestors in the context of domestic ritual associated with corporate forms of social organization, such as lineages. Echoes of earlier Preclassic practices can be seen in both of these later contexts.

Classic Maya Royal Ancestors

After the appearance of ancestors in the Preclassic, ancestral practices diverge along two paths coincident with the widespread appearance of divine kings across the Maya Lowlands. One path is that of kingship and promotion of the royal ruler; the other appears to be focused on kinship and corporate groups (e.g., McAnany 1995:126–144). Each is rooted in the importance of ancestors, yet has distinctive foci and ideologies and is materialized in similar ways.

Evidence of ancient ancestral practices, in the form of seating, the *pop* motif, the *axis mundi*, and the reopening of existing burial loci are all found among Classic Maya royalty. However, Classic kings were buried in supine rather than seated positions. Although seated burial is unusual among Classic royalty, the seated position of the living ruler is directly linked with power and authority, the regal position of a king on a mat (*pop*) or a throne (McAnany 1998:276). In addition, the Classic Cholan word used to describe accession to rulership is *chum*, "to be seated" (Montgomery 2002:66–68). Being seated on a mat echoes the appearance of the *pop* sign on carved deer bones during the Preclassic at Cuello (e.g., Hammond 1999). The seated burial position of the Preclassic, associated with creating (or "seating") an otherworldly ancestor, was used in association with the rite of passage that created a Maya king, investing the ruler with a power previously reserved for a privileged subset of the deceased. This and other unique behaviors identify those who live less like ordinary mortals and more like deceased ancestors (Helms 1999:64; see also Kopytoff 1971).

The Royal Ancestral House

Pyramids were built to house kings after their deaths. Freidel and Guenter (2006) argue that, in the Preclassic, the seated or flexed burial represents a sacred bundle in which the "soul force" of the deceased is preserved or maintained in conjunction with the body, allowing the veneration of specific deceased individuals at their burial places. Among Classic royalty, however, the container for the deceased expanded to become the pyramid itself, essentially a bundle containing the "soul cache" of the deceased. The soul of the deceased gave life and meaning to the pyramid. These buildings "impart a notion of sacralization of place in that the construction of an artificial hill or *wits* converts a portion of the built environment into purely ritual space" (McAnany 1998:278). The burials of the ancestors within pyramids established and defined an *axis mundi* and made the deceased available for consultation (1998:281). Temples atop the pyramids evoked the basic Maya dwelling and provided symbolic entranceways into the underworld (Chase and Chase 1998:300). The four corner posts of the house/temple represented the four directional trees supporting the heavens (Taube 1998:432). The four sides of the temple modeled the structure of the universe, embodying and channeling some of the most basic principles of the cosmos (Taube 1998:428; Webster 1998:29). This is the Classic era architectural manifestation of the quadripartite principle represented by the Preclassic cross motif and tetrapod bowls at Cuello, K'axob, and the Belize River valley.

By linking themselves to the center of cosmic creation using symbols associated with portals to otherworldly realms as part of public ritual, Maya lords asserted their role in the creation and maintenance of the world. Many of the rituals performed by the king in association with this imagery reenacted creation events (Bauer 2005:28; Fields and Reents-Budet 2005:21; Freidel 2008). Many royal ceremonies invoked, or were held in honor of, deceased ancestors. In some cases, interaction with ancestors was explicitly sought through visions, while in others the presence of ancestors observing a particular event is made clear through scenes and texts carved on stone monuments. Finally, the physical remains of ancestors were the focus of ceremonies conducted by living rulers.

Visions

Maya kings and queens interacted with their ancestors as part of royal activities, and the most comprehensive representations of these appear in Classic (AD 250–900) art. Examples of this interaction include bloodletting rites where ancestors appeared to the living in visions. Yaxchilán's Temple 23 features three lintels depicting a queen, Lady K'abal Xook, interacting with ancestors. On Lintel 24, dedicated in AD 709, she pulls a thorn-studded rope through her tongue, with the blood dripping into a paper-lined basket at her feet (Martin and Grube 2008:125). Lintel 25 shows her celebrating her husband's seating as king in AD 681 by conjuring a vision of the king as defender of the city (figure 9.3). The king emerges from the mouth of a serpent, which in turn rises from scrolls of smoke emanating from a bowl filled with burning blood-spattered paper (Martin and Grube 2008:125). The scrolls and serpent recall the reptilian image and smoke scrolls depicted on bone tubes from Preclassic Cuello.

Ancestors Observing

Ancestors are also thought to have been present during the day-to-day activities of the rulers, drawing them close and "embody[ing] their presence within the space shared by the divine ruler" (Herring 2005:222). Auspicious occasions, such as accession to the throne or the marking of a *katun* (twenty-year) cycle, were recorded on carved monuments, with the ancestors or locally important deities looking on. Tikal Stela 31 depicts the ruler Sihnaj Chan K'awiil II (Stormy Sky) ascending to the throne in AD 411 (figure 9.4). His attire is purposely archaic, dating to an era some 150 years earlier, and includes the name of the first known ruler of Tikal, from AD 100. Additional imagery links him to his grandfather and his father, with an ancestral sun god hovering above (Martin and Grube 2008:34). The text on the reverse of the monument is an appeal to an ancestral line for legitimacy by claiming to complete or fulfill the works of past rulers, cementing Sihnaj in the context of Tikal's traditions and history (Stuart 2011).

Figure 9.3. Yaxchilán Lintel 25. Gift of Ian Graham. Drawing by Ian Graham; © President and Fellows of Harvard College, Peabody Museum of Archaeology and Ethnology, PM#2004.15.6.22; digital file #99200047.

Figure 9.4. Tikal Stela 31. Originally published in Tikal Report 33 (Jones and Satterthwaite 1982, fig. 51). Image courtesy of the University of Pennsylvania Museum, Philadelphia.

Another example comes from Caracol, where Knot Ajaw scattered incense in AD 603. Stela 6 describes this scattering as observed by his deceased father, Yajaw Te' K'inich II (Fitzsimmons 2009:142). Much later, Tikal Stela 11 (AD 869) depicts Jasaw Chan K'awiil II with two Paddler Gods floating above him amid scrolls signifying smoke or clouds (Montgomery 2001:218). The Paddler Gods are created or born when a Maya king lets blood; they frequently occur in the smoke created when blood is dripped on paper and ignited (Miller and Taube 1993:128–129). The text refers to Tikal's founder and to the thirtieth successor, Jasaw Chan K'awiil II. Stela 11 was placed alongside stelae from the glorious and more prosperous past (Martin and Grube 2008:53). This placement may also be in homage to Jasaw Chan K'awiil I, his renowned, eponymous forebear, and the hallowed burial ground of his ancestors (Rice 2004:156).

In addition to passive "observing," deceased rulers were depicted in contexts directly legitimating the rulership of the living king. Copán Altar Q is a square monument depicting four of Copán's sixteen rulers on each of its sides. The altar is supported by four circular pillars, with each king sitting on his name glyph and holding the baton of office (Agurcia and Fash 2005:234–236; Sharer et al. 2005:149) or a flaming wooden item (Fitzsimmons 2009:152; Taube 2004:267) in his hand. The sequence begins with the dynastic founder, K'inich Yax K'uk' Mo,' handing a baton or burning dart to the sixteenth ruler and sponsor of the monument, Yax Pasaj Chan Yoaat. The altar itself is located in front of the largest pyramid at the site (Str. 10L-16). Excavations revealed several earlier structures within this pyramid, each with evidence of ceremonies based on fire and homage to K'inich Yax K'uk Mo.' The quadripartite architectural features and symbolism of the building denote its centrality as an *axis mundi* (Taube 2004:266); evidence of smoke generation indicates its use as a portal where the ancestors and gods were contacted through fire rituals. At Copán, the rulers connected themselves personally to K'inich Yax K'uk' Mo's remains and architectural programs (Fitzsimmons 2009:111).

Interaction with Physical Remains

Finally, direct interaction with deceased rulers via their remains, though not universal among the royalty, was one of the most widely practiced (or at least one of the most archaeologically visible) modes of Late Classic ancestor interaction. Evidence comes from six sites and represents at least eleven occurrences. Piedras Negras Stela 40, for example, depicts Ruler 4 in AD 746, kneeling while scattering blood or incense into a vent leading to a sub-plaza tomb. The body in the tomb is dressed in Teotihuacan-style clothing and described in the text as Ruler 4's mother (Martin and Grube 2008:148). As McAnany (1998:286–287) notes, the barrier between the deceased ancestor and the living ruler is not sealed and separate but open and permeable. The upper tomb in Caracol Structure A34 yielded a single long bone fragment with a ceramic bowl cache at the chamber entrance, which had been left after the removal of several bones and all grave goods. The lower tomb was in use for approximately a century. It was completed in the late sixth century, and a single individual appears to have been interred at this time, witnessed by the ruler of Caracol, who was buried above. The lower tomb was entered at least once after its initial use to add at least three more individuals (Chase and Chase 1996:76, 1998:313).

Ancient texts and archaeological evidence indicate the periodic opening of royal tombs and physical interaction with ancestors also occurred at Copán (Sharer et al. 1999) and Piedras Negras (Fitzsimmons 2009). At Copán, the tomb of the wife of city founder K'inich Yax K'uk' Mo' was entered repeatedly and the bones were painted with cinnabar and hematite (Sharer et al. 1999:11), recalling the inclusion of red ocher in the seated burials of Preclassic Cuello.

Butz' Chan, the eleventh ruler of Copán, died in AD 628. In AD 730, Waxaklajuun Ubaah K'awiil, the thirteenth Copán king, conducted a *susaj baak* ("cutting or slicing of bones") rite, thought to involve exhuming bones from the tomb of Butz' Chan for use as relics. The interval between the two events is close to two cycles of the fifty-two-year calendar round and is similar in length between interments identified for the lower tomb of Caracol Structure A34 (Chase and Chase 1996:76; Freidel et al. 1993:279; Grube and Schele 1993:5; Martin and Grube 2008:200).

At Piedras Negras, texts describe Ruler 2 reopening and censing the tomb of Ruler 1 in AD 678, some thirteen days prior to the one-*katun* (twenty-year) anniversary of the latter's death. Ruler 2 also let blood thirteen days later. This blood was spread on bark paper and ignited, and the storm god Chaak and the Jaguar God of the Underworld were invoked. Subordinate lords from nearby kingdoms attended this event. In the presence of both the deities and subordinates, Ruler 2 received a helmet that linked the king to Teotihuacan in central Mexico—a foreign symbol proclaiming power and legitimacy (*sensu* Helms 1998). Later, in AD 706, Ruler 3 received a burning "long thin object" (Fitzsimmons 2009:152) from a deceased Ruler 2; Ruler 4 eventually received a similar item from a deceased Ruler 3. After a period in which rulers 5 and 6 were relatively weak, Ruler 7 entered and censed the tomb of Ruler 4 in AD 782. Archaeological investigations have identified the tomb of Ruler 4. Bones were scattered, the tomb chamber was blackened and burned, and upon completion of the rite the tomb was resealed and covered by a new plaza floor (Houston et al. 1998; Fitzsimmons 2009:154–155). Piedras Negras kings are described on carved stone panels and stelae as having "censed" the tombs of their predecessors to maintain links to the past and legitimize their power in the present (Fitzsimmons 2009:147–155). Stuart (1998:417–418) suggests that the bringing of fire into a tomb could "revivify" the dwelling of the deceased ancestor. Not only was the liminal door to the supernatural world opened through the use of smoke in a tomb, but a powerful and highly charged political drama was played out through contact with the deceased ancestor-king. In addition, this pattern of a major interment, followed by the sealing of the burial with a new plaza floor, is identical to that practiced at Cuello in the Preclassic.

Tikal Altar V depicts Jasaw Chan K'awiil I, king of Tikal, and a ruler of "Maasal" (likely Naachtun) conducting a ritual in AD 711 over a stack of bones surmounted by a skull (figure 9.5). The ritual likely took place at Topoxte, deep within territory controlled by Tikal's rival, Calakmul. Jasaw Chan traveled through enemy territory to meet with an enemy lord and retrieve the remains of a deceased woman, Lady Tuun Kaywak. Excavations beneath Stela 16, associated with Altar V, yielded a human skull and bones in a cache (Jones and Satterthwaite 1982:37), though the sex of the skeleton is not mentioned. Several scholars (e.g., Fitzsimmons 2009:165; Martin and Grube 2008:46; Montgomery 2001:155; Schele and Grube 1994:4–5; Stuart 1998:408; Weiss-Krejci 2011:28–29) have proposed that the bones are those depicted on Altar V.

The importance of ancestral bones to descendant kings also made the remains of royal ancestors in large pyramids targets in warfare. Naranjo Stela 23, dedicated in AD 710 by K'ahk' Tiliw Chan Chaak, describes a military victory over the nearby site of Yaxha. Yaxha was burned and its king captured; a recently deceased Yaxha ruler (Yax Bolon Chaak) was exhumed and his bones were "scattered" on an island, likely Topoxte (Martin and Grube 2008:76; Schele and Grube 1994:148). K'akh' Tiliw of Naranjo defeated the polity of Sakha' in AD 714, and Naranjo Stela 28

Figure 9.5. Tikal Altar V. Originally published in Tikal Report 33 (Jones and Satterthwaite 1982, fig. 23). Image courtesy of the University of Pennsylvania Museum, Philadelphia.

describes a similar tomb desecration at Sakha' in AD 716 (Martin and Grube 2008:76).

Royal tombs were reopened and entered to add bodies, sometimes at calendrically important intervals. Rituals involving red pigments as well as smoke speak to the importance of interaction with royal remains, perhaps to shore up the legitimacy of rulers whose position was precarious without ancestral intervention. The power or importance of royal ancestral bones was such that they could be exhumed and distributed as relics or could be retrieved at great risk, even by a trip behind "enemy lines."

Conversely, the power of royal ancestral bones could be diffused or destroyed by exhuming and scattering them away from the tomb, dispersing the soul force of the pyramid bundle.

While many Preclassic themes associated with the creation of ancestors appear among Classic Maya royalty, some do not persist and a few undergo a reversal. Where men appeared more often in positions of power at Cuello, K'axob, and the Belize valley, for example, images representing both men and women interacting with ancestors became quite common through the Classic, particularly in the Usumacinta region. It appears that, among the royalty, ancestors linked rulers with established, recognized, and revered lines. In the context of several aspirants to the mat, the ability to demonstrate royal descent from both maternal and paternal lines would have been extremely useful (McAnany 1998:292–293). Preclassic burials from Cuello and K'axob do not exhibit the Classic frequency of reentry and degree of manipulation of the primary interment, and not all Classic tombs were reentered. Still, the importance of interacting with the bones of deceased royal relatives represents a shift from the earlier Preclassic pattern, where the primary interment appears to have been undisturbed.

In sum, a significant shift in the treatment of certain deceased occurs from the Preclassic to the Classic. Monumental sculptures depict ancestors observing royal practices, while others portray the result of royal agency—intentionally conducting and participating in rituals whose intent, at least in part, was to bring ancestors back to the world of the living for formal interaction. Maya royalty recognized that the essential identity or persona resided in the head (and by extension, skull) (Houston et al. 2006:60; Duncan and Hofling 2011:203), and rituals were conducted across the Maya Lowlands to help propitiate the goodwill of—as well as to destroy the power of—particular royal ancestors. Among royalty, variation exists in the practices associated with interaction with the deceased. In some cases, bones were painted with cinnabar and hematite, while other tombs were censed. Some tombs had bodies added, others had bodies (or parts of bodies) removed; some of these removed bones became the focus of royal ritual. What these practices have in common is the manipulation of skeletal remains for political and religious ritual by and for the living.

The royals conducting these rituals made a point of recording their activities in monumental stone carvings. Several of the depicted activities left no other recovered archaeological signature (tomb reentry being an exception). Absent the epigraphic record, the types and kinds of archaeologically identifiable ancestral practices are likely fewer in number. In switching to an examination of nonroyal (and nonliterate) Maya populations, we must consider how the absence of a written record may impact our ability to identify a similarly rich body of ancestral practices.

Classic Ancestors among Maya Commoners

Comparatively little attention has been paid to ancestors among the nonroyal Maya until recently. Much of our understanding of Classic Maya ancestors is derived from studies of Maya royalty—focusing on religious practices serving royal interests—rather than on the remaining 90–98 percent of the population (Marcus 2004; Sanders 1992). Still, the work that has been done suggests ancestral practices among commoners focused on kinship and corporate groups (e.g., McAnany 1995). Though the commoner focus on ancestors is in some ways similar to that of the royals (e.g., the importance and legitimacy of what has gone before), the ideology and some of the material manifestations vary from the royal pattern (see Weiss-Krejci, this volume, for a European example of how noble ancestors differ from commoners).

Royal houses are not merely larger versions of commoner social structures. Cross-cultural studies of divine kingship indicate that royalty employ symbols identifiable by any commoner but that these symbols are contextualized in markedly different ideologies and practices. Divine kings are not only above society but also *beyond* it due to their royal status. In fact, among the royalty many activities carried out by kings are described as *inversions* of common practices and often are prohibited among other members of society—the power and privilege of divinity sanctions their practice. In contexts of divine kingship, royalty are so different they are considered in the same category as strangers or foreigners (Feely-Harnik 1985; Houston and Stuart 1996:290; Sahlins 1981:111–113; Valeri 1985:147).

McAnany (1995:125–144) argues that ancestor veneration in general was subverted by elites. Where ancestors once linked families and land, elites manipulated the ideology to validate royal lines, legitimize tributary systems, and sanction kingly prerogative. Divine kingship creates two social classes: a semidivine royal minority and a commoner majority. Kingship is also extractive and seeks to appropriate land from other groups through domination and alienation. Houston and Stuart (1996:299–300) note that, since nobles as well as royals could impersonate Maya deities, the divine basis for elite power was distributed widely among the Maya nobility.

Classic Maya royalty are marked by a distinct ideology, including the appropriation of ancestral attributes and privileges by living rulers as marks of distinction (e.g., Helms 1998, 1999:64). Given the deliberate differences created and maintained by royalty to perpetuate their unequal status within society, we cannot assume that the royal ideology was shared by the entirety of the Maya population. Some of the rituals described above were likely royal perquisites, though symbols were shared between royals and commoners. McAnany (2002:119) notes that rituals among commoner populations are "highly reflective, cosmologically informed, and far more prevalent than state-sponsored rituals." Though the symbols and structures used in both subsets of the population may appear similar or even identical, the commoner rituals may operate (to varying degrees of visibility and success) in cooperation with, as well as resistance against, the state ideology (Ek 2006:13–14).

Homes of the Ancestors

One shared symbol across ancient Maya society was the pyramid, located in the monumental centers populated by royalty and present among commoners throughout the suburban and rural Late Classic Lowlands. Commoner pyramids, however, are usually referred to as "shrines." Shrines have the same square plan as pyramids—all four sides are about the same length—but are much smaller in size (figure 9.6). Shrines usually lack a temple on their peak. One of the most common manifestations of the shrine is as part of a residential unit described at Tikal as the Plaza Plan 2, or PP2 (Becker 1999). This consists of three or more buildings surrounding a courtyard, with a shrine as the eastern structure. Subsequent labels for this residential configuration include "eastern shrine group" (Chase and Chase 1994:53) and "east-focused patio group" (Lohse 2004:130). Though the labels differ, the plan is identical.

Available data suggest the PP2 configuration may have its origins in the Late Preclassic Mirador basin, but began to expand across the lowlands in the Early Classic and proliferated throughout the Late Classic. PP2 is found across the lowlands, at Tikal as well as in northwestern Belize

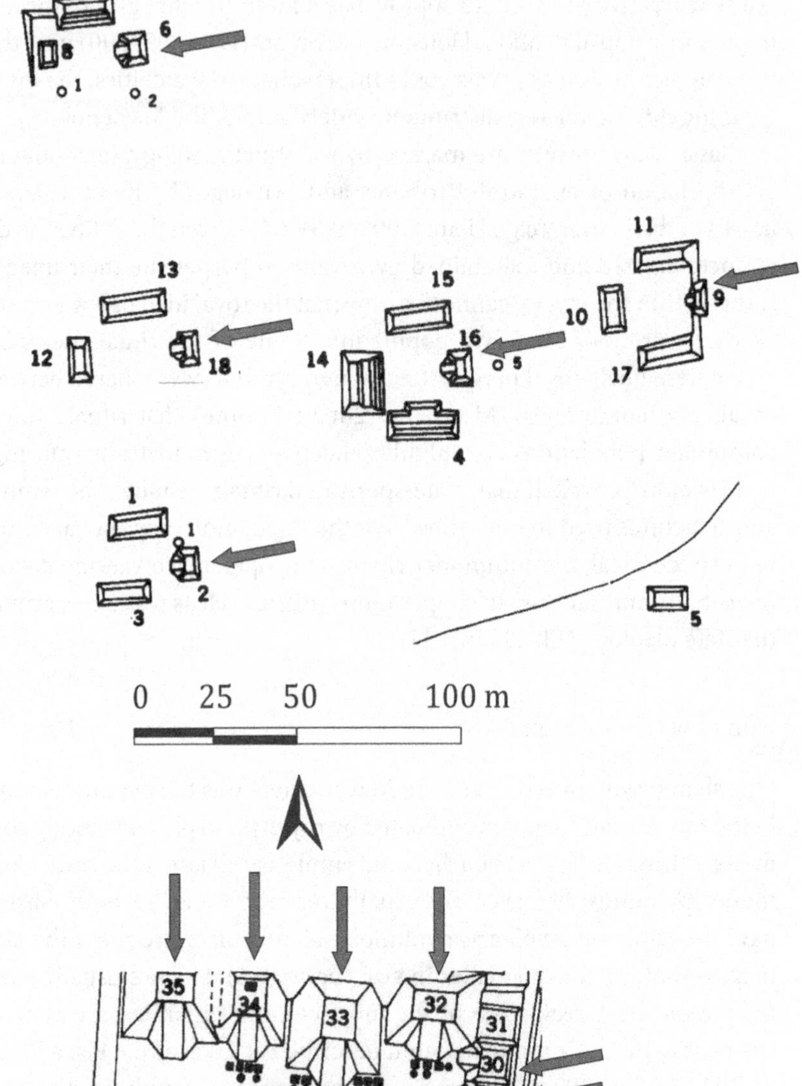

Figure 9.6. Arrows indicate shrines (*top*) and pyramids (*bottom*) at Tikal. Originally published in Tikal Report 13 (Puleston 1983, figs. 2b, 2a). Image courtesy of the University of Pennsylvania Museum, Philadelphia.

(Hageman 2004; Hageman and Lohse 2003; Hammond et al. 1998; Lohse 2004; Tourtellot et al. 1993; Tourtellot et al. 2003), the Belize valley (Awe et al. 1992; Conlon and Moore 1998, 2003; Connell 2003; Glassman et al. 1995; Goldsmith 1993; Iannone 2003; Powis 1993), the Maya Mountains (LaPorte 1991, 1994), northeastern Petén (Bullard 1960), Calakmul (Folan et al. 2001), the Petén Lakes (Rice and Rice 1980), Caracol (Chase 1992; Chase and Chase 1994, 2004), Quiriguá (Jones and Sharer 1980; Leventhal 1983), Chunchucmil (Hutson et al. 2004), Dzibilchaltún (Kurjack 1974:75), Cobá (Benavides Castillo 1987), Quintana Roo (Harrison 1981), Seibal (Willey et al. 1975:37; Tourtellot 1983:41), and Dos Pilas (Palka 1997; Wolley and Wright 1990).

For the Maya, east is linked with *kin*, "day" or "light," and west is *akbal*, or "darkness." The location of the shrine on the east side of the courtyard corresponds to the solar cycle of life and death (Mathews and Garber 2004:52). This sacred space was consistently used for one or more burials (Becker 1999; Ek 2006). Also, ceramics from associated middens suggest that these locales were the sites of feasts (LeCount 2001; Hageman 2004), an important cross-cultural component of ancestor veneration (Fortes 1976). The burials of ancestors within these shrines established and defined an *axis mundi* (McAnany 1998:281) and appear to have been celebrated through periodic group ritual.

In a fashion similar to that of their royal counterparts, the four sides of shrines model the structure of the universe—embodying and channeling some of the most basic principles of the cosmos—and bundle the souls of those interred within (Freidel and Guenter 2006; McAnany 1998:279; Taube 1998:428). As with the Preclassic contexts at Cuello, K'axob, and the Belize valley, shrines contain multiple burials (as many as ten; e.g., Conlon and Moore 1998, 2003). With the Classic shrines, however, the locus of burial is above-ground in a visible, privileged, sacred building. The individual burials within the square building are derivative of the individuals buried in association with the cross and tetrapod motifs found on vessels in the Preclassic. Like Preclassic K'axob plaza Burial 1-2 (Storey 2004:128–129), Late Classic shrines were reopened and resealed for the burial of additional ancestors.

Shrines served not only as reminders of mortuary ritual but also as durable visual symbols of group identity and longevity and maintenance of a jointly held estate (Ek 2006:13; Hageman and Lohse 2003). The pyramid and shrine are both artificial hills, or *witzob*. The burial chambers within these structures have been described as caves or entrances to the underworld (Becker 1992; Brady and Prufer 2005; Prufer and Brady 2005). They house the ancestors of the ethnographically known Tzotzil Maya of highland Guatemala, who emphasize that the ancestors live in caves in the mountains above the village (Nash 1970:23; Vogt 1969:594).

Ensouling the Ancestral Home

The earliest burial within the shrine may have been associated with its initial construction (Schwake 1996). At Tikal, several such "founding" burials in PP2 shrines were excavated into the bedrock, capped with a lens of *saskab*, or white marl, and the shrine built directly over the burial (Becker 1999). In northwestern Belize, the earliest shrine burial at the Barba Group was dug into the bedrock, then sealed with a lens of *saskab*, which was in turn followed by the construction of the shrine (Hageman 2004). This is similar to the marl layer over K'axob burial 1–45 (Storey 2004:128–129). The use of *saskab* has been suggested by Wagner (2002:63–66) to be indicative of ritual purity, regeneration, and fertility. She argues that the wrapping of a burial in *saskab* is a form of bundling, protecting the interred and marking the contents of the burial as a focus of veneration.

At Zubin Structure A-1a, in the Belize valley, some shrine burials were associated with a new construction phase, while others were overlain by chert debitage (Schwake 1996). Layers of debitage have also been identified by Coe (1975) atop royal tombs in large site centers. Debitage and a new construction phase may be analogous to the construction fill and new plaza floor placed atop the Preclassic mass burials at Cuello, while the *saskab* may be the later structural equivalent of the lime plaster floor of the plaza.

Associating a new building or construction phase with a burial may have given a soul to the building (Mock 1998; Vogt 1976). Ensouling individual construction phases using human burials appears to be an important difference between pyramids in monumental site centers and shrines in residential or rural areas. In comparing numbers of burials from pyramids in the North Acropolis of Tikal and shrines in PP2 residences, Ek (2006) found that PP2 shrines have a greater average number of burials per structure (5.5) and per construction phase (1.6) than did their North Acropolis counterparts (0.6 and 0.4). This suggests a difference in the meaning of these buildings: while the royal pyramids of the North Acropolis focus on commemorating the individual buried within, the shrines of PP2 groups instead emphasize the collection of ancestors interred inside and the continuing prosperity of the group (Ek 2006:11; McAnany 1998:278). This is consistent with McAnany's (1995) distinction between kingship and kinship and suggests a corporate association for shrines in contrast to the glorification of individual kings. Whereas the royal pyramid was the container for the "soul force" of the ancestral ruler and a portal to this otherworldly ancestor, the commoner shrine housed the souls of group members and was a locus of festivals for ancestor celebration.

Ancestors, Gender, and Group Status

The relationship between gender and ancestors among nonroyals can also be examined through shrines. Joyce (2000:88) suggests that, in the Classic period, ritual among the royals was characterized by an "encompassment of distinctions in gender." This reflects an ideology in which the gods exhibited both masculine and feminine aspects and may be linked to the desirability of bilateral descent in royal lineages. In contrast, the extent to which commoner women were invested with symbols linking them to the cosmos and to authority is unclear. McAnany et al. (1999:143) note that only males are found with quadripartite motifs at K'axob once flexed and seated burials appear in the Late Preclassic. Contemporary burials of women lack this motif, suggesting some form of as-yet unrecognized ideology behind this gender differentiation.

Late Classic shrine burials exhibit patterns of sex differentiation similar to those described at Preclassic K'axob. Sex was estimated for 17 individuals in a survey of burials ($n = 38$) recovered from eight Late Classic shrines in Belize and Guatemala (Becker 1999; Hageman 2004; Maar and Varney 1993; Schwake 1996); 16 were male, and 1 was female. The single female burial, Tikal Burial 72, comes from Tikal Structure 5G-8. The deceased was interred within a cist excavated in the bedrock; the burial was subsequently capped by a layer of *saskab*. The shrine was then constructed over the cap. Other burials of this type at Tikal contain male skeletons and usually three to six vessels of varying form (e.g., cylinders, bowls, and plates). Burial 72, however, contains an adult female skeleton and a single vessel, a polychrome bowl with glyphs identifying it as the chocolate drinking cup of Ah Wosal, a king of the site of Naranjo (Culbert 1993:figure 42c; Martin and Grube 2008:70–72; Schele and Freidel 1990:177–178).

The members of the social group that buried the woman with the bowl were distinguishing themselves from their neighbors. This group of commoners exploited an unclear yet visible royal link by consciously working against commoner practice—they buried an adult female, rather than an adult male, in a founding cist and included a single vessel associated with a king rather than a collection of plates, bowls, and cylinders. Perhaps this represents someone aspiring to royalty, or an individual or family fallen from grace, symbolically recalling a lost heritage. In either case, Burial 72 combines elements of commoner ancestral burial practice (bedrock cist capped by *saskab*) with royal burial practice (interring women with texts). While royal burials of women may contain several polychrome vessels and hundreds of jade, shell, and obsidian artifacts (e.g., Gonzalez-Cruz 2000; Sharer et al. 1999), Burial 72 has no grave goods beyond the single bowl. The burial replicates royal practice (and ostensibly, status), but does so from within a commoner idiom. The interment of commoner ancestors seems to have focused exclusively on males, making Burial 72 an exception and perhaps the first woman identified as an ancestor in a commoner context. The commoner pattern of interring ancestors in shrines strongly suggests that the beliefs and practices linking males to the organizing principles of the cosmos originating in the Preclassic continued to be important among nonroyal populations in the Classic. Royal ideology, however, emphasized bilateral descent, an effective strategy to support authority and resource control.

Distribution of the PP2 form became much more widespread during the Late Classic. This period was also when populations experienced unprecedented growth in the Maya Lowlands (Santley 1990). Increasing population density and concomitant demand for land may have stimulated the formation of corporate groups, such as lineages, claiming land rights founded on real or fictive claims of ancestors (Hageman and Lohse 2003; McAnany 1995; see also Shipton 1994). At the Zubin Group in the Belize valley and at Guijarral in northwestern Belize, for example, Early Classic shrines were solitary buildings rather than parts of residential plaza groups. At both sites, by about AD 700, new shrines were constructed only a few meters away from the earlier ones as part of larger residential courtyard groups. In each site, an intrusive burial was placed in each of the two old shrines at about the same time that burials were deposited in the new shrines. These new residential groups were associated with important economic resources nearby, including several quarries at Zubin (Iannone 1995) and about 140 agricultural terraces at Guijarral (Sullivan et al. 2008).

Conclusions

Among the Preclassic and Classic Maya, ancestors were a subset of the deceased created through rites of passage conducted by their living descendants, real or fictive. Ancestors figured prominently in the lives of the living, whether through their presence in the form of a memorial monument or in the periodic celebrations held in their honor. Living descendants also leveraged their ancestors to create and maintain social inequalities, both within and between groups. Finally, Maya ancestors were associated with symbols invoking the most fundamental and powerful principles of the cosmos and were links between the natural and supernatural worlds. Descendants appealed to ancestors for benefits and prosperity by honoring and memorializing them through ritual practices conducted at shrines.

Evidence for early Maya ancestors appears in the Preclassic. Interments of bundled adult males in public areas with symbols of cosmological centrality and liminality invested ancestors with a degree of power and authority inaccessible to the living. In later periods, square pyramids marked space in city centers as well as in the hinterlands and served as the sacred containers for the soul force of elect deceased. In urban areas, kings and queens appropriated symbols, such as the *pop*, previously reserved for ancestors. Royal men and women were depicted in Classic Maya art as having visions of ancestors, being observed by them, and interacting with ancestral remains. These practices were a fundamental component and perquisite of royal power (see Campbell, this volume). Conversely, rulers could be disempowered through the desecration of ancestral bones by victorious rival rulers.

In contrast to the depiction of women as ancestors among the royalty, ancestor-oriented activities among commoners appear to have focused on men. Adult males were buried in shrines much more often than adult females, suggesting a strong link between sex (if not gender) and ancestorhood. The interments of these men are often correlated with initial construction or major refurbishment of shrines and are symbolically linked to the initial ensoulment of the building and its continuing renewal and prosperity. Among commoners, data suggest less direct interaction with ancestors compared with royals. This is likely due to the shrine representing and symbolizing the corporate nature of the group, in stark contrast to royal pyramids established to glorify the individual ruler buried within. Rituals, motifs, objects, and architecture linked people with place, tangibly and durably marking a long line of descent and occupation, real or fictive, of an area. These signals were parts of commoner strategies in competition for natural resources, particularly agricultural land.

The continuities and changes in the meanings and uses of potent symbols reflect emphases and processes of ancient Maya creation of ancestors. Multiple lines of archaeological evidence, including body position, sex of the interred, location of interment, architecture, grave goods, symbols, and stratigraphic elements associated with the interment ground the ancestors in the cosmos. The Classic era saw the broadest divergence of ancestral meaning from a pool of common symbols, with royals pursuing strategies that invoked both male and female generative qualities, whereas commoners continued the Preclassic pattern of associating men with cosmological symbols. The available evidence indicates that ancestor veneration was a long-lived phenomenon among the ancient Maya, with both royalty and commoners manipulating practices, beliefs, and symbols to achieve desired objectives.

Acknowledgments

I'd like to thank Norman Hammond for assistance with figure 9.2, as well as Bill Duncan and three anonymous reviewers for their comments.

References Cited

Agurcia Fasquelle, Ricardo, and William L. Fash

2005 The Evolution of Structure 10L-16, Heart of the Copán Acropolis. In *Copán: The History of an Ancient Maya Kingdom*, edited by E. W. Andrews and W. L. Fash, pp. 201–237. School of American Research Press, Santa Fe.

Ahern, Emily M.

1973 *The Cult of the Dead in a Chinese Village*. Stanford University Press, Stanford, California.

Aimers, James J., Terry Powis, and Jaime J. Awe

2000 Preclassic Round Structures of the Upper Belize River Valley. *Latin American Antiquity* 11:71–86.

Awe, Jaime J., Julián Vinuales, M. Velasco, and R. Novela
1992 Investigations at the Cas Pek Group in the Western Periphery of Cahal Pech, Belize. *Progress Report of the Fourth Season (1991) of Investigations at Cahal Pech, Belize*, edited by Jaime J. Awe and Mark D. Campbell, pp. 51–58. Department of Anthropology, Trent University, Peterborough, Ontario.

Bauer, Jeremy R.
2005 Between Heaven and Earth: The Cival Cache and the Creation of the Mesoamerican Cosmos. In *Lords of Creation: The Origins of Sacred Maya Kingship*, edited by V. M. Fields and D. Reents-Budet, pp. 28–29. Scala, London.

Becker, Marshall J.
1992 Burials as Caches; Caches as Burials: A New Interpretation of the Meaning of Ritual Deposits among the Classic Period Lowland Maya. In *New Theories on the Ancient Maya*, edited by E. C. Danien and R. J. Sharer, pp. 185–196. University Museum Monograph 77. University of Pennsylvania, Philadelphia.
1999 *Excavations in Residential Areas of Tikal: Groups with Shrines*. Tikal Report no. 21, University Museum Monograph 104. University of Pennsylvania, Philadelphia.

Benavides Castillo, Antonio
1987 Arquitectura Domestica en Cobá. In *Analysis de Dos Unidades Habitaciones Mayas del Horizonte Clasico*, edited by L. Manzanilla, pp. 26–35. Instituto de Investigaciones Antropológicas, Serie Antropológica 82. Universidad Nacional Autónoma de México, México, D.F.

Brady, James E., and Keith M. Prufer (editors)
2005 *In the Maw of the Earth Monster: Studies of Mesoamerican Ritual Cave Use*. University of Texas Press, Austin.

Brown, Clifford T., and Walter R. T. Witschey
2014 Electronic Atlas of Ancient Maya Sites. http://MayaGIS.smv.org (accessed June 23, 2013).

Bullard, William R., Jr.
1960 The Maya Settlement Pattern in Northwestern Peten, Guatemala. *American Antiquity* 25:255–272.

Chase, Arlen F.
1992 Elites and the Changing Organization of Classic Maya Society. In *Mesoamerican Elites: An Archaeological Assessment*, edited by D. Z. Chase and A. F. Chase, pp. 30–49. University of Oklahoma Press, Norman.

Chase, Arlen F., and Diane Z. Chase
1994 Maya Veneration of the Dead at Caracol, Belize. In *Seventh Palenque Round Table, 1989*, edited by V. M. Fields, pp. 53–60. Pre-Columbian Art Research Institute, San Francisco.

Chase, Diane Z., and Arlen F. Chase
1996 Maya Multiples: Individuals, Entries, and Tombs in Structure A34 of Caracol, Belize. *Latin American Antiquity* 7:61–79.
1998 The Architectural Context of Caches, Burials, and Other Ritual Activities for the Classic Period Maya (as Reflected at Caracol, Belize). In *Function and Mean-*

ing in Classic Maya Architecture, edited by Stephen D. Houston, pp. 299–332. Dumbarton Oaks, Washington, D.C.

2004 Archaeological Perspectives on Classic Maya Social Organization from Caracol, Belize. *Ancient Mesoamerica* 15:139–147.

Coe, Michael D.

1975 Death and the Ancient Maya. In *Death and the Afterlife in Pre-Columbian America*, edited by E. P. Benson, pp. 87–104. Dumbarton Oaks, Washington, D.C.

Conlon, James F., and Allan F. Moore

1998 The Bedran and Atalaya Plazuela Groups: Architectural, Burial, and Cache Complexes as Indices of Social Status and Role within the Ancient Maya Community of Baking Pot, Belize. *The Belize Valley Archaeological Reconnaissance Project: Progress Report of the 1997 Field Season*, edited by James M. Conlon and Jaime J. Awe, pp. 81–101. Institute of Archaeology, University College London.

2003 Identifying Urban and Rural Settlement Components: An Examination of Classic Period Plazuela Group Function at the Ancient Maya Site of Baking Pot, Belize. In *Perspectives on Ancient Maya Rural Complexity*, edited by G. Iannone and S. V. Connell, pp. 59–70. Cotsen Institute of Archaeology, University of California, Los Angeles.

Connell, Samuel V.

2003 Making Sense of Variability among Minor Centers: The Ancient Maya of Chaa Creek, Belize. In *Perspectives on Ancient Maya Rural Complexity*, edited by G. Iannone and S. V. Connell, pp. 27–41. Cotsen Institute of Archaeology, University of California, Los Angeles.

Culbert, T. Patrick

1993 The Ceramics of Tikal—Vessels from the Burials, Caches, and Problematical Deposits. Tikal Report 25A. University of Pennsylvania Press, Philadelphia.

Duncan, William N., and Charles Andrew Hofling

2011 Why the Head? Cranial Modification as Protection and Ensoulment among the Maya. *Ancient Mesoamerica* 22:199–210.

Ek, Jerald

2006 Domestic Shrines, Ancestor Veneration, and the Ritual Production of Group Identity. In *Maya Ethnicity: The Construction of Ethnic Identity from Preclassic to Modern Times*, edited by F. Schause, pp. 165–181. Acta Mesoamericana vol. 19. Verlag Anton Saurwein, Markt Schwaben, Germany.

Feely-Harnik, Gillian

1985 Issues in Divine Kingship. *Annual Review of Anthropology* 14:273–313.

Fields, Virginia M., and Dorie Reents-Budet

2005 The First Sacred Kings of Mesoamerica. In *Lords of Creation: The Origins of Sacred Maya Kingship*, edited by V. M. Fields and D. Reents-Budet, pp. 21–27. Scala, London.

Fitzsimmons, James L.

2009 *Death and the Classic Maya Kings*. University of Texas Press, Austin.

Folan, William J., Laraine A. Fletcher, Jacinto May Hau, and Lynda F. Folan
2001 Las Ruinas de Calakmul, Campeche, Mexico, un Lugar Central y su Paisaje Cultural. Universidad Autónoma de Campeche, Campeche.
Fortes, Meyer
1953 The Structure of Unilineal Descent Groups. *American Anthropologist* 55:17–41.
1976 Introduction. In *Ancestors*, edited by William H. Newell, pp. 1–16. Mouton, The Hague.
Freedman, Maurice
1958 *Lineage Organization in Southeastern China*. Athlone Press, University of London.
Freidel, David
2008 Maya Divine Kingship. In *Religion and Power: Divine Kingship in the Ancient World and Beyond*, edited by N. Brisch, pp. 191–206. Oriental Institute of the University of Chicago, Chicago.
Freidel, David, Linda Schele, and Joy Parker
1993 *Maya Cosmos: Three Thousand Years on the Shaman's Path*. William Morrow, New York.
Freidel, David, and Stanley Paul Guenter
2006 Soul Bundle Caches, Tombs, and Cenotaphs: Creating the Places of Resurrection and Accession in Maya Kingship. In *Sacred Bundles: Ritual Acts of Wrapping and Binding in Mesoamerica*, edited by J. Guernsey and F. K. Reilly, pp. 59–79. Boundary End Archaeology Research Center, Barnardsville, North Carolina.
Glassman, David M., James M. Conlon, and James F. Garber
1995 Survey and Excavations at Floral Park. In *The Belize Valley Archaeology Project: Results of the 1994 Season*, edited by J. F. Garber and D. M. Glassman, pp. 58–70. Department of Anthropology, Southwest Texas State University, San Marcos.
Goldsmith, A. Sean
1993 *Household Archaeology in the Belize Valley: An Analysis of Current Issues*. Unpublished MA thesis, Department of Archaeology, University of Calgary.
Gonzalez-Cruz, Arnoldo
2000 The Red Queen. http://www.mesoweb.com/palenque/features/red_queen/01.html (accessed August 20, 2013).
Grube, Nikolai, and Linda Schele
1993 *Naranjo Altar 1 and Rituals of Death and Burials*. Texas Notes on Precolumbian Art, Writing, and Culture 54. University of Texas, Austin.
Guernsey Kappelman, Julia
2001 Sacred Geography at Izapa and the Performance of Rulership. In *Landscape and Power in Ancient Mesoamerica*, edited by R. Koontz, K. Reese-Taylor, and A. Headrick, pp. 81–111. Westview Press, Boulder, Colorado.
Hageman, Jon B.
2004 The Lineage Model and Archaeological Data in Northwestern Belize. *Ancient Mesoamerica* 15:63–74.

Hageman, Jon B., and Jon C. Lohse

2003 Heterarchy, Corporate Groups, and Late Classic Resource Management in Northwestern Belize. In *Heterarchy, Political Economy, and the Ancient Maya: The Three Rivers Region of the East-Central Yucatan Peninsula*, edited by V. Scarborough, F. Valdez, and N. Dunning, pp. 109–120. University of Arizona Press, Tucson.

Hammond, Norman

1991 *Cuello: An Early Maya Community in Belize*. Cambridge University Press, Cambridge.

1999 The Genesis of Hierarchy: Mortuary and Offertory Ritual in the Pre-Classic at Cuello, Belize. In *Social Patterns in Pre-Classic Mesoamerica*, edited by D. C. Grove and R. A. Joyce, pp. 49–65. Dumbarton Oaks, Washington, D.C.

Hammond, Norman, Gair Tourtellot, Sara Donaghey, and Amanda Clarke

1998 No Slow Dusk: Maya Urban Development and Decline at La Milpa. *Antiquity* 72:831–837.

Harrison, Peter D.

1981 Some Aspects of Preconquest Settlement in Southern Quintana Roo, Mexico. In *Lowland Maya Settlement Patterns*, edited by W. Ashmore, pp. 259–286. University of New Mexico Press, Albuquerque.

Headrick, Annabeth

2004 The Quadripartite Motif and the Centralization of Power. In *K'axob: Ritual, Work, and Family in an Ancient Maya Village*, edited by P. McAnany, pp. 367–377. Cotsen Institute of Archaeology, University of California, Los Angeles.

Helms, Mary

1998 *Access to Origins: Affines, Ancestors, and Aristocrats*. University of Texas Press, Austin.

1999 Why Maya Lords Sat on Jaguar Thrones. In *Material Symbols: Culture and Economy in Prehistory*, edited by J. E. Robb, pp. 56–69. Occasional Paper no. 26, Center for Archaeological Investigations, Southern Illinois University, Carbondale.

Herring, Adam

2005 *Art and Writing in the Maya Cities, AD 600–800: A Poetics of Line*. Cambridge University Press, New York.

Houston, Stephen, Hector Escobedo, Donald Forsyth, Perry Hardin, David Webster, and Lori Wright

1998 On the River of Ruins: Explorations at Piedras Negras, Guatemala, 1997. *Mexicon* 20:16–22.

Houston, Stephen, and David Stuart

1996 Of Gods, Glyphs, and Kings: Divinity and Rulership among the Late Classic Maya. *Antiquity* 70:289–312.

Houston, Stephen, David Stuart, and Karl Taube

2006 *In Memory of Bones: Body, Being, and Experience among the Classic Maya*. University of Texas Press, Austin.

Hutson, Scott R., Aline Magnoni, and Travis W. Stanton
2004 House Rules? The Practice of Social Organization in Classic-Period Chunchucmil, Mexico. *Ancient Mesoamerica* 15:75–92.
Iannone, Gyles
1995 One Last Time among the Thorns: Results of the 1994 Field Season at Zubin, Cayo Distict, Belize. In *Belize Valley Archaeological Reconnaissance Project: Progress Report of the 1994 Field Season*, vol. 1, edited by G. Iannone and J. M. Conlon, pp. 11–122. Institute of Archaeology, University College London.
2003 Rural Complexity in the Cahal Pech Microregion: Analysis and Implications. In *Perspectives on Ancient Maya Rural Complexity*, edited by G. Iannone and S. V. Connell, pp. 13–26. Monograph 49, Cotsen Institute of Archaeology, University of California, Los Angeles.
Jones, Christopher, and Robert J. Sharer
1980 Archaeological Investigations at the Site Core of Quirigua. *Expedition* 13(1):11–19.
Jones, Christopher, and Linton Satterthwaite
1982 *The Monuments and Inscriptions of Tikal: The Carved Monuments*. Tikal Report no. 33, University Museum Monograph 44. University of Pennsylvania, Philadelphia.
Joyce, Rosemary
2000 *Gender and Power in Prehispanic Mesoamerica*. University of Texas Press, Austin.
Kopytoff, Igor
1971 Ancestors as Elders. *Africa* 41:129–142.
Kurjack, Edward B.
1974 Prehistoric Lowland Maya Community and Social Organization: A Case Study at Dzibilcháltun, Yucatan, Mexico. Middle American Research Institute Publication 38, Tulane University, New Orleans.
LaPorte, Juan Pedro
1991 Reconocimiento Regional in el Noroeste de las Montañas Mayas, Guatemala: Segundo Reporte. *Mexicon* 13(2):30–36.
1994 Ixtonton, Dolores, Petén: Entidad Política del Noroeste de las Motañas Mayas, Atlas Arqueológico de Guatemala no. 2. Escuela de Historia, Universidad de San Carlos, Guatemala.
LeCount, Lisa
2001 Like Water for Chocolate: Feasting and Political Ritual among the Late Classic Maya at Xunantunich, Belize. *American Anthropologist* 103:935–953.
Leventhal, Richard M.
1983 Household Groups and Classic Maya Religion. In *Prehistoric Settlement Patterns: Essays in Honor of Gordon R. Willey*, edited by E. Z. Vogt and R. Leventhal, pp. 55–76. University of New Mexico Press, Albuquerque.
Lohse, Jon C.
2004 Intra-Site Settlement Signatures and Implications for Late Classic Maya Com-

moner Organization at Dos Hombres, Belize. In *Ancient Maya Commoners*, edited by J. C. Lohse and F. Valdez, pp. 117–145. University of Texas Press, Austin.

Looper, Matthew

2006 Fabric Structures in Classic Maya Art and Ritual. In *Sacred Bundles: Ritual Acts of Wrapping and Binding in Mesoamerica*, edited by J. Guernsey and F. K. Reilly, pp. 80–104. Boundary End Archaeology Research Center, Barnardsville, North Carolina.

Maar, Marion, and Tamara Varney

1993 Preliminary Analysis of the Human Skeletal Remains from Structure 2 of the Zotz Group, and Structure A-1 of the Zubin Group, Cahal Pech, Belize. In *Belize Valley Archaeological Reconnaissance Project: Progress Report of the 1992 Field Season*, edited by Jaime J. Awe, pp. 121–129. Department of Anthropology, Trent University, Peterborough, Ontario.

Marcus, Joyce

2004 Maya Commoners: The Stereotype and the Reality. In *Ancient Maya Commoners*, edited by J. C. Lohse and F. Valdez, pp. 255–283. University of Texas Press, Austin.

Martin, Simon, and Nikolai Grube

2008 *Chronicle of the Maya Kings and Queens*. Rev. ed. Thames and Hudson, London.

Mathews, Jennifer P., and James F. Garber

2004 Models of Cosmic Order: Physical Expression of Sacred Space among the Ancient Maya. *Ancient Mesoamerica* 15:49–60.

McAnany, Patricia A.

1995 *Living with the Ancestors: Kinship and Kingship in Ancient Maya Society*. University of Texas Press, Austin.

1998 Ancestors and the Classic Maya Built Environment. In *Function and Meaning in Classic Maya Architecture,* edited by Stephen D. Houston, pp. 271–298. Dumbarton Oaks, Washington, D.C.

2002 Rethinking the Great and Little Tradition Paradigm from the Perspective of Domestic Ritual. In *Domestic Ritual in Ancient Mesoamerica*, edited by Patricia A. Plunket, pp. 115–119. Cotsen Institute of Archaeology, University of California, Los Angeles.

McAnany, Patricia A., Rebecca Storey, and Angela K. Lockard

1999 Mortuary Ritual and Family Politics at Formative and Classic K'axob, Belize. *Ancient Mesoamerica* 10:129–146.

McCall, John

1995 Rethinking Ancestors in Africa. *Africa* 65:256–270.

Miller, Mary E., and Karl Taube

1993 *The Gods and Symbols of Ancient Mexico and the Maya: An Illustrated Dictionary of Mesoamerican Religion*. Thames and Hudson, London.

Mock, Shirley B. (editor)

1998 *The Sowing and the Dawning: Termination, Dedication, and Transformation in the Archaeological and Ethnographic Record of Mesoamerica*. University of New Mexico Press, Albuquerque.

Montgomery, John
2001 *Tikal: An Illustrated History of the Ancient Maya Capital.* Hippocrene Books, New York.
2002 *Dictionary of Maya Hieroglyphs.* Hippocrene Books, New York.
Nash, June
1970 *In the Eyes of the Ancestors: Belief and Behavior in a Maya Community.* Yale University Press, New Haven, Connecticut.
Palka, Joel
1997 Reconstructing Classic Maya Socioeconomic Differentiation and the Collapse at Dos Pilas, Peten, Guatemala. *Ancient Mesoamerica* 8:293–306.
Powis, Terry G.
1993 Special Function Structures within Peripheral Groups in the Belize Valley: An Example from the Bedran Group at Baking Pot, Belize. In *Belize Valley Archaeological Reconnaissance Project: Progress Report of the 1992 Field Season*, edited by Jaime J. Awe, pp. 212–224. Trent University, Peterborough, Ontario.
Prufer, Keith M., and James E. Brady (editors)
2005 *Stone Houses and Earth Lords: Maya Religion in the Cave Context.* University Press of Colorado, Boulder.
Reilly, F. Kent
1995 Art, Ritual, and Rulership in the Olmec World. In *The Olmec World Ritual and Rulership*, edited by Jill Guthrie, pp. 27–46. Princeton University Press, Princeton, New Jersey.
2006 Middle Formative Origins of the Mesoamerican Ritual Act of Bundling. In *Sacred Bundles: Ritual Acts of Wrapping and Binding in Mesoamerica*, edited by J. Guernsey and F. K. Reilly, pp. 1–21. Boundary End Archaeology Research Center, Barnardsville, North Carolina.
Rice, Don S., and Prudence M. Rice
1980 The Northeast Peten Revisited. *American Antiquity* 45:432–454.
Rice, Prudence M.
2004 *Maya Political Science: Time, Astronomy, and the Cosmos.* University of Texas Press, Austin.
Robin, Cynthia
1989 *Preclassic Maya Burials at Cuello, Belize.* BAR International Series 480, Oxford.
Robin, Cynthia, and Norman Hammond
1991 Ritual and Ideology: Burial Practices. In *Cuello: An Early Maya Community in Belize*, edited by N. Hammond, pp. 204–225. Cambridge University Press, Cambridge.
Sahlins, Marshall
1981 The Stranger-King, or Dumézil among the Fijans. *Journal of Pacific History* 16:107–132.
Sanders, William T.
1992 Maya Elites: The Perspective from Copán. In *Mesoamerican Elites: An Archaeological Assessment*, edited by D. Z. Chase and A. F. Chase, pp. 278–291. University of Oklahoma Press, Norman.

Santley, Robert S.

1990 Demographic Archaeology in the Maya Lowlands. In *Precolumbian Population History in the Maya Lowlands*, edited by T. P. Culbert and D. S. Rice, pp. 325–343. University of New Mexico Press, Albuquerque.

Schele, Linda, and David Freidel

1990 *A Forest of Kings: The Untold Story of the Ancient Maya*. William Morrow, New York.

1994 The Workbook for the XVIIIth Maya Hieroglyphic Workshop at Texas, with Commentaries on the Tlaloc-Venus Wars from 378 AD to 730 AD. Department of Art, University of Texas, Austin.

Schele, Linda, and Mary E. Miller

1986 *The Blood of Kings: Dynasty and Ritual in Maya Art*. Braziller, New York.

Schwake, Sonja

1996 Ancestors among the Thorns: The Burials of Zubin, Cayo District, Belize. In *The Social Archaeology Research Program: Progress Report of the Second (1996) Season*, edited by G. Iannone, pp. 84–105. Department of Anthropology, Trent University, Peterborough, Ontario.

Sharer, Robert J., David W. Sedat, Loa P. Traxler, Julia C. Miller, and Ellen E. Bell

2005 Early Classic Royal Power in Copán: The Origins and Development of the Acropolis (ca. AD 250–600). In *Copán: The History of an Ancient Maya Kingdom*, edited by E. W. Andrews and W. L. Fash, pp. 139–199. School of American Research Press, Santa Fe.

Sharer, Robert J., Loa P. Traxler, David W. Sedat, Ellen E. Bell, Marcello A. Canuto, and Christopher Powell

1999 Early Classic Architecture beneath the Copán Acropolis: A Research Update. *Ancient Mesoamerica* 10:3–23.

Shipton, Parker

1994 Land and Culture in Tropical Africa: Soils, Symbols, and the Metaphysics of the Mundane. *Annual Review of Anthropology* 23:347–377.

Storey, Rebecca

2004 Ancestors: Bioarchaeology of the Human Remains of K'axob. In *K'axob: Ritual, Work, and Family in an Ancient Maya Village*, edited by P. A. McAnany, pp. 109–138. Cotsen Institute of Archaeology, University of California, Los Angeles.

Song, Rhan-Ju, Bobbi Hohmann, Denise Mardiros, and David Glassman

1994 All in the Family Circle: A Second Interim Report of the Human Skeletal Remains from Tolik, Cahal Pech, Belize, 1993. In *Belize Valley Archaeological Reconnaissance Project: Progress Report of the 1993 Field Season*, edited by Jaime J. Awe, pp. 147–63. Institute of Archaeology, University College London.

Stuart, David

1998 "The Fire Enters His House": Architecture and Ritual in Classic Maya Texts. In *Function and Meaning in Classic Maya Architecture*, edited by Stephen D. Houston, pp. 373–425. Dumbarton Oaks, Washington, D.C.

2011 Some Working Notes on the Text of Tikal Stela 31. *Mesoweb*, www.mesoweb.com/stuart/notes/Tikal.pdf.

Sullivan, Lauren A., Jon B. Hageman, Brett A. Houk, Paul Hughbanks, and Fred Valdez Jr.

2008 Structure Abandonment and Landscape Transformation: Examples from the Three Rivers Region. In *Ruins of the Past: The Use and Perception of Abandoned Structures in the Maya Lowlands*, edited by T. W. Stanton and A. Magnoni, pp. 91–111. University Press of Colorado, Boulder.

Taube, Karl

1998 The Jade Hearth: Centrality, Rulership, and the Classic Maya Temple. In *Function and Meaning in Classic Maya Architecture*, edited by Stephen D. Houston, pp. 427–478. Dumbarton Oaks, Washington, D.C.

2004 Structure 10L-16 and Its Early Classic Antecedents: Fire and the Evocation and Resurrection of K'inich Yax K'uk' Mo.' In *Understanding Early Classic Copán*, edited by E. E. Bell, M. A. Canuto, and R. J. Sharer, pp. 265–295. Museum of Archaeology and Anthropology, University of Pennsylvania, Philadelphia.

Tourtellot, Gair

1983 An Assessment of Ancient Maya Household Composition. In *Prehistoric Settlement Patterns: Essays in Honor of Gordon R. Willey*, edited by E. Z. Vogt and R. M. Leventhal, pp. 35–54. University of New Mexico Press, Albuquerque.

Tourtellot, Gair, Amanda Clarke, and Norman Hammond

1993 Mapping La Milpa: A Maya City in Northwestern Belize. *Antiquity* 67:96–108.

Tourtellot, Gair, Francisco Estrada-Belli, John J. Rose, and Norman Hammond

2003 Late Classic Heterarchy, Hierarchy, and Landscape at La Milpa, Belize. In *Heterarchy, Political Economy, and the Ancient Maya: The Three Rivers Region of the East-Central Yucatan Peninsula*, edited by V. Scarborough, F. Valdez, and N. Dunning, pp. 37–51. University of Arizona Press, Tucson.

Valeri, Valerio

1985 *Kingship and Sacrifice: Ritual Society in Ancient Hawaii*. University of Chicago Press, Chicago.

Vogt, Evon Z.

1969 *Zinacantan: A Maya Community in the Highlands of Chiapas*. Harvard University Press, Cambridge, Massachusetts.

1976 *Tortillas for the Gods: A Symbolic Analysis of Zinacanteco Rituals*. Harvard University Press, Cambridge, Massachusetts.

Wagner, Elizabeth

2002 White Earth Bundles—The Symbolic Sealing and Burial of Buildings among the Ancient Maya. In *Jaws of the Underworld: Life, Death, and Rebirth among the Ancient Maya*, edited by P. R. Colas, G. LeFort, and B. L. Persson, pp. 55–70. Verlag Anton Saurwein, Markt Schwaben, Germany.

Watson, James L.

1982 Chinese Kinship Reconsidered: Anthropological Perspectives on Historical Research. *China Quarterly* 92: 589–622.

Webster, David

1998 Classic Maya Architecture: Implications and Comparisons. In *Function and*

Meaning in Classic Maya Architecture, edited by Stephen D. Houston, pp. 5–47. Dumbarton Oaks, Washington, D.C.

Weiss-Krejci, Estella

2011 The Role of Dead Bodies in Late Classic Maya Politics: Cross-Cultural Reflections on the Meaning of Tikal Altar V. In *Living with the Dead: Mortuary Ritual in Mesoamerica*, edited by J. L. Fitzsimmons and I. Shimada, pp. 17–52. University of Arizona Press, Tucson.

Willey, Gordon R., A. Ledyard Smith, Gair Tourtellot, and Ian Graham

1975 *Excavations at Seibal. 1. Introduction: The Site and Its Setting*. Memoirs of the Peabody Museum of Archaeology and Ethnology no. 13. Harvard University, Cambridge, Massachusetts.

Wolley, Claudia, and Lori Wright

1990 Operación DP7: Investigaciones en el Grupo L4-4. In *Projecto Arqueológico Regional Petexbatun, Informe Preliminar* no. 2, edited by A. A. Demarest and Stephen D. Houston, pp. 44–65. Vanderbilt University, Nashville.

Contributors

Carla Antonaccio is professor of archaeology at Duke University. Most recently her research has focused on the archaeology of identity and on diaspora and colonization among ancient populations in the Mediterranean of the first millennium. She is the author of *An Archaeology of Ancestors: Greek Tomb and Hero Cult* (Rowman and Littlefield, 1995) and coeditor (with Donald Haggis) of *Classical Archaeology in Context* (De Gruyter, 2015) and (with Jane Carter) *The Cambridge Companion to the* Greek *Iron Age* (in preparation).

Roderick Campbell is assistant professor of East Asian archaeology and history at the Institute for the Study of the Ancient World at New York University. His research has focused on theorizing ancient social-political organization, social violence, and history in late second millennium BC (Shang) north China. He has published in *Current Anthropology* and *Antiquity* and most recently authored *Archaeology of the Chinese Bronze Age: From Erlitou to Anyang* (Cotsen Institute of Archaeology, 2014).

Jon B. Hageman is associate professor of anthropology at Northeastern Illinois University and research associate at the Field Museum. He has directed excavations at Maya sites in Belize and Guatemala for several years. His work has been published in the *Journal of Archaeological Science, Ancient Mesoamerica*, and several edited volumes. He is currently compiling an online Mesoamerican ethnobotanical database.

Erica Hill is associate professor of anthropology at the University of Alaska Southeast. She studies Moche iconography, the archaeology of human-animal relations, and the prehistory of the Bering Sea region. Her work has been published in *Antiquity, Cambridge Archaeological Journal,* and *Arctic Anthropology*. She is the editor of *Iñupiaq Ethnohistory* (University of Alaska Press, 2012).

Charles Mather is associate professor of anthropology at the University of Calgary. His current research focuses on anthropology of sport and medical anthropology. He has carried out research on shrines, the anthropology of pharmaceuticals in North America and Ghana, and the cultural determinants of decision making among patients suffering from cardiovascular disease. He has published in *Social Science and Medicine*, the *Journal of Anthropological Research*, and *Africa*.

Matthew L. Murray is instructional associate professor of anthropology in the Department of Sociology and Anthropology at the University of Mississippi. His primary research interest is the investigation and interpretation of mortuary and settlement practices in southern Germany from the Early Neolithic to the Late Iron Age. His research has been published in the *Journal of European Archaeology*, *Antiquity*, and the *Journal of Archaeological Science*. He is currently preparing a monograph with Bettina Arnold about the "Landscape of Ancestors" project in southwest Germany.

Estella Weiss-Krejci is a researcher at the Institute for Oriental and European Archaeology of the Austrian Academy of Sciences in Vienna. She also holds a *venia docendi* in the Department of Social and Cultural Anthropology at the University of Vienna. Her research interests are mortuary behavior and political use of the dead in medieval and post-medieval Europe, Neolithic and Copper Age Iberia, and among the ancient Maya. Her work has been published in the *Journal of Social Archaeology*, *Latin American Antiquity*, *Antiquity*, and several edited volumes.

Index

Page numbers in *italics* refer to illustrations.